Marilyn Monroe

Hollywood Legends Series
Carl Rollyson, General Editor

MARILYN MONROE

A Life of the Actress

REVISED AND UPDATED

Carl Rollyson

University Press of Mississippi / Jackson

www.upress.state.ms.us

The University Press of Mississippi is a member
of the Association of American University Presses.

Illustration on page ii: Marilyn Monroe (c. 1952)

All illustrations are from the author's collection.

First printing 2014
∞
Library of Congress Cataloging-in-Publication Data

Rollyson, Carl E. (Carl Edmund)
Marilyn Monroe : a life of the actress / Carl Rollyson. — Revised and updated [edition].
     pages cm. — (Hollywood legends series)
Originally published: Ann Arbor, Michigan : UMI Research Press, 1986.
Includes bibliographical references and index.
Includes filmography.
ISBN 978-1-61703-978-2 (pbk.) — ISBN 978-1-61703-979-9 (ebook) 1. Monroe, Marilyn,
1926–1962. 2. Motion picture actors and actresses—United States—Biography. I. Title.
PN2287.M69R65 2014
     791.4302'8092—dc23   2013042774

British Library Cataloging-in-Publication Data available

Contents

Acknowledgments

Several interviews were valuable owing to the insights Monroe's friends and business associates were able to supply concerning the shaping of the actress's life and attitude toward her art. Bruce Minnix, my friend and professional colleague, helped to arrange the initial interviews with Ralph Roberts and Steffi Sidney, the daughter of Hollywood columnist Sidney Skolsky. Sidney made a significant contribution to this biography by shrewdly commenting on an early draft and by questioning some of the "facts" included in other books on Monroe. Because her father was ailing and no longer able to grant interviews, she relayed a few of my questions to him. She also discussed her own perceptions of a Monroe who delighted in carefully crafting her career in an almost conspiratorial way that included Skolsky as her confidant. For example, when Ben Hecht had a draft of *My Story* ready for Monroe to check, she read passages from it over the phone to Skolsky, asking his opinion on how they sounded. Although Skolsky wrote a great deal about the actress, he revealed very little about those things she confided to him in strictest confidence. As a result, even his daughter could not say for sure how much she believed in the stories her father and Monroe concocted together. And Monroe—precisely because she held on to parts of herself that were not for distribution—becomes a more complex figure.

Ralph Roberts kindly reviewed what had been written about him in other sources and responded readily to questions about the actress's development of her talent. He conveyed a solid impression of Monroe's working life as an actress and of her fervent desire to educate herself. Our discussions of the Method led him to recommend an interview with Ellen Burstyn, who generously shared with me her experience as a movie actress. She suggested ways in which Stanislavsky would be particularly relevant to Monroe, and she helped to work out an approach to life and art partly based on our discussion of Audrey Flack's painting of Monroe.

A long conversation with Audrey Flack suggested that what she had painted was what I wanted to write. For over three years Flack was a constant source of support, corresponding with me regularly, commenting on drafts of the biography, and introducing it to friends and associates. My attention has shifted somewhat in this new edition of my biography, and I have deleted a section devoted to Flack's work, but its spirit continues to inspire what I write about Marilyn Monroe.

Norman Rosten consented to several interviews in person, on the phone, and by correspondence. He patiently responded to my pleas for advice and shrewdly assessed several chapters of this book. I am grateful, as well, to his wife, Hedda, who took the time to review her memories of Monroe—especially those concerning *The Prince and the Showgirl*.

Rupert Allan's recollections of Monroe's career, early and late, have proved indispensable. Allan first knew Monroe in his capacity as a writer for *Look*. Then he worked as her press representative. Through it all he remained her close friend. He checked several sections of my manuscript and answered numerous questions in person and on the phone. Stanley Flink, like Allan, first met Monroe when he was working as a writer— in Flink's case, for *Life*. As Richard Meryman suggested to me, Flink's memory of Monroe's early career remained vivid. The wit and enormous vitality she displayed during her first Hollywood years were still reflected in Flink's amusing stories.

Meryman generously made available several hours of his tape-recorded *Life* interview with Monroe. He wanted to demonstrate how easily one could get caught up in her style, in the incredible energy of her laugh. John Springer, the actress's press representative on the East Coast during the last three years of her life, was also very helpful in characterizing the kind of professional life Monroe pursued in New York. Like Meryman and Rupert Allan, he helped me get in touch with others who could confirm Monroe's intelligence as an artist.

Susan Strasberg made astute comments on my manuscript that led to further revisions. She gave me a clearer sense of her mother's part in Monroe's preparations for the screen than can to be found elsewhere. Susan Strasberg's father was not available for an interview, but Fred Guiles supplied a tape-recording of his sessions with Lee Strasberg, as well as other material that made a crucial difference in writing this biography. Both Guiles and Maurice Zolotow read my early drafts and answered many queries. Without them, several important leads would have been missed.

Milton Greene was available for a brief interview, and he clarified several points about the actress's working life and discussed her attitude toward *My Story*. It was a flawed autobiography, she thought, but one worth preserving. Almost everything she ever did, Greene noted, was tinged with regret over not having been able to do it better. I came away from this encounter with Greene impressed with his sober and—it seemed to me—subdued demeanor, which conveyed a sense that he still found it difficult to discuss his fruitful but fraught relationship with Monroe.

Rose Steinberg Wapner yielded insights on Monroe's movie set behavior, and a short talk with Patricia Newcomb clarified aspects of the actress's professional plans in her last year. Newcomb was cordial but guarded, and I regret that I could not penetrate the barrier of her discretion.

I also regret that several other important sources were not available to be interviewed. Joe DiMaggio's fierce refusal to deal with biographers of Monroe is legendary. He once walked out of the room when Fred Guiles tried to put a question to him about her. I had a similar experience with Arthur Miller. I wrote to him asking for an interview. I did not receive a reply. At a reception for him at the University of Michigan I introduced myself and said I was writing a biography of Monroe and would like to ask him some questions. He stared at me and said, "What is your question?" As I began to formulate one, a woman, book in hand, interrupted and asked him for his autograph. Miller turned toward her (his back to me), signaling the end of my "interview." Later, I sent him my manuscript for comment. He replied that he had done with my work what he always did with material that did not included a stamped return envelope: He threw my book in the waste basket. As a result, I have had to make do with his by turns reticent and revealing autobiography, *Timebends*.

I want to express my appreciation to Gary Vitacco-Robles for sharing with me the manuscript of his forthcoming two-volume biography of Marilyn Monroe, in which, at the last minute, I discovered those revealing notes by Joe DiMaggio that show how much he regretted treating her badly during their marriage and how he vowed to make every effort to make amends.

Several librarians were instrumental in finding obscure sources and suggesting fruitful areas of research: Mary Corliss in the Film Stills department of the Museum of Modern Art; Maxine Fleckner and her assistant Nancy Cieki at the Wisconsin Center for Film & Theatre Research; Geraldine Duclow in the Theatre Collection of the Free Library of Philadelphia; and Nancy Goldman of the Pacific Film Archive. For their patient and prompt handling of my requests, I wish to thank the staffs of the Los Angeles Police Department and the city's district attorney's office; the Theatre Arts Library, University of California, Los Angeles; the Doheny Library, University of Southern California; the Margaret Herrick Library of the Academy of Motion Picture Arts and Sciences; the American Film Institute in Hollywood and Washington, DC; the New York Public Library at Lincoln Center; the Library of Congress; the Columbus Public Library; the Cincinnati Public Library; and the Detroit Public Library. The Museum of Modern Art, Robert Rosen of the University of California, Los Angeles, the Library of Congress, and Films Incorporated all provided opportunities to screen Monroe's films. Although I was not able to visit the Film & Theatre Collection at the Humanities Research Center of the University of Texas at Austin, Edwin Neal kindly made available information on the library's considerable holdings of Monroe material, and Robert W. Daum and Paul M. Bailey arranged for a copy of Natasha Lytess's memoirs to be sent to me. And for advice about selecting photographs I am indebted to David Wills. His book *Marilyn Monroe/Metamorphosis* is an incomparable collection of photographs. Jeff Mantor of the Larry Edmunds Bookshop, a wonderful supporter of the Hollywood Legends series, was also instrumental in providing important photographs.

Several friends, relatives, and acquaintances were invaluable in keeping track of the enormous output of Monroe items: Bridget Allen, George and Barbara Barnett, Judy Bischoff, Kristin Brady, JoAnna Dutka, Avrum Fenson, Mary Lee Field, Joan Fiscella, Cyril Forbes, Ken and Geraldine Grunow, Mike Harmel, Charles Harte, Paul and Jeanne Hauben, Judy Hodge, Gloria House, Mary Hrabik-Samal, M. Thomas Inge, David Jacobs, Ella Johnson, Julie Klein, Patty Mallon, Jim Michels, Bette Z. Olson, Paul Orlov, Lisa Paddock, Hope Palmer, Amy Perrone, Noel Polk, Bob Reinhard, Seymour Riklin, Virginia Rock, Bernie Rodgers, Betty Rollyson, Beulah Rollyson, Frances Saunders, Bette Savage, Roslyn Schindler, Vickie Siegal, Andy Silber, Hugh Stilley, June Taboroff, Brian Tremain, Tomasz Warchol, Rea Wilmshurst, Saul Wineman, Pat and Bob Young, and Bill Zick. For their encouragement and advice, I thank T. H. Adamowski, Shaye Areheart, Michael Daher, Susan Feinberg, Scott Feltman, Brad Field, Joe Gomez, Barry and Sondra Gross, Barbara Lounsberry, Penelope Majesky, Michael and Jane Millgate, David Saunders, and Pat Trickey.

Bob Reinhard, Paul Orlov, David Jacobs, Joan Fiscella, Jim Michels, Joe Gomez, Anthony Summers, and Joyce Engelson all made searching comments about various drafts of my biography. Some of the drafts were presented at the American Literature Symposium II, University of Warsaw (1980), a Popular Culture of the South meeting (1981), joint meetings of the Popular Culture and American Culture Associations (1982, 1984), the Feminist Research in the Eighties Conference at Northern Illinois University (1982), a Midwest Modern Language Association meeting (1982), and a Modern Language Association convention (1983).

Rea Wilmshurst typed an early draft of the manuscript and through careful editing saved me from committing many embarrassing errors. I owe the biggest debt of all, however, to my wife, Dr. Lisa Paddock. Every page of this book reflects her precise editing; every passage is richer because she helped me to imagine it.

Foreword

Discovering Marilyn Monroe

I discovered Marilyn Monroe in the late 1970s while working on Norman Mailer. His biography of Marilyn Monroe excited my admiration. Mailer shrewdly drew on previous work by Maurice Zolotow and Fred Lawrence Guiles, Monroe's first two important biographers, to portray a proactive person he deemed Napoleonic. To this day, no one seems to have recognized how his insight into this ambitious actress catapulted Monroe biography to a different level.

To explain, I need to summon the dark days of Monroe biography, the pre-Norman Mailer period, when she was viewed as a rather pathetic figure—a victim of Hollywood, a vulgar popular cultural figure, generally a messed up human being. Of course, there were exceptions to this view. Diana Trilling wrote a sensitive piece about Monroe's artistry, and other writers and artists who met Monroe were impressed with her wit. Maurice Zolotow had the advantage of actually knowing the actress and reporting vividly on her movie set behavior. Then Fred Lawrence Guiles, author of the first comprehensive Monroe biography, probed deeply into her early years, especially her experiences with foster families. But Zolotow and Guiles treated Monroe mainly as a woman who all too often succumbed to the pressures of her career and rarely seemed in control of what was happening to her. Embedded in their narratives, however, was another Monroe, one far more canny and cunning. But this side of the actress was still overwhelmed by stories of how many takes it took for her to say "It's me, Sugar," in *Some Like It Hot.*

In 1978, I published an article about Mailer's book in a new journal, *Biography*, explaining that with his work our understanding of Marilyn Monroe had turned a corner. A year later, a small press offered me a contract to produce a bio-bibliography of Monroe. Only then did I seriously consider what I could contribute to the already voluminous literature about her. I spent the summer of 1980 re-reading Guiles, Zolotow, Mailer, and other biographies. And I realized two things: 1) I was getting bored reading and summarizing what others had written about her, which is what I was supposed to be doing in a bio-bibliography, and 2) Her three best biographers knew next to nothing about acting and had missed what should be the focus of Monroe biography. In my view, her biographer needed to address two questions: 1) Why did she turn to acting as a way of finding an identity and fulfilling herself, and 2) To what extent—on the screen—did she actually achieve her goal? Previous biographers had no vocabulary to describe her acting, and thus were at a loss when it came to discussing the nexus between her life and her art.

I doubt that I would have recognized the deficiencies of earlier biographies if I had not been a trained actor, one who at a very early age turned to acting for many of the same reasons that Monroe was attracted to the art. In brief, acting allows you to be someone even before you know who you are or what you want to become. And as an actor, you can't just say you are so and so; that so and so has to arise from a complex arrangement of gestures, postures, and mannerisms that are developed both in privacy and in front of fellow actors, audiences, crews, and directors. Monroe began to form a self in the absence of a "mirror," a parent who could acknowledge and validate her. Her mother was mentally ill, and Monroe was never sure about the identity of her father, so she turned to acting as a kind of compensation—as I did after my father died when I was thirteen.

Because of my own voracious reading and commitment to acting, I also understood why Monroe built an impressive library of works on psychology and physiology, keeping copies of Mabel Elsworth Todd's *The Thinking Body*, as well as an edition of Freud's letters on her bedside table. But what interested me as a younger man in the 1980s was Monroe's battle with concentration. When she remained focused, she created an extraordinary range of performances: from the introvert in *Bus Stop* to the extrovert in *The Prince and the Showgirl*. Watch just those two films, and you will see why she is a great actress. Each performance is a de novo creation built through a vocabulary of gesture and movement that is inimitable. In her major roles, Marilyn Monroe did not repeat herself.

Tired of simply reading about Marilyn Monroe during that long summer of 1980, I decided to contact people who actually knew her. Biography is history made palpable. I wanted to forge the human chain of evidence, not just read books and write about them. Not having worked on a biography before, I sought out both Guiles and Zolotow for inspiration and guidance. Both of them welcomed my focus on Monroe's acting and seemed delighted that a young academic (I was then an assistant professor of humanities at Wayne State University in Detroit) took them seriously. Zolotow became a friend and advisor. Guiles greeted me from a hospital bed, having just suffered a heart attack. He supplied me with a recording of his interview with Lee Strasberg discussing Monroe's work at the Actors Studio. Mailer wished me well, but pleaded overwork and the claims of friends asking for his help and endorsement. In a memorable letter, he referred to their supplications as part of his "guilt impost pile." Later, I was gratified to learn from George Simson, editor of *Biography*, that Mailer told him I had published the best discussion to date of his Monroe book.

Do you know what it was like for a biographer like me in the early 1980s? You don't unless you understand what academia was like then. It was all right to write a book about a Hollywood or a foreign film director. After all, this was the heyday of the auteur theory, when certain directors were treated like authors. But to write about a movie star? Find a biography of a movie star published by a university press before the year 1986. My female colleagues looked askance at my work, although most were polite enough not to come right out and say my subject was unworthy. I say most, because at a popular culture conference in the mid-1980s a prominent feminist scholar told me that next time I should pick a "strong woman to write about." That scholar could have been Lois Banner. In her Monroe biography, she confesses that her own attitude toward Monroe has gone through a sea change. Indeed, both in conversation with me and in her book, Banner singles out my work for showing her just how serious and accomplished an actress Monroe was.

It is not an exaggeration to say that in the mid-1980s I was in the wilderness. In Detroit, I would pick up the phone and call editors in New York, pitching my book. I got polite responses but no takers. Now I'm astonished that those editors even deigned to talk to me. In frustration, I turned to Matthew Bruccoli, a professor at the University of South Carolina who had all sorts of contacts in publishing. A friend had recommended him. The brusque Broccoli suffered my importuning telephone call for several minutes before finally coughing up a name: Shaye Areheart. She was an editor at Doubleday he thought would be receptive to my approach to Monroe. And she was, but she could not get the publisher's editorial board to buy my book. "It fell between two stools," I was told. It was written in an engaging style, but it was also "serious" and "scholarly." The question of how to market that kind of book puzzled them.

Eventually, through Shaye, I found an agent who convinced me no trade house would publish my book. But if I persuaded UMI Research Press, publisher of my revised dissertation on William Faulkner, to take the book and limit their rights to a three-year deal for the hardcover, I could launch my biography. Then she could get deals for paperback and foreign publication. And that is what happened. Souvenir Press published the hardcover in England, then Hodder & Stoughton came out with a paperback, followed by Da Capo Press with the American softcover—proving not only that a market existed for my book, but that readers were eager to see more facets of Marilyn Monroe than had been on display in the earlier biographies.

I asked readers to consider what Marilyn had been confronted with: the prospect that she was going to portray basically the same character, the so-called "dumb blonde," in picture after picture. If she took herself seriously, then she had to find a way to make each of her characters live within the very narrow range the sex symbol occupied. By describing Monroe's impressive repertoire of gestures—from *Bus Stop* to *The Misfits*—I showed that she was, indeed, a consummate professional and more. She was a great artist. When Gloria Steinem read my book, she concurred: "More than anything else in her life, Marilyn Monroe wanted to be taken seriously as an actress. Rollyson has done just that in *Marilyn Monroe: A Life of the Actress*, the first and only book that is entirely an analysis and appreciation of her work. It will be important to both film historians and to Marilyn's fans—it would have made Marilyn feel honored and worthwhile."

Steinem also authored an important feminist analysis of Monroe in a book published the same year as mine. Steinem wondered whether Marilyn might have been heartened by the second wave of the women's movement, which would have put her plight into historical context and made her protest against male chauvinist moviemaking all the more powerful. Perhaps—although Banner, who is sympathetic to this argument, also wonders if Monroe, as a male-identified actress, would have been able to make the transition to a new era. On balance, I side with Steinem because of what I know about Marilyn Monroe. She never stopped reading and learning and arguing. Hers was not a closed mind.

At the same time I was writing my interpretative Monroe biography, I encountered Anthony Summers, then involved in researching the star's life—especially her connection with the Kennedys. He called me at the urging of one of our mutual friends, Steffi Sidney. I exchanged information and ideas with Summers and agreed with his assessment that we were writing very different kinds of books. When his book *Goddess* appeared in 1985, it was highly praised and roundly denounced. In over six hundred interviews, he had amassed an astounding record of testimony that some deemed gossip, while others found his work suggestive evidence that considerably widened and deepened our understanding of the incredible range of Monroe's appeal. It is not too much to say that Summers's work made the endeavor to comprehend Marilyn Monroe into a Napoleonic campaign that attracted other ambitious biographers. Without Summers's spadework, I don't see how the noteworthy biographies of the 1990s by Donald Spoto and Barbara Leaming would have been published.

For a long time, I resisted revising this book. I felt it had its place in the history of Monroe biography, and short of discovering new material and conducting extensive new interviews—a daunting prospect because of my commitments to other projects—I did not see the point. But then two books of primary source material appeared, providing fresh insight into both the young woman preparing herself to become Marilyn Monroe, and the star struggling to maintain her focus on her art. *Fragments* and *MM-Personal* reveal her acute self-consciousness, a Virginia Woolf-like obsession with watching herself and scrutinizing her relations with others. Monroe did not keep diaries as faithfully as Woolf did, and she did not have Woolf's literary gifts, but Monroe had a sensibility like Woolf's that relentlessly pursued itself to the point of extinction. In short, it was not the traumatic childhood, not the factory-like production of movies, not the failed marriages—not her even her disappointed hopes—that led to Monroe's demise, but rather her unrelenting focus on herself. This self-consciousness appeared at least as early as her first marriage, years before she became a star or even had an acting career.

In this new edition, I have drawn on the discoveries and commentaries made since my book first appeared in 1986. I have also provided a bit more of the social and historical context in which Marilyn Monroe made her fateful choices. Virtually every page also reflects, I hope, my development as a writer of better sentences. But mainly I have sought to flesh out the story that shaped my initial narrative: the struggle of a great artist to realize herself and her talent.

Marilyn Monroe

CHAPTER ONE

Childhood (1926-38)

On the Outside of the World

On February 11, 1924, Gladys Pearl Baker married Martin E. Mortensen. She already had two children (then not living with her) by a previous marriage to John Newton Baker, from whom she was divorced. She was a quiet woman who worked as a film cutter at one of the Hollywood studios. Gladys kept to herself most of the time, and friends and family never seem to have fathomed what went wrong in her second marriage to Mortensen, a union that lasted only sixteen months. Although they were not divorced until June 1, 1927, Gladys left him two years earlier on May 25, 1925. When her daughter, Norma Jeane, was born on June 1, 1926, the birth certificate listed her last name as Mortensen, although Mortensen almost certainly was not her father.

Gladys never told Norma Jeane who her father was, although the mother confided to her daughter a few things about him, including a story about his death in an auto accident that the child refused to believe. Many years later, when Norma Jeane became the starlet Marilyn Monroe, she said she learned that her father was Stanley Gifford, one of her mother's co-workers in the film industry. Gifford refused to acknowledge her efforts to contact him, and she took his rejection bitterly. It gave her one more reason to think of herself as a waif.

Norma Jeane never had anything like a normal relationship with her mother. Just twelve days after her birth, Gladys took her daughter to Wayne and Ida Bolender's home in Hawthorne, California. The Bolenders were neighbors who would look after the baby for more than six years while Gladys worked. Gladys apparently doubted her capacity to handle a child full time, because even when she was not working she seemed more like an aloof visitor to the Bolender home than a mother who missed her child. She did not respond to her daughter's use of the word "mama." Instead, as Monroe later recalled, her mother stared at her and gave no sign of affection. She did not even hold her daughter, and she barely spoke to the expectant little girl. On visits with Gladys, Norma Jeane was frightened and spent most of her time in the bedroom closet hidden among her clothes. Gladys cautioned Norma Jeane not to make "so much noise." It was as if the child were an intruder. Even the sound of Norma Jeane turning the pages of a book made her mother nervous. In sum, the child had few opportunities to behave in a free, spontaneous, and autonomous fashion.

Norma Jeane looked for a way to fill the void in her visits with her mother. She noticed on the wall of Gladys's room a photograph of a rather jaunty looking man with a lively smile and a Clark Gable mustache, and she was thrilled to learn from her mother that this robust figure was her father. No more was said about the photograph, but Norma Jeane dreamed about it constantly, probably because it exemplified the exuberance of spirit stilled in herself.

Norma Jeane spent several months with an English couple, movie extras who had rented part of the bungalow from Gladys. Then Grace McKee, Gladys's friend and co-worker, was named the child's guardian. But McKee kept her ward for only a brief period, and Norma Jeane found herself in her first foster home with the Giffens family before being sent to an orphanage on September 13, 1935. She spent nearly two years there. When she finally left the institution in June of 1937, she stayed temporarily with two foster families before settling again with Grace in January or February of 1938.

In her years as a starlet, Marilyn Monroe would treat her childhood like a Dickensian story involving a dozen or so foster homes, the drudgery of washing and cleaning dishes in an orphanage, sexual molestation, and even her attempted murder, when her grandmother Della tried to smother her with a pillow. These shocking tales derived from Marilyn's feeling that she had been deprived, exploited, and violated at a very early age. The normal pattern of growth had been disrupted, and she had trouble making the connections between herself and the world that children from stable families take for granted.

Norma Jeane had to discover some way of building and controlling her self-image in a world that could easily wipe away her attachments to it. She turned to daydreaming and to the movies as a means of self-fortification, for she was a child who "often felt lonely and wanted to die." As Monroe later put it, fantasizing exercised her imagination: "[I]n a daydream you jump over facts as easily as a cat jumps over a fence." Daydreams provided her with an effortless, instantaneous attractiveness: "I daydreamed chiefly about beauty.... Daydreaming made my work easier." She dreamed of appearing naked in church for "God and everyone else to see." This confession in *My Story* seems circumspect compared to a reflection she later recorded in a private notebook, noting her "strongly sexed feeling since a small child."

Movies also filled in the gaps in her identity. Films made her feel more alive and more conscious and better able to visualize the world that otherwise excluded her. There was nothing she could not follow on the screen, and nothing that could diminish the intensity of her perceptions: "I loved everything that moved up there and I didn't miss anything that happened—and there was no popcorn either." Her phrasing dramatically recaptures the child's awestruck love of human experience as magnified on film, seemingly compensating for the diminution of her own experience outside the movie house.

Grace McKee, who had worked alongside Gladys in a film laboratory at a movie studio, never lost touch with Norma Jeane and often came to her rescue. Twice divorced and with a 1920s figure and stature that made it easy to share clothes with Gladys, Grace found the little girl adorable and apparently responded to that "strongly sexed feeling," telling Norma Jeane that someday she would be a movie star, another Jean Harlow (1911–37). Grace, who liked the bootleg liquor available during the years of Prohibition (1920–33), often joined Gladys on nights out with various men. So it is little wonder that Harlow, who played the quintessential platinum blonde and good time girl in both silent films and talkies, should appeal to Grace as a desirable role model for Norma Jeane.

By the early 1930s, Harlow had become a superstar. Paired in six films with Hollywood's premiere leading man, Clark Gable, she enchanted audiences with her gift for comedy and her sexual allure—precisely the qualities that audiences would find so appealing in Monroe. Harlow's shocking death at the age of twenty-six, just after Norma Jeane's eleventh birthday, made a deep impression not only on Harlow's fans but also on a nation of moviegoers. This shimmering platinum blonde presence, a spirited woman who held her own on the screen with seasoned leading men such as Spencer Tracy and William Powell, left a void that no other actress of her generation seemed able to fill. Grace mesmerized Norma Jeane with the promise of Hollywood stardom, a dream that countless young American girls would pursue in the aftermath of Harlow's death. Later, in *My Story*, Monroe would allude to this generation of Hollywood hopefuls she eventually joined, saying of herself, "I was dreaming the hardest."

Occasionally, incidents in Norma Jeane's childhood seemed to presage her later envelopment in image building. A sign that included the RKO movie studio water tower, which she could see from a large dormitory room, reminded her of the Hollywood dreams Grace had instilled in her. Norma Jeane had been on a movie lot with her mother, and that glamorous world still seemed within reach when, every week, Grace visited with gifts of lipstick and rouge and played dress up with the young girl. The actress later remembered the time she was returned to the orphanage after she tried to run away. She feared punishment, but instead she was greeted by the compassionate superintendent, Mrs. Dewey, who took Norma Jeane in her arms, telling her she was pretty, and powdered the child's face with a powder puff. No doubt the actress could not resist dramatizing this incident, and in another version she went on to describe how Mrs. Dewey had her look in the mirror and observe her face, soft and alabaster smooth like her mother's. "This was the first time in my life I felt loved—no one had ever noticed my face or hair or me before," Monroe told a publicity woman at Twentieth Century- Fox. A letter Mrs. Dewey wrote many years later to Grace clearly shows that she did take an interest in Norma Jeane and wanted to know how the child was doing. Grace proudly replied that the "orphan" had become a movie star.

Norma Jeane was "buoyant for days" after the recognition scene with Mrs. Dewey, but when nothing resembling it was repeated, she began to doubt that the events had actually taken place. Like so many of her other experiences, this one was fragmentary. It seemed to lead her nowhere. She felt incomplete, as orphans and adopted children often do. She really did not know what to expect from one moment to the next from people who did not have time for her. Since the gratification she did receive seemed equivocal, she apparently divided her personality in two. In her dreams, she was naked and unsullied, an immaculate figure. In reality, she submitted to degrading experiences—such as having to bathe in water her foster family had already used. She always came last—or so it seemed to her.

Norma Jeane needed to see herself reflected in her mother's eyes and mirrored in her mother's concerns. A child who cannot find herself in her mother's face suffers from the same alienation that prevents the mother from truly recognizing her own child. As a result such a child, in Alice Miller's words, "would remain without a mirror, and for the rest of his life would be seeking this mirror in vain."

There have been cases of such children who become mirrors to themselves. R. D. Laing describes one who actually used a mirror as a way of becoming "another person to himself who could look at him from the mirror." Monroe turned toward mirrors for self-confirmation, as she mentions doing in *My Story*, and she may have experienced the duality felt by others who fail to have their beings confirmed by their mothers or fathers. Such individuals consequently look for a means to make themselves seen as "real live persons." Certainly Monroe suffered from the "persecutory features" that have been identified in persons who split themselves into two parts. They feel threatened with the disappearance whenever others fail to endorse their presence.

Monroe's guardians provided contradictory role models. What could she make of her various "homes"? The Bolenders were fundamentalists and teetotalers; the English couple drank and allowed Norma Jeane to play with their liquor bottles; and Grace McKee, married to Erwin "Doc" Goddard when Norma Jeane returned to her in early 1938, ran a household considerably more easygoing than the strict Bolenders. Mutually exclusive environments were discordant. Norma Jeane could not confidently validate her feelings or believe that anyone trusted her. In *My Story* Monroe says, "I knew people only told lies to children—lies about everything from soup to Santa Claus."

Of course, Norma Jeane was not entirely without resources or mentors. In fact, for nearly four years, beginning in 1938, she could count not only on her guardian, Grace, but also on Grace's aunt, Ana Lower, a devout Christian Scientist. Until Ana Lower died in 1948, Norma Jeane and then the starlet Marilyn Monroe tried to follow the teachings of a religion that emphasized the power of "right thoughts" in allaying pain and suffering. Illness and sin were illusions that could be overcome by the power of the mind. Christian Science functioned as a welcome mental hygiene in Monroe's early life and as a way of practicing self-reliance, like her daydreams. "I dreamed of myself walking proudly in beautiful clothes and being admired by everyone and overhearing words of praise," Monroe later recalled in *My Story*. The energy of what may have been an incipient erotic desire saved her from the severest feelings of self-loss, in which a person lacks not only the customary sense of "personal unity," but also, R. D. Laing suggests, a "sense of himself as the agent of his own actions . . . of being the agent of his own perceptions." At a very early age, Monroe seemingly invested her dream self with an attractiveness that at least partially transcended her public humiliation. Fantasies are often used to replenish a depleted identity. In acute cases, they become increasingly delusional, but as Monroe entered her adolescence, her craving for attention coincided with her growing physical beauty. Her fantasies were soon realized, as she captivated her first male audiences.

CHAPTER TWO

Adolescence to Adulthood (1938–45)

Suddenly Everything Opened Up

By the age of eleven or twelve, Norma Jeane began wearing tight clothing that accentuated her rapidly developing figure. This sexual exposure was exhilarating, and she seemed to revel in the attention of schoolboys, workers, and other people on the street. Adulation made her feel a part of things for the first time in her life. She could drop the oppressive, inhibiting sense of belonging to nobody, exchanging it for an exuberant, sensual contact with the elements of life itself—with the wind that caressed her as she zoomed along on a bike borrowed from an admiring group of boys. She felt, however, like "two people," the neglected Norma Jeane and some new being who "belonged to the ocean and the sky and the whole world." She grasped for the grandeur of life even as she was riddled with anxiety about her rootlessness and failure to locate herself in a specific world. The mature Monroe reflected that her emerging sexuality "was a kind of double-edged thing." It got her the attention she craved, but it also resulted in "overly friendly" advances. Her guardians worried about her high spirits, which could be so easily misinterpreted as hysteria. This shy girl had found a way to impress herself on others as soon as she realized just how pleased they were with her presence. But what ties would she make in a world that had suddenly become so accessible? And how could Norma Jeane handle these new companions when she had so little family, properly speaking, to guide her in her choices?

Grace, now married to "Doc" Erwin Goddard, seems to have been the first to suggest to Norma Jeane, some time in the early spring of 1942, the idea of marrying James Dougherty. An ailing Ana Lower, no longer able to provide a home for Norma Jeane, apparently concurred with Grace's belief that the twenty-one-year-old Dougherty would bring stability to this fifteen-year-old girl's life. Grace apparently saw no contradiction between marrying Norma Jeane to an eligible young man and encouraging the young woman to dream of a career in movies—even though few husbands were prepared to marry women who dreamed of becoming film stars.

James Dougherty drove Norma Jeane to Van Nuys High School as a neighborly gesture. He would later claim that it never occurred to him to marry her, but he certainly took to the idea when Grace and others suggested it. But what about Norma Jeane? Dougherty would later claim that the early years of their marriage were happy. And initially, Norma Jeane—still very uncertain about her own place in the world—clung to Dougherty in grateful appreciation of his genial effort to be, in his words, "her lover, husband, and father." She would join with him in establishing the first home of her own. They were married on June 19, 1942, just three weeks after her sixteenth birthday.

In the early 1940s, a good wife took care of her husband—fed him, did the household work, and in general tried to make a pleasant and loving home. The couple settled into a small four-room house in Van Nuys. The young wife seemed to enjoy the comfortable conventions of domesticity. This was, after all, the first time she could set some of her own terms for living. A kind and gentle Jimmy really seemed to appreciate Norma Jeane's efforts to become the model housewife. She had his meals ready for him when he returned from his work at the Lockheed aircraft plant. She appeared fresh and eager to please, cheered by her first efforts to furnish her own home.

But conflicting accounts make it difficult to determine the compatibility of husband and wife. Was Norma Jeane daunted by the sexual demands of her husband, or did she more or less take this new aspect of adulthood in stride, as Dougherty insists in his memoirs? In *My Story*, written just as the movie star Marilyn Monroe was emerging, the marriage is portrayed in dreary terms. Although the memoir's version has been challenged, a remarkable personal note the young wife wrote—perhaps late in 1943—is startling because it sounds like it issued from an older woman looking back on the early years of her marriage: "[M]y relationship with him was basically insecure from the first night I spent alone with him." She found him attractive but unsure of his ability to please her. She wanted to feel she belonged to someone and to follow the lead of her

Norma Jeane (c. 1942)

elders who had encouraged the marriage. A part of her wanted the marriage to work, but she also felt stifled, since she had not given up on her dreams of becoming a model and an actress.

Norma Jeane's adjustment to marriage and adulthood was complicated by what she described as her introverted personality. She was shy and found her greatest pleasure in reading. She questioned her own motives. Was she in love, or just thrilled that her husband wanted her? Like so much of what she would write throughout her life, the note she wrote about her marriage is full of self-doubt. Already, the makings of a deeply self-conscious identity are apparent. This awareness of her own weaknesses stimulated her desire to improve, even as her acknowledgment of her failings debilitated her. She had a striking grasp of the self's mixed motivations, which led her to question not only herself, but those close to her—in this case making her wonder if her husband had been unfaithful. She also knew that too much self-examination could harm her: "Everyone needs a little conceit to carry them through & past the falls." This line, with its misspellings, is characteristic, and other parts of the note reflect the shaky syntax of a high school dropout. But the introspective quality of this seventeen-year-old is powerfully present in this six-page document.

Judging by her "personal note," and his memoir, Dougherty never discovered the depths of the young woman he married. He always professed amazement that his Norma Jeane metamorphosed into Marilyn Monroe. "I never knew Marilyn Monroe," he liked to say. He did not realize, however, that he never knew Norma Jeane either.

Dougherty took on too much. After the United States entered the war, he was eager to participate and deferred his decision to enlist only to placate his young wife, terrified at the prospect of losing the sense of permanence marriage represented. He was there, in part, to bolster her confidence, and she may have regarded overseas duty in the merchant marine in early 1944 as an attack on the marriage itself. In her calmer moods, she did not resent his war service, but during emotional periods she blamed him for wrecking their relationship. His departure seems to have been a direct blow to her sense of self-worth, to her own reason for living, so she had to find another way of surviving. As Arthur Miller observes in *Timebends*, she deeply feared abandonment. Abandonment was what people did to her, sooner or later: They left.

According to Dougherty, the night before he was to ship out Norma Jeane became hysterical and pleaded with him "to make her pregnant," so that she would have a part of him if he did not return. She dreaded his leaving, refusing to talk about it, and in desperation announced that she planned to call her father. This was evidently the first occasion on which she tried to contact him, and she may have been trying to certify her existence in still another way. When he failed to respond to her call, to accept his paternity, she was devastated. Norma Jeane exhibited terrible anxiety about being alone. There were too many gaps in her life, and like other women of her age and troubled background, she panicked easily. She was not depressed or sad; rather, she was out of control and absolutely at a loss when contemplating the absence of her husband's attention.

She was far from inconsolable, however, and she quickly took up war work as a paint sprayer and parachute packer in an airplane factory. She wanted to feel needed and recognized. A diligent worker, she managed to cope with her husband's departure quite well. The marriage itself may have seemed less crucial to her well being—more like an interim identity, the first substantial role in which she had invested herself.

As an aircraft employee, Norma Jeane had no trouble getting noticed. On June 26, 1945, David Conover came to the factory to photograph young women engaged in war work. He found Norma Jeane fascinating. He marveled at how easily she performed for his camera over the course of three days. A quick study, she welcomed the new world opening up to her. She began to make suggestions about how she should be positioned for shots at various factory locations. Norma Jeane's encounter with Conover confirmed her sense of destiny, which had been dormant since those early days with Grace and conversations about Jean Harlow. From then on, no matter what her disappointments, Norma Jeane was on her way. With Conover's encouragement, a modeling and movie career seemed possible, and her commitment to Dougherty diminished. She wrote him fewer letters and single-mindedly pursued her new goal. On his return he tried to win her back, but he had very little interest in her dreams of stardom and could not identify with the success she had made of herself while he was away. Although they were not officially divorced until September 13, 1946, the marriage was surely over by late 1945, when Emmeline Snively's modeling agency employed Norma Jeane.

Reflecting on her first marriage in *My Story*, Monroe bitterly regretted years that held her back. She dismissed the significance of her feelings for Dougherty, as though her real life only began with her photographed incarnation. She stressed that she had come to Hollywood after the breakup of her marriage seeking more than fame and adulation; she was came in a spirit of self-interrogation. She intended to live by herself so that, at nineteen, and she could "find out who I was." Dougherty would have kept her from even attempting this daring discovery of an identity.

In 1945 and 1946, a reborn Norma Jeane mastered new images of herself the camera helped her find, just as an infant manipulates images of

The mirror-gazing Marilyn (c. late 1940s)

itself duplicated in a mirror. Could a fully realized self emerge from posing for the camera? By focusing a lens on herself, she learned to hold the world in her gaze. Perhaps the intense drama of her photographic sessions could make up for the insufficiency, the dullness, of her life up to that point.

Both Emmeline Snively and David Conover recall Norma Jeane's persistent scrutiny of photographic prints. She wanted to be able to recognize her mistakes and to make each shot as perfect as possible. This hardworking apprentice was far more inquisitive than Snively's other models; Norma Jeane wanted to know as much as possible about the powers of projection.

Andre de Dienes, who photographed Norma Jeane against various landscapes in early 1946, captures her ingenuous youthfulness and self-assurance. With her frizzy brown hair, uneven jawline, somewhat bulbous nose, and slightly protruding front teeth she is hardly ready to metamorphose into Marilyn Monroe. But she gazes directly at the camera, conveying the impression of a willing, malleable subject. Her sexual playfulness and the organic sensuousness of the scenes she is placed in are happily congruent. She is a pliable performer, utterly at ease whether she rests against a rustic fence railing or clings to the side of a mountain slope.

Norma Jeane's work habits were admirable. Punctual and well prepared for each day's shooting session, she also exhibited extraordinary resilience. Yet de Dienes observed that she seemed curiously frail and that she would "curl up in the front of the car and fall asleep" after an assignment. It is not surprising, of course, for a performer to behave this way after the excitement of a performance, but to de Dienes, Norma Jeane seemed out of focus when she did not have the camera's attention. His impressions echo what other photographers would later notice: "Her hours passed in a state of dreaminess that left her oblivious of the environment, and this began to irritate him."

De Dienes had illusions that this young woman would fall in love with him, but she seemed bent on demonstrating her independence, dating several young men who shared her ambition to be successful in Hollywood. Bill Burnside, one of Norma Jeane's dates, remembers her liking for Shelley and Keats and that what she most wanted from him was his education. She built up a considerable library and a small circle of friends who could help her with reading she thought essential to the development of herself as a person and a professional actress. No man during this period excited her special devotion. De Dienes's photographs—like countless others she would pose for in this period—were not definitive for her. Instead, they served as her threshold to a larger world.

CHAPTER THREE

Early Career (1945-50)

*It was the creative part that kept me going—
trying to be an actress.*

On August 26, 1946, after about a year of working as a professional photographer's model, Norma Jeane Dougherty signed her first movie contract—as Marilyn Monroe. Modeling had been a crucial step toward an acting career, but it was only a step. She posed for department stores and industrial shows, wearing a variety of clothing—ranging from sports outfits to negligees—diligently took lessons in makeup, grooming, and posing at Ms. Snively's school, and appeared on the covers of several magazines.

But Norma Jeane had no clear idea of how to go about learning to become an actress. Of course she had to spend most of her time acquiring modeling skills, which to some extent propelled her toward acting, and she had to spend the rest of her time supporting herself through modeling jobs. Nevertheless, over the next three years—while under studio contract and taking classes in acting, dancing, and singing—she showed little promise as an actress. She had virtually no acting experience when signed to her first contract, with Twentieth Century-Fox, yet acting, she insisted in *My Story*, "was this secret in me . . . something golden and beautiful . . . like the bright colors Norma Jean[e] used to see in her daydreams." It was not an art but a game about "worlds so bright they made your heart leap just to think of them." Acting was her compulsion, "a thing in me like a craziness that wouldn't let up." Acting would eventually become a transformative process capable of expanding the boundaries of her small and lonely being.

The year before Norma Jeane signed her first studio contract, Emmeline Snively told her, "You're very girl-next-doorish." Her face and figure were pleasing, sometimes provocative, but not yet compelling as perfect sexual shapes. She had to learn to smile with her upper lip drawn down in order to help minimize the length of her nose and to hide her gum line. This adjustment resulted in a wavering of her lips, first glimpsed at the end of her second scene in *The Asphalt Jungle* and then emphasized in close-ups in *Gentlemen Prefer Blondes,* where her undulating lip seems to mimic the movement of her whole seductive body. So that she could adapt to a variety of modeling assignments, her hair had to be cut short, straightened, bleached honey blonde, and styled in a "sophisticated up-sweep."

Such changes imposed a welcome redefinition of her person; now she had a specific role to play. Yet she had not chosen this identity, and she resisted, momentarily, Hollywood's highlighting techniques. Emmeline Snively had to persuade the young woman to consider both a screen name and the physical changes that would make her a negotiable prospect in the modeling agency's dealings with the studios. Thus a role was grafted onto her, and she had to attach herself to it—which she did by joining Monroe, Gladys's maiden name, to Marilyn, the first name proposed for her at the studio by Ben Lyon, the executive in charge of new talent. Lyon had been so deeply impressed with Norma Jeane's youth and beauty that he immediately arranged for a screen test on July 17, just five weeks before she signed the contract he had promised her at their first meeting.

She was good visual material—this was the verdict on the silent screen test, shot in color. She was directed to "walk across the set. Sit down. Light a cigarette. Put it out. Go upstage. Cross. Look out a window. Sit down. Come downstage and exit." She is supposed to have looked and acted like "one of those lush stars of the silent era." On screen she appeared palpable, kinetic, "all fire" one witness to the test exclaims.

Yet what to make of "Marilyn Monroe" seemed to puzzle both the actress and her studio. In fact, she would not legally change her name for another ten years. Publicity shots of the period 1946–48 reveal nothing about her intense desire to act or about what kinds of roles might suit her. The arbitrariness of the shots is most striking. Monroe is there to make the poses, fulfill the assignments in a makeup session, in a series of yoga-like exercises, in skimpy bathing suits, in low-cut evening gowns, in a potato sack, in a babysitting sequence, in an acting lesson, in tights, in sultry poses, night gowns and tee shirts, and playing baseball. This miscellany provides no apparent unity of image, no archetypal Monroe—although her vibrancy does make some of these ephemeral shots captivating.

Early publicity shot (c. late 1940s)

After about six months of appearances as an extra, she performed a brief bit in *Scudda Hoo! Scudda Hay!* Editing eliminated her close-ups, and she survives only in a long shot in which her face is undistinguishable. Rose Steinberg Wapner, a script assistant on several of Monroe's films, beginning with *Scudda Hoo! Scudda Hay!*, remembered a Monroe sweetly and innocently committed to dreams of stardom. "How do you become a star?" she asked Wapner, as the two of them traveled by car to a movie set. At twenty-one, this starlet did not seem anything like a stunning, provocative female personality. Instead, she was like "many girls," Wapner remarked, eager to fit herself into the proportions of stardom.

On August 25, 1947, after a year that saw little film work, Fox cancelled Monroe's contract. She continued to take acting lessons and to play a few stage roles. She did not create much of an impression in her theatrical debut at the Bliss-Hayden Miniature Theatre in Beverly Hills, where she appeared in *Glamour Preferred* from October 12 to November 2, but she was remembered for her subsequent willingness to play whatever role was assigned to her.

Monroe had not yet made friends with the kind of people who could promote and guide her career, although she would start to do so in December of 1947, when she signed a personal management contract with the husband and wife tam of John Carroll and Lucille Ryman, who would be instrumental in securing her first featured role in *The Asphalt Jungle*. To Carroll, an actor who bore a slight resemblance to Clark Gable, and to Ryman, who headed the talent department at MGM, Monroe seemed like the waif she specialized in impersonating. "We didn't think of her as a star for MGM," Ryman recalled, "not when the studio had great beauties like Greer Garson, Katharine Hepburn and Lana Turner. We signed Marilyn to keep her off the streets because she was hungry, like a little kitten looking for food."

Even as a model Monroe sometimes failed to demonstrate talent. John Engstead remembered her pose for a *Photoplay* photograph entitled "How a Star is Born." Against a background of velvet draperies "the starlet would stand in an elaborate gown with her hands outstretched with an isn't it wonderful expression." A reticent Monroe arrived promptly for her assignment, "put up her arms, smiled, and that was that." Engstead was impressed with her pretty face, but he could not account for what "transformed this sweet young thing into the superstar and sex symbol of a generation." Indeed, her "isn't it wonderful" photograph is lifeless; she looks like a mannequin, a stiff-limbed waxworks "star." Posing for this photograph was not so wonderful, her lack of focused expression implies. Aimlessness pervades the whole composition; nothing about the frozen figure sustains attention.

Monroe's earlier photographs—especially those taken by Conover and de Dienes—were probably successful because a certain degree of improvisation was encouraged, and she remained free to invent a repertoire of poses against informal settings that dispelled her anxieties. In the series with Conover she performed against the background of her working life in a factory. For de Dienes she had landscapes to which she could respond. What could she place herself against in the brief session with Engstead? Her arms are held up in this photograph, but they lack the force of a genuine uplifting gesture. Her mechanical posture may well be related to the absence of continuity in the conditions of her employment.

At this point, Monroe's first powerful mentor began to shape for her a sense of what a whole career would look like. Sometime during the end of her first year at Fox she met Joseph M. Schenck, an executive producer and one of the founders of the studio and of the star system. Schenck took an early interest in Monroe for her "offbeat personality." In *My Story*, she describes herself sitting around his fireplace listening to him talk wisely about "love and sex" as though he were a "great explorer." His visage fascinated her: "It was as much the face of a town as of a man. The whole history of Hollywood was in it." These were lean days for her, and both Schenck's food and his dinner guests fed her ambitions. She believed Schenck would secure her status at the studio, and while Fox did not keep her, Schenck persuaded Harry Cohn, head of Columbia pictures, to sign her to a contract in March of 1948. Marilyn denied the gossip that she was "Joe Schenck's girl" and that she performed sexual favors for him in return for his support of her career. She was secretive about her sex life, but several of her friends believe she used sex as a way of saying thank you to men who had helped her.

In her first months at Columbia in the spring of 1948, Monroe struggled to find herself as an actress. Natasha Lytess, an acting coach, was instructed by her boss, Max Arnow, to see what could be done. In Lytess's bitter and self-serving memoir, she recalls that her pupil "was more than inhibited, more than cramped. She couldn't say a word freely." Singlehandedly, Lytess would have readers believe, she shaped Monroe into the semblance of an actress. Lytess tried to make Monroe her protégée, even taking her into her home several years later during the making of *Clash by Night*. As a result, the actress became increasingly dependent on her coach for advice and insisted that Lytess accompany her on movie sets.

Under Lytess's supervision, Monroe would read scripts several times and underline words that ought to be emphasized. She also marked scripts to indicate character traits or questions of interpretation she wanted to discuss with Lytess. Monroe developed a sense of deliberateness that simply would not allow her to be rushed. She began to treat her own body, her own strenuously acquired sensitivity, as instruments—a point she emphasized in her last recorded interview. Finally, with Lytess, a former student of the great Max Reinhardt, a legendary director and producer of modern theater and film, Monroe could talk over the world of ideas without sounding pretentious. On movie sets male directors had been skeptical of her intellectual curiosity and ridiculed her reading of writers like Rilke and Tom Paine. But with Natasha, Marilyn could explore the Russian classics, the Stanislavsky school of acting, and, more generally, a world of European learning that World War II émigrés brought to Hollywood.

In Fred Karger, Monroe discovered a mentor and lover to whom she could devote her passion and determination to become a star and a woman of importance. Karger, a musical coach, became an exemplar of elegant style and clear performances. *My Story* describes him as a handsome man with a compelling smile. His compact physique perfectly complemented his neat and efficient handling of a song. Nothing was wasted on this immaculate figure with whom Monroe quickly fell in love. Although Karger responded warmly to Monroe, introducing her to his mother and sister and frequently taking her out, he also had reservations about her curious blend of immaturity and raw ambition. He was put off by her "embryonic" mind, which was also "inert" and barely conscious of the life around her. He hurt her, but she valued his honesty and his objective appraisals. At his urging, for example, she submitted to plastic surgery and dental work that removed the imperfections visible in the Conover and de Dienes photographs. She progressed steadily under Karger's professional supervision and gradually withdrew from his equivocal courting.

Karger had shown Monroe that she could work according to a rigorous, concentrated schedule and produce a convincing performance. Natasha Lytess might be preparing her for her future as a serious artist, but Karger had gotten Monroe ready in a very short period for her immediate assignment, second lead in *Ladies of the Chorus* (1948). This was her first sizable role, and she performed well. In *Motion Picture Herald*, Tibor Krekes noted that "one of the bright spots is Miss Monroe's singing. She is pretty and, with her pleasing voice and style, she shows prom-

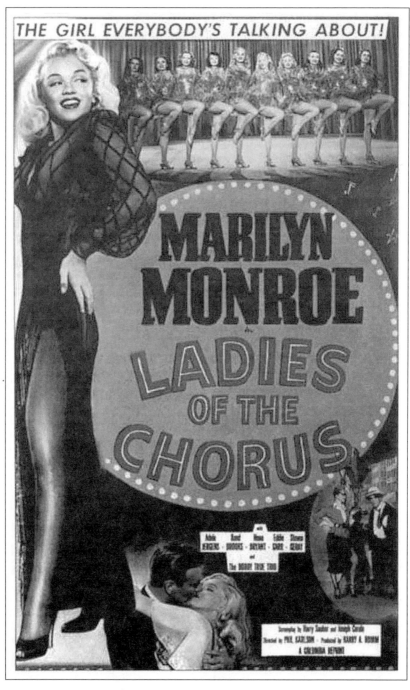

Ladies of the Chorus (1948)

ise." The movie—shot in eleven days—seems to have been designed to be forgotten, for the plot, the characters, and the songs are bland and barely credible. The movie received few reviews, and Monroe was not able to impress the studio with her performance. And indeed, Columbia terminated her contract after the first six months. This eventuality was hardly her fault, since her role had so little room for subtlety of characterization. She plays a chorus girl, Peggy, engaged to marry a wealthy young man (Rand Brooks). She is fearful that his family will reject her as soon as it learns of her lowly show business background. Her fears are happily dissolved when her fiancé's mother (Nana Bryant), convinced Peggy loves her son, pretends in front of guests at an engagement party to have a secret show business background of her own in order to ease Peggy's entrance into high society.

For Monroe, this trite movie was a manifestation of her new life. She had finally been able to follow herself across a movie screen as she had followed so many stars in her childhood. That gloomy childhood—or at least her somber sense of her early years—was lightened by the glowing sign of her success. She had managed to have an impact on the world—at least briefly—in the enlarged brightness of her own image. No wonder she repeatedly drove past the theater featuring her film, for it was like watching the announcement of her new identity—an announcement even more exciting than the fifty-foot tall skirt flying likeness of herself, an advertisement for *The Seven Year Itch*, that later appeared on the front of the State Theatre Building in New York City.

With no more than this token of success in hand, she was forced into other work after the expiration of her Columbia contract on September 8, 1948. Dress designer Jean Louis, who worked on the film, saw nothing remarkable in Monroe: "She was just a baby then." No one at Columbia pictured her potential, he told interviewer John Kobal. In late August and early September she appeared in a production of *Stage Door* at the Bliss-Hayden Theatre, and she is reported to have worked briefly as a stripper at the Mayan Theatre in downtown Los Angeles.

Now an actress unattached to a studio contract, she was able to land only very small roles in *Love Happy* and *A Ticket to Tomahawk*, both released in 1950. The latter, in which she has one song-and-dance number with Dan Dailey and a few incidental appearances with three other dance hall girls, is almost as forgettable as *Ladies of the Chorus*. But the former, a Marx Brothers production with a built-in audience, features her in an extremely brief but highly visible walk-on wearing a tight, low-cut sequined gown. Slinking into Groucho's office (he is playing a detective), she asks for his help. After he answers "What can I do for you?" she saunters directly toward the camera as in an aside he comments, "As if I didn't know." Then in mock seriousness he inquires, "What seems to be the problem?" She replies, "Well, men keep following me all the time!" The scene received extraordinary attention, which the film's producer, Lester Cowan, helped generate by putting Monroe on a cross-county publicity tour. For the first time, she had been really noticed, in a film that revealed a crucial aspect of her screen persona, a curious blend of innocence and maturity. She has a puzzled, naïve quality, so she is the perfect target for Groucho's wisecrack. But her voluptuous body, which sweeps across the screen with such aplomb, suggests that she knows the answer to her "problem." She rests her right hand on Groucho's upper chest and leans against him. Then her fingers move slowly up his shoulder in command of him. Her eyebrows are slightly arched, as she sways past the camera with lowered lids. Surely a woman who can handle herself in such a deliberately provocative manner is conscious of the power of her sexuality. Her saucy hips playfully belie her sweet voice—that is part of the joking nature of her appeal.

Of course, there was no way to know if what Monroe could project for less than a minute could be sustained for a whole film. She was still a figure, not even a face in films. With her anonymity still intact, and with a desperate need for some ready cash (fifty dollars) to make a car payment, she consented to pose for a couple of nude calendar illustrations, shot by Tom Kelley on May 27, 1949. Like her role in *Love Happy*, the two nude poses, "Golden Dreams" and "A New Wrinkle," emphasize her body, not her face, as a decorative item. Neither the movie nor the calendar photographs identify Marilyn Monroe. Indeed, it would be a few years before her calendar shots would make news. She escaped immediate recognition because she modeled as a type of figure popular on such calendars at the time. Yet, as in the case of *Love Happy*, she brought an added dimension to the type. Her pose stands out from other "girlie" pictures of that era.

Like Monroe's screen test, one of the calendar shots—in which she lies across a red velvet background—became an exercise in creating striking visual effects and a composition that has been called a work of "perfect symmetry." The overall picture is one of harmonious interplay between the model and her background. Her long blonde hair cascades across the flowing diagonal folds of red velvet drapery. Sexual tension is suggested by her right hand, thrust into her hair, and a bit of coyness in her seeming to glance back at the viewer from her twisted pose. A vivid, self-directed personality is portrayed in this photograph. Note, for example, how the model has framed her face with her right arm, tilted her head upward and to her right, opening her red lips slightly—her upper front teeth are showing—and shifted her eyes to the right. Although girlie pictures ordinarily depict passive women who expose themselves to lascivious inspection, Monroe's calendar shot seems a new wrinkle indeed, for the model is nothing if not active and in control of the sight lines in this pose.

Did Monroe intend precisely these effects? Was she conscious of compositional techniques? Her photographer, Tom Kelley, recalled that he was "convinced that she had a genius for sensing what the camera saw as she posed." She worked for two hours without any specific coaching from Kelley: "She was as graceful as an otter, turning sinuously with utter naturalness." The inhibitions Lytess had observed in the young actress "vanished as soon as her clothes were removed," Kelley remembered. In *My Story*, Monroe says the "striking [of] joyous poses" while nude reminded her of childhood dreams and momentarily saddened her, until "after a few poses" she realized how much she liked her body. As usual, the star ties up the loose ends of her life by transforming them into an integral narrative of her self's slow emergence. Yet it is also likely that Monroe's absorption of the photographic medium was having a cumulative impact upon her, so that she could begin to gather her experience together and express it coherently.

Monroe's work on *Love Happy* and the nude calendar suggests she was learning how to attract professional notice. She gained confidence from Carroll and Ryman, who were well connected to studio executives, and who also provided the affection and support Monroe craved. She may have had a brief affair with Carroll, and for a short period she lived with the couple. In their company, she also met the powerful Hollywood agent, Johnny Hyde.

Shortly after the release of *Love Happy* in March 1950, Hyde, charmed by her scene with Groucho, decided to represent her. He was the first influential professional who expressed unreserved faith in her star quality. He did not take her apart in Karger's merciless fashion, he did not follow Lytess's dictation of how an actress should carry herself, and he did not emulate Schenck's reserved counsel. Instead, he seemed to reach inside of her as he would reach inside himself for an organic understanding. Monroe notes in *My Story* that after her success in *The Asphalt Jungle*,

Hyde was beaming and acting "as if he had made good on the screen, not me." Certainly she made good as his client, his discovery, but he was also happy for her, Monroe insisted. He was a deeply kind man without any selfishness in his treatment of her because, according to Monroe, "he not only knew me, he knew Norma Jean[e] too. He knew all the pain and all the desperate things in me." Hyde's primary contribution was to get her to see herself without always relying on the evaluation of others, to have faith in her own genius. Paradoxically, she could only sense her autonomy by imagining how great his need was for her. They became lovers, but she was not in love with him. She refused several offers of marriage from the ailing agent, even though such a union would have given her financial security.

On the advice of Lucille Ryman, Hyde had convinced John Huston to test Monroe for the part of Angela in *The Asphalt Jungle* (1950). The actress secluded herself with Natasha Lytess in order to explore every facet of Angela's personality and to understand her character's relationship to the film as a whole. At the audition Monroe felt sick and had to remind herself of her years of study in preparation for her "first chance at a real acting part with a great director." She doubted that she would be any good, but Huston was kind and patient and allowed her to do her lines lying on the floor to simulate Angela lounging on a couch. As soon as the scene was finished, Monroe asked to do it again. Huston said that was not necessary—he had already decided to give her the part—but he allowed her to do so anyway.

This version of Monroe's breakthrough moment has been disputed. Only in retrospect, reports Donald Spoto, did Huston accord himself the distinction of spotting Marilyn's genius. In fact, he had another actress in mind: Lola Albright, sultry, stylish, beautiful, and Kirk Douglas's co-star in *Champion* (1949). Lucille Ryman goes even further, rejecting Huston's story altogether, insisting that Hyde had not been able to persuade Huston to test Monroe. Ryman and her husband, she continued, confronted the director, who owed the couple a considerable sum for training and housing his horses. Carroll told Huston, who loved horses as much as he loved to spend money, that Huston's debt would be cancelled in exchange for testing Monroe. "Otherwise, I'll have to sell your horses," Carroll told him. "Well, Huston blew up," Ryman recalled. "He said, 'She gets to everybody, doesn't she?'"

The tactic worked, but Monroe was one of seven actresses auditioned for the part. The next day Monroe told Ryman that the audition had been "wonderful. I was good. I was awfully good." Did the director say so? Ryman asked. No, Marilyn admitted, but instead of making her repeat the scene several times, as he had done with the other actresses, he simply said her work was "fine." She did not realize that Huston's thank you was a "brush-off," Ryman said. "Marilyn was so naïve." Ryman then gave her version of what really happened:

> I called Cotton Wharburton, an editor at MGM, and I asked him if I could see the tests the next day before Huston saw them, even though the director is supposed to see the tests before anyone else. I called Mr. Mayer and got him out of a meeting. I told him it was urgent. I said, "I want you to look at this film that just came up, the tests for the part of Angela we've had so much trouble casting." As he watched all the girls, he pointed to the screen and said, "There's the girl." It was Marilyn.

Did Ryman ever tell Monroe this story? Ryman did not say. It is not likely that Huston ever revealed how Monroe obtained the part, for after all she did it well, and Huston had no reason for regret. However, his comment, "She gets to everybody, doesn't she?" is tantalizing. He seemed to be alluding to a power—a kind of political savvy—Monroe employed, which made people want to help her. And perhaps Huston felt a certain frustration at being defeated by such a low-ranked actress. Was Marilyn so naïve after all? And hadn't Ryman and Carroll, too, been taken in by the waif?

Whatever the case, Monroe believed that Huston was sensitive to her requirements—she praised him for that. It was typical of her to ask for a retake of the scene, and her need for retakes would grow as her roles in films expanded. She kept pushing herself long after her directors and fellow actors were satisfied. The retakes had to do with her perfectionism, which was linked with her dread of incompleteness, of leaving a role unfinished. She had thought of herself as having been born a second time through her Hollywood career. That second birth had to be better; each role had to be in some way an advance over the previous one—an impossible demand to realize in Hollywood.

Huston had a sense of the entirety of a production that in Monroe's experience most directors lacked. To her, other directors seemed more concerned with photographing the scenery than the actors. Superb shots and set-ups, framing techniques and editing, were their major interests.

They wanted to please the front office, whereas Huston worked for his actors and seemed, indeed, a part of their acting. Even though she had a small role, he treated her like an important performer. Monroe shared with her fellow actors many complaints against directors. Huston was unusual because he showed her that everything an actor feels—including a bad case of nerves—contributes to the energy of a scene. She needed to know the whole script, not just her lines, he insisted. For "acting was also reacting—listening to other actors, losing herself." Each piece of advice had its incremental effect, until she could see how all of it was integrated into a systematic approach to the art of film. He had objectified a process of creation for her that had been previously narrowed by her nervous preoccupation with herself, or by the constricted concerns of less talented professionals.

Monroe found the role of Angela in *The Asphalt Jungle* deeply satisfying. Although she had only a few lines and two scenes, her character was indispensable to both the plot and the themes of the film. As in the famous calendar pose, the first shot of Angela shows her sleeping in "the twisted posture" which emphasizes her enticing figure and her attention to her body, "one hand entangled in her hair." She is in a position of extreme passivity and is startled by the staring face of the attorney, Emmerich (Louis Calhern), who has been her lover, but who now manifests what is to her a "puzzling mixture of desire and contempt." In her sybaritic waiting upon him she represents a significant aspect of the corrupt lifestyle he has grown to deplore, but from which he cannot seem to extricate himself. She is one of his collectibles, an extravagant example of what he calls his "absurd" lifestyle.

Angela will lie for him and provide an alibi to cover his involvement in a jewel robbery only so long as she is under his direction, but when he fails to supply her with her cues she is uncertain, meek, scared, and finally devastated by harsh police interrogation. When Emmerich bids her to tell the truth, she quickly offers the last bit of evidence that will convict her lover. She has her moment of anguish when she says, "I . . . I tried . . . I'm sorry, Uncle Lon." He expected her to acquiesce to whomever controls the situation, and so he replies, "You did pretty well—considering." Considering what? Considering that she did lie for him, that she was loyal to him for at least a few moments under intense police pressure? She did pretty well considering the kind of amoral, conniving creature she is? Such questions seem appropriate, given that she immediately asks him if she will still be able to go on the trip he has promised her. She knows he

The Asphalt Jungle (1950)

will be going to jail, but she thinks only of herself. His answer, "(shaking his head) 'Some sweet kid,'" ironically exposes just how self-preoccupied she is in pursuit of her happiness. She lowers her eyes and moves away to dictate her statement to the police. Is she disappointed, or is she aware that she has asked an inappropriate question? She is easily cowed by circumstances and willing to shift with the momentum of the scene.

The role of Angela deserved the keen concentration Monroe gave it because it was meant to suggest one of four choices made by women in an asphalt jungle dominated by hard, brutal, and greedy men. Emmerich's wife (Dorothy Tree) seeks refuge in invalidism. She hopes that she will be able to ensure her husband's affection and keep him in the home. Emmerich simply installs Angela in another "home." Doll Conovan (Jean Hagen), in love with stick-up man Dix Handley (Sterling Hayden), tries to keep her man by observing strict loyalty to masculine codes of toughness, which means she refrains from overt displays of affection and from openly confessing her need for Handley lest he regard her as an obligation. He softens under her tactful care, and she discovers why he has adopted such a mean exterior. Maria Ciavelli (Teresa Celli) is the faithful housewife and mother who knows nothing about her husband's job (he is expert at cracking safes) and is bewildered by his sudden death in the jewel robbery, since she has been so cut off from the realities of his life.

As the most beautiful of these women, Angela has room in which to maneuver and to manipulate men, but she is also undermined by her own youthful stupidity, which makes it difficult for others to take her seriously. As a very young woman she has not yet learned how far her scheming can take her. She does not size up situations well and, as a result, she can appear to be ridiculous, as in her response to the policeman who knocks on her locked door: "Haven't you bothered me enough you big banana head?" In such a role Monroe had to portray an unusual variety of emotions. Her character is shallow, but Angela's behavior is devious enough to allow for a full play of gestures and facial expressions. If she was acting a type, the kept woman, Monroe nevertheless was interpreting lines and script directions that gave her the opportunity to fashion a whole person. Angela had to be passive, seductive, innocent, solicitous, puzzled, vulgar, scared, angry, stupid, nearly hysterical, anguished, and calculating in just two brief scenes. There was plenty of room for mistakes, for missing the transitions from one emotion to another, but Monroe was flawless in her fulfillment of the script's demands.

In *The Asphalt Jungle*, Monroe gave her first thoroughgoing performance, one that would finally lead to significant roles. Hadn't she shown an impressive authority as an actress, an especially important matter for one who struggled so grimly to be creative? Joseph Mankiewicz, impressed with her work, took Johnny Hyde's advice and cast her as Miss Caswell in *All About Eve*. Monroe welcomed another chance to work with a fine director. This small but conspicuous part presented her with the opportunity to make a vivid impression in a film sure to receive wide distribution and publicity.

The role of Miss Caswell solidified Monroe's dumb blonde stereotyping. The variation on the type, in this case, is Miss Caswell's absence of innocence. She is hard, ambitious, and corrupt, in spite of her youthful beauty. She is less dependent on men for her cues than Angela is, although she is just as ignorant. When she fails to get a part in a stage production, she asks whether they have auditions for television. Rather than cultivating her own talent, she entertains important producers whom she hopes will help her acting career. Her understanding of success is couched in crass materialism. Seeing a fur coat she admires, she says, "Now there's something a girl could make sacrifices for." Although the character is vulgar, Monroe plays her in a fairly restrained manner, with no awkward gesturing, no obvious attempt to render Miss Caswell's lack of subtlety in visual terms. Yet Monroe shows Caswell—in her first appearance in the film—always on the verge of smirking, suggesting the wanton attitude just behind her soft, beautifully displayed figure. In other words, Monroe employs a sensitive tactfulness in portraying a tactless character. The point of such restraint is to prepare for the right dramatic moment, when Miss Caswell's predatory sexuality can emerge in its most appropriate form. Monroe saves Caswell's exaggerated use of sexual innuendo for a brief scene with a producer, in which she drops her eyelids, smiles provocatively—her lips almost pucker—and delivers a heavily suggestive thank you while lowering her voice.

Monroe's three brief appearances in this film amounted to something less than she was given to work with in *The Asphalt Jungle*, and Miss Caswell's range of emotions is constricted compared with Angela's. So it is difficult to say what a shrewd professional observer might have been able to make of Monroe's performance in November 1950 when *All About Eve* was released. Monroe wisely took Natasha Lytess's advice to understate the character's mannerisms. Her coach exhorted her "not to act," so as not to destroy the credibility of Caswell's simple insights into people. As Fred Guiles suggests, one of the best lines in the script is Caswell's perceptive description of a producer (Gregory Ratoff) she is encouraged to cultivate: "Why do they always look like unhappy rabbits?" It is very easy to laugh at this blonde, and it would have been easy for Monroe to turn the character into a kind of cartoon. Instead, she endowed Caswell with a complete personality, and in doing so she contributed to our understanding of Eve, the main character in the film.

Eve (Anne Baxter) is a sophisticated, truly successful version of Miss Caswell. Eve wants to become a star in the theater, and she does so by ingratiating herself into the lives of the most important theater people. She is adept at dissembling, at making herself indispensable to others. She is always careful to prepare for her exploitation of others, and for the sexual advances she hopes will help secure her success. She is able to fool nearly everyone, and she achieves her career goals, for she has assumed the role of acolyte to the famous actress Margo Channing (Bette Davis), telling Channing that acting has made up her life. Margo misses the irony of the statement. Not only does Eve mean she has become obsessed with the stage and with following its stars, she also means that she is acting, making herself into a kind of character who will trample the lives of those who help her. Everything Eve does is an act; she is nothing as a person,

All About Eve (1950)

everything as an actress. She plays the role of Margo's secretary, so she can grasp the role of the star, later insinuating herself into the role of Margo's understudy and then seeing to it that Margo misses one of her performances. It is essential that Miss Caswell also audition for the understudy role, to show that only Eve's shrewd kind of "acting" can prevail. Miss Caswell lacks Eve's insight into the necessity for ubiquitous acting.

In many ways this film about the actor's personality had great relevance for Monroe's life and career. Many people in Hollywood already equated her with Angela and then with Miss Caswell. She was given credit for skillfully playing parts according to her type, not for imaginatively exploring a type according to her talent. As in *The Asphalt Jungle*, she was featured as a blonde siren who could not possibly perform any of the other female roles.

It would seem to be an elementary observation that an actor who performs a part well need not be just like the part she or he plays, and yet particularly in the case of film the person and the role often become interchangeable for both the audience and for film professionals. Various aspects of Angela and Caswell seemed similar to aspects of Monroe.

Both characters were under the protection of older men, just as Schenck and Hyde had protected Monroe. Monroe, like Miss Caswell, was viewed by some as a schemer. Nunnally Johnson, who would later write parts for Monroe, saw her as one of the "eager young hustlers" of Hollywood. She was "Johnny Hyde's girl," not worth talking about outside Hyde's presence. Natasha Lytess, speaking in rancor after Monroe rejected her, claims in her memoirs that her pupil found Hyde an "expedient" tool in her rise to stardom. Monroe acknowledged this questioning of her motivations in *My Story* when she complained that no matter how truthfully she spoke or how honestly she behaved, most men and women "believed I was trying to fool them."

On others, Monroe made little impression. Celeste Holm, one of the stars of *All About Eve*, recalls that she "saw nothing special about [Monroe's] Betty Boop quality. I thought she was quite sweet and terribly dumb, and my natural reaction was 'whose girl is that?'" On a visit to the home of Dana Andrews, then one of Hollywood's leading men, Monroe, in the company of agent Charles Feldman, showed no star power at all. At the time, Andrews found her indistinguishable from the other Hollywood hopefuls he met. Later, he expressed bafflement that he detected nothing at all in her manner that presaged her fame.

Two reporters for *Life* and *Look*, Stanley Flink and Rupert Allan, witnessed other sides of Monroe that reflected a young woman making the transition from obscurity to stardom, a transition that inevitably provoked conflicting responses in the subject and in her observers. Flink's memories of late 1949 or early 1950, when he first met Monroe, center on how she seemed to be caught "in the swirl" of Hollywood glamour and publicity. She was not absolutely sure she wanted to be an actress, but the possibilities of such a career dazzled her and seemed better than anything else she could imagine. She was quite willing to take direction; indeed, he remembers a highly nervous young woman who seemed, whenever he visited her movie sets, quite dependent on her directors. Her peculiar combination of innocence and ambition charmed Flink much more than her appearance, which he found "pleasant but not startlingly pretty."

Rupert Allan, a soft-spoken, Oxford-educated American, was immediately impressed with the actress's stunning beauty and dedication to her craft, as well as to her physical fitness program. She lifted weights, a very unusual activity for a woman then. But as Lois Banner reports, on Catalina Monroe "became friends with Howard Corrington, a former Olympic weightlifting champion who was in her husband's unit, and she studied weight lifting with him." Allan worked hard to prevent *Look* from turning his article about her into the typical celebrity piece. Instead, he wanted to impress readers with her intelligence and wit. He had no doubts about the great career she was about to begin, and he looked forward to the fulfillment of the youthful promise he detected in early 1950. In a few years he would work for her as a press representative. They remained close friends for the rest of her life.

Allan provides the best evidence of a complex performer learning how to inhabit many roles—including her assumption of injured innocence—behind which (as Lytess claims in her memoir) Monroe hid a hardened shrewdness and guile: "It was always like that. When you disagreed with her she was like a little flower in the grass, a poor thing whom no one loved. At the smallest suggestion she might be wrong, she could make you feel guilty." Lytess might as well be describing the clear-eyed sharpness of Miss Caswell that is so strikingly different from the soft, droopy-eyed vagueness of some of Monroe's later roles. The tableau shot from *All About Eve* that is often reproduced shows Caswell's vivid focus on Eve as Eve aggressively focuses on the critic Addison DeWitt. This was a tough, competitive period for Monroe, as she implies in her description in *My Story* of Hollywood parties she would attend for purposes of self-advertising. Such behavior clearly labeled her a young woman on the make. She was much more than that, however, judging by Lytess's intriguing description of Monroe's behavior: "Whenever she explained something her right hand darted forward, weaving to the left and right like a serpent. It was a gesture of evasiveness and survival through expediency." Certainly Lytess's favorite epithet, "a veiled woman," evokes a Monroe far more secretive and devious than Angela or Miss Caswell could ever hope to be.

Films fused Monroe to her personae and standardized responses to her. In the theater, it might have been somewhat different for her because of the distance between the actor and the audience. The actor can increase or decrease that distance, accentuating or diminishing certain features and gestures according to the demands of the role. In film, the camera moves in and away from and around the person of the actor, creating a personality that somehow survives and transcends individual roles, and audiences gather to see how different roles reflect the same film personality. This is basically a tautological process, in the sense that films perform like mirrors throwing back to audiences images of stars that have already been reflected in other films, mirrors. On stage there is no screen—even a stage star does not have to contend with replications deposited, so to speak, onto strips of celluloid. It is easier for the stage actor to outlive earlier roles, since it is merely memories of past performances with which she must contend. Memories are also mirrors, of course, but memories fade and change; celluloid strips, on the other hand, continually refresh reflection. In the images of her face, her figure, her voice, it was easy for Monroe to confirm the impressions of those directors who typed her as a dumb blonde. In other words, they were able to fill in their visions of what a dumb blonde was like by elaborating on those aspects of her that resembled the type. They missed the whole person—or perhaps it is more accurate to say that they were not looking for one. George Sanders recalled that Monroe's conversation had "unexpected depths. She showed an interest in intellectual subjects which was, to say the least, disconcerting."

Although so much attention has been devoted to the resemblances between Monroe and the parts she played, no one has noticed that she experienced the kind of psychological pattern that would prepare her to play Eve's role. Like Eve Harrington, Marilyn Monroe desperately wanted to be a star, and she was willing to sacrifice most of her personal life to attain her goal. She had relatively few friendships other than with those people who were in positions to support her career. She moved in with people who helped her and became intimately involved in their lives, just as Eve moved in with Margo Channing and began to run her life. Monroe appeared to be "kind and soft and helpless. Almost everybody on meeting her wanted to help her. Marilyn's helplessness was her greatest strength," asserts Sidney Skolsky, her Hollywood columnist confidant. Similarly, Eve appears to be a naïve and tender young girl who appeals to the hard-boiled, cynical theater crowd.

Monroe may also have been like Eve in her ability to deceive herself, so that she would not have to admit that she had occasionally deceived others. As Lytess observed in her memoirs, "She cannot face herself, she keeps her back to herself." Certainly Monroe was like Eve in her fanatical belief that only through acting could she be a success, somebody deserving of respect. After recounting several instances of Monroe's thoughtless cruelty, Lytess reports telling her, "You knew how ill I was and you never called . . . . I want to love you, but you make it difficult." Monroe replied, "You don't have to love me, Natasha, as long as you will work with me." This brutal refusal to deal with her coach's feelings of betrayal reveals just how far Monroe's monomania may have taken her toward

Eve's ambitions. She may also have found it necessary to harshly separate her personal and professional feelings regarding Lytess because of the latter's all-consuming interest in her life.

Lytess never seems to have considered that Monroe had to protect herself from a mentor who tried to supervise every aspect of her life. How Monroe evaluated the sincerity of the role she played in relation to Lytess is impossible to determine. *All About Eve* makes this point when its characters accuse one another of playing scenes rather than expressing sincere emotions. To complicate matters further, actors may believe in the characters they create, just as some famous figures—including Monroe—have been suspected of believing their own publicity. Fiction that is intensely conceived, in other words, can replace fact. As Mailer puts it, "[T]he most mysterious property of a factoid [a fiction that masquerades or functions as a fact] is that it is believed by the people who put together the factoid printed next to it."

Perhaps Monroe's work on *All About Eve* made her especially conscious of Addison DeWitt's notion that actors are not like "normal human beings," for they are particularly likely to believe their own fantasies. She may well have thought of herself as belonging to a separate category of human beings. Skolsky points out that Monroe often quoted her own version of DeWitt's remarks: "Once in a while somebody writes an article saying that actors and actresses are just like other people. We're not. It's because we're not that we're actors and actresses." DeWitt's view of the actor's abnormality leads him to conclude that all "theatrical folk" are "the original displaced personalities." Certainly Monroe's own version of her life stressed her displacement, her alienation from the conventions of ordinary life. Acting was a form of compensation for her many deprivations, and the warm response of an audience—which Monroe experienced for the first time in a movie theater showing *The Asphalt Jungle*—replenished her identity. It is easy to imagine Monroe fervently delivering Eve's statement of commitment to acting: "I've listened, from backstage, to people applaud. It's like—like waves of love coming over the footlights and wrapping you up. Imagine . . . to know, every night, that different hundreds of people love you . . . they smile, their eyes shine— you've pleased them, they want you, you belong. Just that alone is worth anything . . . ."

Monroe consulted Sidney Skolsky, just as Eve consulted DeWitt. Monroe even used to leave messages for him signed "Miss Caswell." With Skolsky acting as the crucial manager of her early publicity, she was able to model herself into a strikingly sympathetic and attractive personality who could compel the adoration of audiences in just the way Eve describes. In retrospect, at least, Skolsky insisted on the deliberateness of Monroe's self-creation. She "knew how to sell herself" and had an immediate, intuitive grasp of "the value of publicity." She refined stories about herself that proved colorful, carefully embellishing them to provoke "even more publicity." Skolsky never knew what to believe about "the story of her bleak childhood," but he concluded she was "not quite the poor waif she later claimed to have been." She kept increasing the number of her foster homes, "because she knew it was a good selling point." She had doubts about her identity, but not about how she should portray her biography. It should play like a good movie Similarly, she was remarkably astute about her movies, and she knew far better than the studio executives what a successful Marilyn Monroe movie ought to contain, Skolsky concluded.

Without a definitive sense of herself Monroe was free to engage in endless variations on her biography. Whether she was calculating or relatively unconscious about her fictionalizing, or cynically performing what was expected of her, is difficult to determine. Surely at one time or another she engaged in all of these different behavioral possibilities perhaps mixing them together in ways that cannot be distinguished. It may have become as difficult for her as it was for others to know when she was just being herself.

It is impossible to describe confidently the state at which Monroe had arrived in the evolution of herself and her career in 1950. Norma Jeane, Angela, Miss Caswell, and Marilyn Monroe are some of the shifting phases of her identity. But she (what name is appropriate for her at this point?) cannot be associated too closely with any of these phases. She is not as young as the Angela she played so well. Unlike Miss Caswell, she passes her audition and is praised for her talent. Marilyn Monroe, the star and the mythic figure, had not yet emerged, and Norma Jeane never really had the opportunity to develop as an adult. Clearly, Monroe was tentative about herself and elusive with others. Joseph Mankiewicz remembered her as a solitary actress carrying around an edition of Rilke's *Letters to a Young Poet*. She seemed unsure of herself and in social gatherings of the cast after the filming of *All About Eve*, although she was pleased to be invited to join them, "somehow she never understood or accepted our unspoken assumption that she was one of us. She remained alone. She was not a loner. She was just plain alone."

Monroe put her whole trust in only one person: Johnny Hyde. Although she had lost her first contract with Fox, he was able (on the strength of her performances in *The Asphalt Jungle* and *All About Eve*, plus very small roles in *The Fireball* and *Right Cross*) to get her another Fox screen test with the actor Richard Conte in early December. On December 10, she signed a seven-year agreement with the studio. In the minds of Joseph Mankiewicz and others, Hyde was responsible for whatever self-esteem and professional confidence Monroe could muster.

Troubled by a weak heart for years, Hyde finally succumbed to his ailment on December 20, just ten days after ensuring his client's professional future. Monroe went to pieces and, according to Lytess, tried to kill herself with a pill overdose. Joseph Mankiewicz thought that Monroe never fully recovered from Hyde's death and, in fact, "gave up on herself." Hyde's son remembers her at his father's funeral, where she was overcome with grief, throwing herself on the coffin. She shook everyone, screaming Hyde's name over and over again. Monroe grieved for him as if for herself.

Grief did not prevent Monroe from doing her work, although on the set of her next film, *As Young as You Feel*, she would weep and disappear from the set, according to her director, Harmon Jones. Just two weeks after Hyde's death, Elia Kazan's visit bolstered her. This Group Theatre veteran of the 1930s, an acclaimed film and theater director of the 1940s, liked her unpretentious wit, her reliance on his advice, and her sexual attention. In *Fragments*, Monroe gives just a glimpse of what Kazan meant to her: He was a sounding board and comforter, holding her once through a long night of terror, a not infrequent experience for a woman whose insecurities stimulated men to want to embrace and protect her.

Kazan wanted to introduce Monroe to his friend, Arthur Miller, whose work Kazan had directed on the stage. Kazan had brought the playwright to Hollywood to work on an original screenplay they hoped would be produced. Later that same week, Miller and Monroe met at a party given by Charles Feldman, an important Hollywood agent and producer. Monroe and Miller became involved in an intense conversation about their lives and literature. Although there were relatively few contacts between them until she moved to New York City nearly six years later, it was already clear to Natasha Lytess that Monroe began almost immediately to console herself with the idea of someday joining with this celebrated playwright in establishing the career and identity that Johnny Hyde had promised her.

In *Timebends*, Miller reveals that Monroe's hopes were not misplaced. In fact, her impact was overpowering. She represented to him a seductive free spirit and imagination itself. She was capable of living in the moment with a joy he had never encountered. Just before their departure, they visited a bookshop where she picked up a volume of e. e. cummings's poetry and amused herself with his celebrated poem, "in Just-," which celebrates the "puddle-wonderful" world of spring. Monroe walked out of the bookstore, practically singing the poem's refrain, "and / it's spring." Miller fled Hollywood, realizing not doing so would result in his being drawn into Monroe's irresistible orbit at a time when he still yearned to rejuvenate his moribund marriage.

Miller's testimony is the best evidence of how magnetic Monroe had become, even before her first starring roles. Miller, not one of the jaded Hollywood crowd, thought better of her than she thought of herself. He did not make a pass at her. She took this restraint as a sign of respect. But he admitted in his memoirs that a mixture of fear and moral misgivings prevented him from acting on his desires. Nevertheless, she was for him, as she would become for millions of men, fantasy made flesh. And Miller, no match for the power of this fantasy, faded away, no more equipped to deal with this eruption in his middle class life than Richard Sherman is when he meets "The Girl," the very embodiment of his desire, in *The Seven Year Itch*.

CHAPTER FOUR

Becoming a Star (1950-52)

*And I want to say that the people—
if I am a star—they made me a star—no studio,
no person, but the people did.*

On January 1, 1951, Marilyn Monroe made her first appearance on the cover of *Life* magazine. Throughout the next two years her popularity grew steadily, yet she was given parts that were usually brief and undistinguished versions of what her studio biography called "the blowtorch blonde." Stories about her in *Life, Look, Colliers*, the *American Weekly, Photoplay*, and *Modern Screen* noted her serious pursuit of acting, but the career Hyde had carefully charted seemed about to lose its direction because of her studio's lack of imagination. To Robert Cahn in *Collier's* she appeared to be "the standard Hollywood blonde" with a "vague smile that seems to include everybody." *Life* wondered if she could really achieve "the universal sex appeal of Jean Harlow." Monroe was not taken seriously, perhaps because her photographs and films appeared to be self-contained. They did not put the question—who am I?—that Monroe herself wanted to address. Instead of showing her as the half-finished, fragmented personality she said she was, the photographs often portrayed her in a partially aroused state that stimulated the viewer imaginatively to elaborate on her erotic provocations.

A typical publicity pose displays her with half-closed eyes and half-open mouth, for neither seeing nor speaking—her potential intellectual attributes and capacities—are meant to form part of her appeal. Parts of her body—the darkened lips, the long black eyelashes, the smoothly shaped and elongated eyebrows—are heavily outlined, and other parts, her neck and torso, are ringed with jewelry and clothing that accentuate the roundedness and fullness of her figure. The luminous makeup, the lustrous jewelry, the self-encompassing use of her hands, and the bent–forward attitude of her head and upper body fashion a fully equipped and seductive self-image that contradicts the cryptic off-camera self Monroe was trying to fathom and to define.

Photographs and films projected a dazzling array of Marilyns, an enormously passionate display of a person who wanted to believe that she was a remarkable individual, who wanted to see and hear how she looked and sounded to others. But her replications were, in a sense, all pretense; she was producing shadows of selves and not living out her life in her own way—unless she was willing to have "her own way" dictated by the studio. Like many creative persons, she wanted to reinvent herself, to give birth to herself in her own image. If Kennedy Fraser is right that "women get accustomed to chopped-up images—eyes, nose, and mouth in a powder compact; the back of the head in the hand mirror; the feet and ankles in the sloping glass at the shoe store," then imagine how Monroe became accustomed to polishing parts of her reflected image, so that she was deflected from the deeper sense of self she claimed to be seeking. It was not enough for her to recognize herself in her mirrored image, she said—although this is literally one of the few forms of self-recognition she was allowed in most of the films she worked on from 1950 to 1952.

In *Right Cross* and *The Fireball* (released in October and November 1950, respectively) she plays sexy blondes in roles that gave her no opportunity to develop complete characterizations. Her sexy blonde secretary role in *Hometown Story* (May 1951) is no better, and it is not until her performance in *As Young as You Feel* (June 1951) that she made an impression on the critics. She is a secretary to a corporate executive (Albert Dekker), and as usual her sexual appeal is emphasized. The camera holds on her wiggling walk down a hallway, she takes shorthand in a low-cut dress, and she is prominently featured as a kind of decoration in her boss's office. She's given just a little more to work with in this role, and she is on screen long enough to suggest an alert attentiveness which is quite different from the attitudes of the giddy blondes of some of her later films. Her lines are almost all brief, monosyllabic replies to her boss, yet there is a scene in which she is pictured as very deliberately attending to herself—looking into two mirrors, smoothing her face and dress, arranging her hair, and sticking out her tongue—offering the first direct view of the self-involved figure who emerges in later films. "It is my business to be sexy, that's the way I define myself," Monroe seems to be saying.

Love Nest immediately followed *As Young as You Feel* in October 1951, and it makes clever use of her developing screen persona as a woman with such formidable sexual appeal to men that she belongs in a category all her own. Monroe plays an ex-WAC, Roberta Stevens, the friend of Jim Scott (William Lundigan), a veteran recently returned home to his wife, Connie (June Haver), who has just purchased a building in New York City as a means of supplementing their income. With her first appearance Monroe's character is set up as the kind of provocative female that other women suspect. Connie eyes Roberta suspiciously, even though Roberta behaves quite properly and dresses formally in a business suit and veil. When Jim comes out to meet his old friend—he has offered to rent her a room—he is somewhat ruffled by his wife's insinuations and perhaps overwhelmed by the impact Roberta has made before she even enters his home. He trips over himself as he follows her up the steps. Monroe plays Roberta as a confident, outgoing model, who is mildly amused by Jim's friend, Ed (Jack Paar), who makes enthusiastic passes at her. She laughs at him tolerantly, just as "The Girl" Monroe plays in *The Seven Year Itch* good-naturedly accepts her male companion's sexual gambits. In both cases, Monroe's characters imply a certain degree of sexual knowledge that is never revealed. The quick shots or scenes in which Monroe appears throughout the rest of *Love Nest* excite curiosity about her and convey a personality that never gets fully expressed on the screen in brief glimpses of her in a bathing suit, taking off her nylons, undressing to reveal a silky slip and lacy bra, and wrapped in a towel getting into the shower, then coming out in a bathrobe, smiling seductively at Jim.

June Haver's recollections of working on *Love Nest* provide a fascinating insight into how Monroe regarded herself in the first stages of her stardom. More importantly, Haver touches on the sources of Monroe's universal appeal: her vulnerability, her quick and confident response to an appreciative audience, and her way of eliciting an elemental reaction in others who enjoyed just watching her effortless movements. Monroe was a shy and nervous actress, and she seemed very young and pretty to Haver. She had an "electric something," especially noticeable in a scene "where she was supposed to be sunning in the back yard of the apartment house we all lived in." The entire crew seemed stunned by Monroe's appearance in a bathing suit and stared silently as she walked across the set. Work stopped. Haver had never seen a film crew so impressed, and she marveled at their attention to Monroe, since they were used to seeing actresses in "brief costumes" in musicals and beach scenes. There might be some playful flirtation with actresses, but never this kind of complete devotion. Haver could tell that Monroe loved their reaction, and "in her shy way, she smiled."

Having an audience gave Monroe confidence and made it easier for her to deliver dialogue that was always difficult to get out—just "on the first word or two," Haver observes. Not only did Monroe have to overcome a stammer that dated back to childhood and adolescence, when she could not bring herself to audition for school plays, she believed her hesitations on movie sets would make people "think I'm no good," as she wrote in a note to herself. She dreaded ridicule, especially outright laughter that would belittle her. The very thought of such rejection made her depressed and angry. Her only antidote to such troubling thoughts was to think of the times when she had performed well and of "moments that were excellent."

When Monroe relaxed and warmed up, she "suddenly seemed to be another person," as if she had gone through "a complete metamorphosis; she became completely uninhibited in her movements, the way she sat in that chair—so gracefully, naturally graceful—and seductive at the same time. Suddenly, she seemed to shine like the sun," Haver concludes. But this "naturally graceful" actress worked hard at seeming spontaneous and unself-conscious, writing in her notebook, in separate lines, this mantra:

no attitude
listening to the body for
the feeling
listen with the eyes

Haver's tender reminiscence is similar to what other women felt on the set of *Love Nest*, and it suggests that Monroe could charm both sexes—in spite of all that has been written about her appeal to men. In such moments she attained the goal for which she and Natasha Lytess had striven: "freedom of self."

Movie sets were difficult places for Monroe to practice self-expression, for making movies is often a dull, repetitive, and frustrating business. Scenes are shot over and over again, with checks for lighting, makeup, sound, changes in script, various camera adjustments, and so on. An actress wonders exactly when the crew will really be prepared, when she should give all of her effort to a scene. Filmmaking is guided by rhythms of mechanization, of industry, not by actors' rhythms. Since movies are rarely shot in sequence, there are few opportunities to build toward climaxes that are rehearsed in stage plays.

In spite of these obstacles, Monroe continued to give energetic, humorous, and fully committed performances in forgettable films. For example, in *Let's Make It Legal* (November 1951) her physical appeal—"she is a 'beautiful blonde' who trades on her looks to get what she wants"—is gratuitously used at the beginning, middle, and end of the movie. In 1951 and 1952 she compelled the attention of audiences by honestly playing every bit part as if it really mattered—as it probably did to her, since making movies had become the objective of her life. Such an extraordinary expenditure of creative energy on insignificant roles may very well have damaged her, in the sense that she became less and less able to cope with the fragmentations of herself filmmaking fostered. What was left of Marilyn Monroe once her screen selves were discounted? Very little. She felt "terribly dumb" about many of the things people discussed: painting, music, books, history, geography, sports, and politics. She decided to go to school and enrolled in extension courses at the University of California, Los Angeles. She studied Renaissance art and literature and Freud and other psychologists, and though she did not pursue a degree, she learned enough to see just how superficial her studio upbringing had been. In her class notes, she commented on the politics of art, the way a pope could fund certain kinds of art, and the controlling role of the Medicis. Artists then, as in her own time, struggled with patrons and employers. She also read Machiavelli, who could only have reinforced her determination to be as calculating as the Hollywood princes she worked for.

Through a friend, Jack Palance, Monroe made contact in the fall of 1951 with Michael Chekhov who, along with Lee Strasberg, should be regarded as the major influence on her mature acting style. Palance had suffered from his own inadequacies as an actor and from a cadaverous appearance, and so Monroe, worried over her own professional weaknesses and physical typing, seems to have been prepared to listen carefully to his confident recommendation of Chekhov's acting class. Monroe revered her acting teacher, a descendant of the playwright Anton Chekhov. She called him Russia's "best actor" and a "brilliant man." He was "selfless and saint-like and witty, too," and a heroic figure to be compared with her beloved Abraham Lincoln. In several Hollywood movies he established himself as a premier character actor, and then he retired to write, to garden, and to teach. From him she "learned more than acting. I learned psychology, history and the good manners of art—taste."

Working with Chekhov gave her a sense of tradition; she felt like a carefully chosen and honored disciple. His virtuosity, particularly his ability to play a range of roles, naturally appealed to an actress whose work had been so depressingly limited. Doing a scene with him "was more exciting" than acting on movie sets, for acting became for the first time an art that belonged to the actor, not to the director or producer. Chekhov had an extremely powerful idea of the actor as a disciplined interpreter of life, rather than as an imitator. He encouraged the same blending of intellectual and esthetic interests Monroe had been trying to achieve on her own. His book asks the actor to imagine himself into the psychology of persons from other periods of history and from different nations, and of persons around him toward whom he feels unsympathetic. Chekhov adopts both an esthetic and a moral stance toward acting when he speaks of making the body "sensitive, noble, and flexible."

As Monroe continued to chafe against an inflexible studio system, she was laboring at a set of exercises designed by Chekhov to produce sensations of "freedom" and "increased life." She learned a very concrete way to "open" and "close" the self. After a preliminary series of "wide, broad but simple movements, using a maximum of space," so that the whole body was involved and utilized, there followed an enactment of what might be called Chekhov's organic enrichment of the actor's sensations:

Open yourself completely, spreading wide your arms, hands, your legs far apart. Remain in this expanded position for a few seconds. Imagine that you are becoming larger and larger. Come back to the original position. Repeat the same movement several times. Keep in mind the aim of the exercise, saying to yourself, "I am going to awaken the sleeping muscles of my body; I am going to revivify and use them." Now close yourself by crossing your arms upon your chest, putting your hands on your shoulders. Kneel on one or both knees, bending your head low. Imagine that you are becoming smaller and smaller, curling up, contracting as though you wanted to disappear bodily within yourself, and that the space around you is shrinking. Another set of your muscles will be awakened by this contracting movement.

As part of the same exercise, the actor is to resume a standing position and then employ various thrusting, stretching, throwing, lifting, holding, dragging, pushing, and tossing movements—all of them intended to help him know his body and its capabilities. Command of the space in which the actor works is a way of exerting control over environment. Gradually—as her film roles from *Don't Bother to Knock* to *The Misfits* demonstrate—Monroe would find ways to inhabit more fully the frames of her films and go beyond her early intuitions about proper positioning in the frame.

In Chekhov's view, the actor is a sculptor, a shaper and molder of movement and space, and there are concrete exercises that demonstrate how he can create himself as a "movable form." The fingers and hands are trained separately to combat vagueness and shapelessness. There can be nothing amorphous, aimless, or accidental about the actor's movements. Similarly, his sense of hearing has to be sharpened through deliberate exercise, so that in every sense of the word the actor becomes a finely tuned instrument.

Much of what Chekhov covers about interpreting a role Monroe would have already learned from Lytess, but perhaps his emphasis on the autonomy of the actor was new to her. Chekhov directs actors to work on imagery associated with their characters, and with "images of fantasy" in order to develop imaginative flexibility. He explores in considerable depth the process of perfecting a character's dominant psychological gesture, and he combines his initial physical exercises with certain psychological themes the exercises explore. He then progresses to the principles underlying the composition of a good performance and the structures of plays. At every step, his aim is to broaden the actor's sense of responsibility and insight. Chekhov stresses the organic relationship between life and art. His view is that the same laws of composition govern the universe, "the life of earth and man," and all of the arts. As a corroboration of his insight, he recommended that Monroe study Mabel Elsworth Todd's *The Thinking Body*, which became, Monroe later told her friend Ralph Roberts, her bible. "[N]o looks / body only," she wrote in a notebook. She would take years to absorb *The Thinking Body*, and she never claimed to understand all of its technical information, but she practiced many of its exercises and was influenced by Todd's way of situating the body within the continuum of human psychology and physiology.

In early 1952, Monroe's work with Chekhov—and indeed her very career—seemed in jeopardy when journalist Aline Mosby announced she was about to break the story that the actress had posed for nude calendar photographs that appeared in gas stations, barber shops, and other places where men congregated, participating in a culture that catered to soft pornographic depictions of disrobed females. This was still a period in which the stage striptease was popular and burlesque theaters thrived. Ever since the introduction of the Hollywood production code in 1934, the movie industry had carefully censored the images and the language of sex, so that nothing approaching the explicitness of strippers like Gypsy Rose Lee could be shown on screen. There was, of course, a lively underground economy involving pornographic movies for men, but no legitimate actress would dare to appear in such work. It has long been rumored that Monroe made what used to be called girlie films, but no one has produced an authentic example.

Marilyn Monroe was in trouble. Darryl Zanuck summoned her to a meeting with Harry Brand, head of publicity at Twentieth Century-Fox, the man who perfected sanitized studio biographies of stars emphasizing their wholesomeness. Zanuck warned Monroe that if Mosby published her story, the actress's career might be over. Studios always included a "morals clause" in contracts, giving employers the power to rid themselves of players who offended the public's standard of decency. Marilyn's first reaction was to believe she had destroyed her chance at fame.

Opinion divided on what she should do. Some studio executives expected her to deny the story, reasoning that her partially obscured face left the identity of the poser in doubt. But Harry Brand had watched how well Monroe had worked with the press, and her confidant, gossip columnist Sidney Skolsky, urged her to get ahead of the story by giving Mosby an exclusive interview. Monroe opted for the straightforward approach, telling Mosby she had done nothing wrong and was not ashamed of her work for what she called an "art calendar." As an aspiring actress she needed the money, and the photographer's wife had been present for the photo shoot. "That wasn't a terrible thing to do, was it?" she asked the sympathetic reporter. Treating the scandal as a surprise, Monroe said she had not expected anyone to recognize her. And then she took the journalist into her confidence: "They say it will ruin my career. They want me to deny it's me." The actress's lack of shame about her work, and her defense of it as artistic, won the admiration and sympathy of millions of fans. The public was on her side. Later she would joke when asked about what she had on during her calendar poses. Just the radio, she replied.

Biographers have treated the calendar controversy as a key moment in Monroe's ascent to stardom, and they have lauded her deft handling of the press. They have not, however, paid enough attention to the shifts in American culture that made Monroe's candor possible. The calendar kerfuffle had been anticipated twenty years earlier, in 1931, when Gypsy Rose Lee was arrested after the premiere performance of her striptease act at the Republic Theater on 42nd Street in New York City. "My baby is innocent and pure," her mother told the New York *Evening Graphic*. "I wasn't naked," Gypsy said. "I was completely covered by a blue spotlight." Even the detectives who arrested her said that Gypsy had not committed an obscene act. Telegrams "offered to protect her as if she was a virgin in distress," biographer Rachel Shteir reports. "One tabloid quoted Gypsy as explaining that she made the detective wait outside while she dressed."

Since the early 1940s, Lee had made the striptease not merely popular entertainment, but also a witty art, writes Shteir. No less than Eleanor Roosevelt offered this tribute to Lee: "May your bare ass always be shining." Like Lee, Monroe emphasized both her youthful innocence and her seriousness as an artist and, also like Lee, Monroe liked to talk about her avid reading of serious literature. Lee, in other words, set the precedent for transforming what had been considered a crude and demeaning kind of low entertainment into an esthetic form of self-revelation. Monroe won the public by saying exactly the right thing: "They want me to deny it's me." That a new magazine, *Playboy*, used one of Kelley's nude photographs on its cover consolidated her national appeal.

Just a few days later, Monroe agreed to Sidney Skolsky's idea to announce in his column her blind date with Joe DiMaggio. Not only did this story bury any lingering blowback about the nude calendar, it elevated her into the pantheon of American heroes. DiMaggio, considered one of baseball's greatest players, had just retired from the game. His record of getting at least one hit in fifty-six consecutive games is an achievement that no other player has ever surpassed. Barbara Leaming does not exaggerate when she writes that DiMaggio was "idolized and revered." Graceful on the field, at thirty-seven he was trim, tall, and an elegant dresser. Fastidious and taciturn, he amused Monroe, who is supposed to have asked how he contrived to get the polka dot exactly in the middle of his tie knot. He was circumspect and reminded Monroe of a business executive. If they did not seem to have much in common, the sexual attraction between them momentarily overrode any qualms they had about one another.

With Joe DiMaggio (c. 1954)

The couple had probably met, at least briefly, a few years earlier. And though she was no sports fan, it is hard to believe Monroe's later claim she had not known DiMaggio was a famous baseball player. David March, a mutual friend, had arranged the first date precisely because DiMaggio was a legend, one who had his eye on Monroe when he had seen a picture of her with another baseball player, Gus Zernial. Encouraged by DiMaggio's interest and powerful presence, Monroe began dating him. He seemed to fit the cliché of the strong silent type. That he did not open up easily, though, seemed to entice Monroe, who was used to glib Hollywood men who were showoffs and manipulators. DiMaggio believed he was the one to steady her as she managed her way to the top in Hollywood. He was a tough negotiator and gave Monroe sound career advice. But ultimately he wanted her to quit show business, believing that being Mrs. Joe DiMaggio should be enough for any woman—even Marilyn Monroe. Marilyn Monroe, however, was just beginning the major phase of her fame.

Then yet another journalist seemed to undermine the carefully managed account of her ascent to stardom. A *Los Angeles Daily News* reporter was set to publish a story about Gladys that would contradict the account of Norma Jeane the orphan that Marilyn had carefully nurtured. Monroe had let reporters think that her mother was dead rather than have to explain the sordid details of Gladys's biography. How would the public react when it learned that Marilyn's mother was alive? Repeating what she had done with Aline Mosby, Marilyn called the *Daily News* reporter, Erskine Johnson, and gave him an exclusive interview. She released a statement that cleverly implied that not disclosing the truth about Gladys had been a way of protecting her mother's privacy, not an effort to hide inconvenient facts. "My close friends know that my mother is alive," she began, and then reiterated the sad tale of her times in foster homes and in an orphanage. Gladys, an invalid, had been sent to a state institution while her daughter was still a child, making it difficult for her young daughter to maintain any significant contact, but Marilyn had been supporting her and would always be available to help. As with the calendar scandal, the public found Marilyn's version of her victimhood endearing. As Mailer suggests, she broke through some kind of publicity barrier in this year, so that everything she did was made to seem interesting.

The various views of Marilyn Monroe in 1952 and 1953 in popular circulation and fan magazines, in *Time, Newsweek*, and in the daily newspapers, were nearly all generous. Most reviews of her film acting were approving or tolerant, and beginning with *Clash by Night* (June 1952), a few reviewers began to credit her with acting skill. Unfortunately, her films were not carefully assessed, and most viewers did not see her versatility. In *Clash by Night*, she is forceful as a working class woman, Peggy, who does not feel the urgent need to defer to men, to seduce them, or to complete her life by marriage. She is not a liberated woman by today's standards, but she plays her part with a vigor that is directly attributable to her independent stance, to her awareness of male domination, not just natural vivacity. She is a convincing worker as she plunges her hands into an assortment of fish, a tense determined expression on her mouth. The film still of this scene (which does not appear in the film's final cut) is a study in the concentration of human labor uncharacteristic of most of Monroe's other roles. Yet there is nothing about her aggressiveness that diminishes her sexual attractiveness. Indeed, a study of the different postures she assumes in this movie suggests an upright, bold personality who can also be sensitive and affectionate with women as well as men.

The film exemplifies director Fritz Lang's abiding concern with the dark side of American life. It stars Barbara Stanwyck as a woman ex-

Poster: *Clash by Night* (1952)

hausted by years of fending for herself, who is tempted by the sense of security that marriage to dependable Jerry D'Amato (Paul Douglas) will provide. She nonetheless has an affair with Earl Pfeiffer (Robert Ryan), a more intense, if rather sadistic man. Ultimately, Mae breaks the hold Earl has on her to partner with Jerry, the safer man. Although the film capitulates to a postwar ideology that mandates Mae's subordination to Jerry, who is a strong and kind, if somewhat dull man, *Clash by Night* nevertheless examines with some sharpness the generation of women who grew up in the war and young women like Peggy, who admires Mae's moxie—even though Peggy also accommodates herself to her boyfriend Joe (Keith Andes).

Dressed in jeans, which Monroe liked to wear off-screen, Peggy is nothing like the glamour figure of the actress's later films. She does not walk or talk like Marilyn Monroe. More than any other film in the Monroe canon, *Clash by Night* demonstrates her down-to-earth sensibility, which had to be suppressed in order to be rendered palatable to postwar sensibilities and to her studio's desire to manufacture a fantasy of femininity that appealed to the broadest possible audience. In this respect, the decision to build up "Marilyn Monroe" was a political move by a studio seeking to turn this actress into a brand that could be exploited in film after film.

Monroe's mantra for this film could have been "keep it real." By this point, she was already getting the full treatment as an emerging star—much to the disgust of Paul Douglas, who did not see why a supporting actor should get so much press attention. Others, like Barbara Stanwyck, took a more sympathetic view. A thorough professional, Stanwyck understood the young actress's desire to get her part right even as her publicity tended to overwhelm any consideration of her talent. Monroe herself tried to come to the set with an ally, Natasha Lytess. Lang tolerated Lytess until he discovered that she was interfering with his own direction.

Arriving late and requiring innumerable retakes of her scenes was becoming a pattern with Marilyn Monroe. She did not trust herself or others, but her reliance on Lytess was not quite what directors and studio executives supposed it to be. They regarded Lytess as a kind of guru who treated her pupil as an acolyte. When Monroe requested Lytess's presence on the set of *Don't Bother to Knock*, studio head Darryl Zanuck replied that it was "impractical and impossible." Sideline coaching would be a disaster for her director (Roy Baker), whose creative ideas would be undermined. Zanuck expressed his confidence that she could play the part and concluded, "You have built up a Svengali and if you are going to progress and become as important talent-wise as you have publicity-wise then you must destroy this Svengali before it destroys you." Zanuck's attitude is understandable. How could a movie production company function if actors brought their own staff, which would serve as a kind of alternative authority to the director? But to Monroe, Lytess was a mirror, an ally, a piece of armor she wanted on her side as the studio stamped out its version of what "Marilyn Monroe" was supposed to be. Monroe had her own ideas for roles that she tested out with Lytess, who operated as an advisor, not a dictator—even if the acting coach did try to dominate Monroe.

On all sides, Monroe engaged in a power struggle to determine what her screen identity should be. She was desperate to retain some measure of control over both her talent and her image. To be sure, a more confident actress like Barbara Stanwyck could take care of herself, but Stanwyck, who had had to pay her dues and take roles that were beneath her, surely understood the demeaning conditions of the contract player who was supposed to do as she was told. Surrendering to the studio system paralleled the national mood of conformity to conventional standards of behavior.

In *We're Not Married* (July 1952), Monroe had a role that is much closer to the conventions established by *Let's Make It Legal*, where she is paraded in bathing suits and other costumery of sex. In *We're Not Married* she is a beauty contest winner who is referred to as "that cute little girl." It ought to be easy to condescend to Monroe as the simple-minded housewife whose ambitions hinge on her looks, yet she plays the role with a verve and lack of pretension that make it difficult to dismiss her as simply giddy. Forsaking the sultry posing of her publicity shots, she projects a down-to-earth determination and ambition to be the best, even when that means inconveniencing her husband (David Wayne) by shifting the burdens of housekeeping and child raising to him. All the same, the film typifies the unreal movieland environment that enveloped Monroe, for the housewife dimension of the beauty she plays is never presented. Furthermore, it is impossible to locate her character in a specific locale, even though she is explicitly identified as coming from Mississippi. Of course, none of the characters in the film speaks in regional dialect, yet Monroe suffered more than most actors and actresses from the distortions of moviemaking typified by homogenization of language. So often, her roles centered on her figure, her presence, as if what she said, or what she was as a whole person, could not possibly be as interesting or as impressive as her body.

Twentieth Century-Fox still did not know precisely what to do with Marilyn Monroe. Until a proper vehicle for her stardom could be contrived, she had yet another opportunity to show off her talent in a starring role that called for a textured performance in a film that was not a major release. Zanuck seemed to regard *Don't Bother to Knock* (August 1952) as a way of seasoning Monroe before her huge buildup in the year to follow. Her work in *The Asphalt Jungle, All About Eve,* and *Clash by Night* had received favorable reviews, but could she carry a whole film on her own? Initially, Zanuck had insisted Monroe take a screen test for *Don't Bother To Knock* to confirm her suitability for the role of Nell Forbes, a young woman recently released from a mental institution. Traumatized by her fiancé's wartime death in a plane crash, Nell has a grasp on reality that is tenuous at best, as she shifts deliriously between past and present, confusing an airline pilot she meets in a hotel room with her dead lover. Monroe found preparing for the test an ordeal, although her work with Lytess secured Zanuck's approval.

Barbara Leaming reports that Zanuck thought Monroe's own instability heightened her performance of a mentally disturbed character. She had told stories about how she had thrown herself on Johnny Hyde's coffin in a hysterical scene that suggested she could not come to terms with his death. Other rumors alleged that she had exhausted Hyde with her needs and was "sexually dangerous and not a little mad." It seems improbable that a shrewd businessman like Zanuck would put a production at risk because his leading actress shared some of her character's mental defects. But *Don't Bother to Knock* emerged out of a postwar period during which certain psychiatrists promulgated the idea that women deprived of the conventional support of husbands and families were prone to deviant behavior. Such women had trouble adjusting to "normal" life because they had no man they could serve. Without a "healthy, happy home," the postwar family was in crisis, argued William Menninger in *Psychiatry in a Troubled World: Yesterday's War and Today's Challenge* (1948). In *Modern Women: The Lost Sex* (1947), Ferdinand Lundberg, a sociologist, and Marynia Farnham, a psychoanalyst, characterized women without strong male protectors as "neurotic and maladjusted."

In *Don't Bother to Knock*, Monroe had trouble playing Nell Forbes mostly because the role was poorly written. Unlike the vigorous working class character in *Clash By Night*, Nell is a retiring, waifish introvert. She has a dreamy, unfocused look about her eyes and a rather listless, passive expression about her lips that make her seem blank, out of touch with others. Her primary means of expression is her hands; she grips her fingers together at about waist level as if she is holding herself together. At first the gripping gesture seems normal and casual, or at most a nervous habit occasioned by her first meeting with the Joneses, for whom she will babysit. But later—when her suicidal tendencies become evident, when the camera tilts down to her scarred wrists—it becomes clear that all along she has been trying to get a grip on herself. It is through her hands that Monroe develops what Chekhov calls the "psychological" or "archetypal gesture" conveying the essence of a personality, which "serves as an original model for all possible gestures of the same kind." Monroe plays Nell as an unobtrusive person who is on the edge of insanity, but as Manny Farber points out, Monroe "lulls you into always believing the girl is more normal than she is."

As soon as Nell is alone, she gazes into the mirror while trying on Mrs. Jones's perfume, jewelry, and attractive evening dress. She admires herself in the mirror and suddenly begins to create a whole scene out of her glorious transformation. She behaves—as "Mischief," the Charlotte Armstrong story on which the film was based, suggests—like "some movie star." There is something "perfectly fresh" about the way Nell works her metamorphosis; she does so in the wondering manner of a child, and her apprehensive clutching of her hands gives way to much more forthright hand motions as she deliberately composes herself in the mirror and loses her inhibitions. She really comes alive when Jed Towers (Richard Widmark), who is staying in a hotel room directly across from her, spots her through the open blind of her room dancing with herself. After some hesitation she invites him over, and in response to his admiring glances she says, "You like the way I look." It is the first time that the familiar Monroe appears, with her undulating lips and provocatively lowered voice. She gazes in the mirror as she tells Towers the story of his life, for she has confused him with her lover (a flyer like Towers) who died in the war. She kisses Towers passionately in her desperate attempt to make him her former lover, and with dreamy eyes and lowered lids, she briefly recites the sad details of her abused childhood.

Monroe takes her character through several changes of mood and makes her transitions from lethargy to seductiveness to sadness to desperation compelling. Nell is so self-absorbed, so intent on incorporating Jed into her fantasy life—the only world over which she has control—that she turns murderously on the child she is babysitting, almost pushing it out of a window (Jed stops her) when the youngster interrupts the dream of personal fulfillment Nell has tried to consummate. Similarly, she strikes her uncle (Elisha Cook, Jr.), the elevator operator who has gotten her the babysitting job and who apprehensively checks in on her, because he violates the make-believe atmosphere of her hotel room. When Nell is finally subdued after having again brought herself to the point of suicide, she subsides into the self-effacing mood that characterized her at the beginning of the film—except that now she seems to have been momentarily shocked into recognizing her debilitating tendency to merge her fantasies with reality.

Manny Farber calls Nell "a small-town Alice in the Wonderland of the 'Franklin Hotel,'" an apt phrase, for it captures the way the character is mesmerized by fantasies of her own adventures in front of a mirror. Jed can be anything she likes, so long as she looks at him in the mirror. Jed is

Don't Bother to Knock (1952)

nothing to her as a three-dimensional figure, but he is everything to her as a screen on which she can project her dreams. At first she pretends the hotel room is hers. She makes up a story about why she is there; she even projects the glamorous personality she has created for herself into the future when she talks to him about a trip to South America. But her perceptions of the present and the future tend to be ungrounded, disconnected, and fragmented, just like the flat, distorted surface impressions of a mirror, which supply only the illusion of depth. Nell is a frustrating character to read because there is no sure way to connect with her; she is not lucid enough to invite explorations of her personality. A few more details about her past would clarify the source of her personality disorder, but such details would not explain her person.

While Roy Baker's direction and Monroe's acting are good, Daniel Taradash's screenplay deflects attention from Nell by having Jed conveniently rescue her from another suicide attempt and gently enforce for her the distinction between illusion and reality. Such an ending does more to show how Jed the wise guy has learned to be compassionate than it does to show how Nell will cope—or fail to do so—with her inveterate need to transform her cryptic life into the dream of a whole self.

Monroe told Hedda Rosten that *Don't Bother To Knock* was one of her favorite films. She believed that in it she had given one of her strongest performances. Anne Bancroft, who played a character reacting to Nell's breakdown, said of Monroe's acting in this part, "It was so real, I responded; I really reacted to her. She moved me so that tears came into my eyes. Believe me, such moments happened rarely, if ever again, in the early things I was doing out there." Richard Widmark was less impressed with Monroe's talent, but he conceded her powerful screen impact. In many ways, *Don't Bother To Knock* became a test case for her, a show of strength in which she had to prove she could create a major dramatic character. "Seen in retrospect," David Robinson remarks, her performance "is far from being her least impressive," and it raises pertinent questions about her reactions to a role which appeared to correspond painfully to her own biography. She shared Nell's waif-like attitude, her dreamy mirror gazing, her desire to be glamorous and to dominate her environment by means of that glamour, and her generally fragmented sense of the world and human relationships. On the set of *We're Not Married*, screenwriter Nunnally Johnson observed Monroe's own diffidence and remoteness, the impression she created that she was not "all there."

Most of Monroe's other films from this period merely referred to her own character, breaking it into sexual segments. With no narrative links between the segments, she just appeared and radiated, as if the integument of her person covered everything it was essential to know about her. Thus *O. Henry's Full House* and *Monkey Business* (both released in September 1952) feature her as a showpiece. In the former, she is seen briefly as a streetwalker who is surprised when a gentlemen (Charles Laughton) in the street treats her with respect. "He called me a lady!" she exclaims in wonder, almost in disbelief, as if to indicate what a poor opinion she has of herself. There is perhaps just a hint of plaintiveness in her reaction that can be read autobiographically, since Monroe always sought respect but seemed startled to receive it. But the film's intention is to display rather than probe her personality, so it is impossible to say exactly what the person-to-role relationship is in this instance.

Don't Bother to Knock is an aberration in Monroe's career, although the studio capitalized on her sexual appeal by having her appear in a revealing negligee during romantic scenes with Widmark. Even more than *Clash by Night, Don't Bother to Knock* disrupts the benign presentation of her as a life-enhancing and carefree archetype of American optimism. In *Monkey Business*, on the other hand, the person is completely subordinated to the role. Monroe plays Miss Laurel, a comically stupid secretary, whose special skill is swinging her hips. She never really seems to understand what is going on around her, but because of her buxom figure (accentuated by a bra that thrusts her breasts forward and upward), her competence does not matter. As her boss, Oxley (Charles Coburn) says, "anyone can type." She is allowed an earnest line in which she offers to type for her employer, but he explains that his letter is important, and clearly Miss Laurel belongs to the unimportant side of business. She comes to the office early, she says, because Oxley has been complaining about her "punctuation." She is asked to check all of the Ford dealers in town and find Dr. Fulton (Cary Grant), the inventor of a youth serum, who has gone off on a joy ride after taking his own serum. She asks, "Which should I do first?"

Throughout the film Monroe is photographed and regarded strictly in terms of her sexual parts. She begins this splitting up of herself by ostentatiously raising her dress part way up her thigh and offering one of her nylon-clad legs for Dr. Fulton's close inspection, since he has invented a new kind of acetate stocking. The scene is positioned so that Dr. Fulton is sitting on a couch and Miss Laurel is standing above him. Naturally he has to look up her leg as she smiles encouragingly down at him. Later there is a scene with Fulton in a car lot in which there is a cutaway shot to a pair of legs, and Fulton naturally says, "Hello Miss Laurel," his greeting followed by a shot of her face (still missing her torso). The effect of this shooting style is to dismember Monroe, and to concentrate on her gorgeous face, her slim legs, her rounded behind, or her full breasts. When Oxley catches Fulton gazing at Miss Laurel's leg, Fulton replies that he has been looking at her "acetates." This vulgar way of punning on her anatomy continues with other innuendoes. When Fulton jumps in alongside Miss Laurel in his sports car, she asks, "Is your motor running?" He replies, "Is yours?" During the sports car sequence, in which Fulton recklessly maneuvers his way through innumerable near-accidents, Miss Laurel laughs spontaneously and actually seems to enjoy the danger. She acts like an adolescent (she's taken no youth serum) and

Monkey Business (1952)

is flattered by Fulton's attraction to her. In spite of her obvious interest in him, she never attempts anything like a mature seduction. Indeed, she is the only character in the film who is doomed to be perpetually adolescent, and as such she is the proper target of those adults who momentarily abandon their sense of decorum after swallowing the serum. So Fulton's wife, Edwina (Ginger Rogers) shoots Miss Laurel twice in the behind with a sling shot. Again, this scene is arranged to give maximum exposure to Monroe's body, for Miss Laurel has to twist her torso twice to slap Oxley's face and then Fulton's (she thinks the two men on each side of her have pinched her). Later Oxley, intoxicated with youth serum, chases her and shoots seltzer water at her behind.

Monkey Business was the first film since *Love Happy* to make deliberate sport of Monroe's figure, largely because its director, Howard Hawks, actually believed the actress was "goddam dumb." *The Asphalt Jungle* and *All About Eve* treat her with some humor, but *Monkey Business* stands alone in its exploitation of every opportunity to amuse itself at her expense. As in the case of *Love Nest*, *Monkey Business* spreads what is actually a very small role over several brief sequences, so that the character Monroe plays heightens interest in the film as a whole. In *Love Nest*, Monroe's character has an adult attractiveness; however, in *Monkey Business* she is portrayed with a cuteness that is on the level with that of the monkeys featured in the film.

Monkey Business was a substantial success, and it suggested that Monroe would be good in comedies. She had a sprightly, daffy, perfectly timed insouciance—the breezy sports car sequence shows that much. And she was already a star, not so much because of the movies she had made, as because of the images she was able to impress on the public's consciousness. As a representation of sexual provender, she had arrived.

In *My Story*, Monroe recalls that success arrived in a rush and surprised studio executives—but not her, since she had carefully noted how much publicity her bit parts generated. In her last recorded interview, she acknowledged how strenuously and shrewdly she had worked for public acclaim, yet she wondered if she could carry the load of adulation, if perhaps she had tricked herself into believing she could be greater than she actually was.

CHAPTER FIVE

Fame (1952-54)

*Fame to me certainly is only a temporary and
a partial happiness—even for a waif and I was
brought up a waif. But fame is not really for a daily
diet, that's not what fulfills you. It warms you a bit
but the warming is temporary. It's like caviar, you
know—it's good to have caviar but not when you
have it every meal and every day.*

By the summer of 1952, Joe DiMaggio had taken Marilyn Monroe home to meet his family. The DiMaggios were used to meeting celebrities and welcomed her without a qualm. When she came to dinner at Joe's family home, Marilyn always asked his mother what she could do to help. "Everything she did, she did with gusto," remembered June DiMaggio, one of Joe's nieces. Marilyn did the dishes, spurning Mrs. DiMaggio's offer of gloves to protect the star's lovely hands. Marilyn "would plunge right into the hot dishwater, seeming to enjoy the sensation," June recalled. Marilyn confided in Joe's mother and enjoyed "girl talk" with June. Marilyn impressed June by reciting from memory passages from Emerson. The family's Burmese cat, Minka, snuggled next to Marilyn anytime she slept in the DiMaggio home. Tommy, the family's cockatiel, would fly to the front door to meet Marilyn. When a startled neighbor happened on her at the DiMaggio front door and saw the bird perched on the star's head repeating, "Mari-lyn Monroe," Marilyn turned to the neighbor and with a deadpan expression said, "It's okay. This is my son and he's here to greet me." Marilyn worked hard at pleasing Joe, downing wild duck even when it nearly made her gag, and fishing with the DiMaggios even though she became seasick. They would play cards, gin rummy and canasta, betting a dime a game.

Often in a rush, Marilyn would show up in the most casual kind of clothing. One time she appeared in pajamas covered by a mink coat. "I didn't have time to change," she told June. Other times, Marilyn would go clothes shopping with Joe's mother. In her downtime from the screen, Marilyn braided her hair and looked like the "sweetest little Dutch girl." On one outing to get birdseed for Tommy, Marilyn traveled without a disguise. A crowd gathered, instantly recognizing the star. "Everyvun sinks I'm Marileen," she said in a thick Scandinavian accent, "but my name is Eve Lindstrom." She even signed an autograph with that name. Marilyn and Joe's mother nearly laughed themselves sick over their little adventure.

In some of her pessimistic moods, Monroe gave the impression that she might relinquish her quest for fame. That she was a beautiful person—not simply a coveted image or an approximation of a desirable woman—is what counted with Joe DiMaggio. It counted heavily with Monroe, too, since others had seldom been able to comprehend the nexus between her self and her roles.

Associating with DiMaggio also instilled confidence in her and a growing sense of her public prominence. Even as her relationship with him promised to pull her clear of the film role/person dichotomy, her first major film, *Niagara* (February 1953), made her face, her figure, her voice, and the way she employed them the screen's subject. To cast Marilyn Monroe in the part of a femme fatale was not, however, an obvious choice. After the success of *Monkey Business*, Howard Hawks assured Darryl Zanuck that he could make Monroe a star in light comedies. True, Monroe had excelled in a dramatic role in *Don't Bother to Knock*, but box office receipts had been disappointing, and as Nell Forbes the actress had projected vulnerability more than menace. Nevertheless Zanuck knew he had, in the parlance of the time, a hot property, judging by Monroe's burgeoning fan mail and publicity. Before Hawks found the right role for her, Hathaway convinced Zanuck that *Niagara* would make her a star. Hathaway believed in Monroe's intelligence and wished she would rely more on herself since she was so eager to learn. Like most directors, he disliked the interfering Natasha Lytess. Hathaway believed that the studio, Joe DiMaggio, and nearly everyone who got close to Monroe did not accord her the respect she deserved. When John Kobal interviewed the director, Kobal sensed that Hathaway had fallen in love with Monroe. Certainly his comments to Kobal suggest he was one of the few men in Hollywood who seemed capable of appreciating the person and the actress.

Niagara is a Technicolor film noir, almost a contradiction in terms. Such films, shot in black and white, usually featured a wanton woman who corrupted a male hero. She had to be punished for her crime (murder or abetting a murder). Although the genre emerged during the 1940s in films such as *The Maltese Falcon* (1941) and *Out of the Past* (1947), it became a staple of low budget thrillers emphasizing the seamier side of American life, the nightmare chiaroscuro of cops and criminals who battled over the hearts and minds of communities determined to overcome lawless elements threatening core American values of justice and fair play. Henry Hathaway had excelled in the genre with films like *The Dark Corner* (1946) and *Kiss of Death* (1947). In *Niagara*, he amplified the sexuality of the femme fatale, thereby magnifying one of the underlying themes of the genre: the American male's concern about his own masculinity and his worry that he was not up to the job of subduing the postwar woman, who emerged from the war confident of her own abilities but also disenchanted with her prospects. Fritz Lang had explored this theme in *Clash by Night*, but not with the kind of brio and flamboyance that Hathaway brought to the screen by making Monroe the screen siren par excellence. She is Rose Loomis, a seductress who plots to murder her husband (played by Joseph Cotten), a returning war veteran, who finds it hard to adjust to civilian society and to a powerfully sexualized wife.

After all those World War II films that featured a man's world, the return home became an anxious journey for men who wondered how they would be received by wives and lovers. This male dilemma is epitomized in films like *The Best Years of Our Lives* (1946), when Fred Derry (Dana Andrews), a bombardier in the war, is mocked by his sassy wife, played with appropriate cruelty by Virginia Mayo. How could Fred demonstrate his masculinity any more powerfully than with a war record? And yet, like George Loomis, Fred is at a loss as to how to please and impress his wife. As Frank Krutnik notes in *In a Lonely Street: Film Noir, Genre, Masculinity*, the "more prominent the woman, the more difficult it becomes to validate the masculine ethos."

How can the male hero compete with the celebrated cinemascope tracking shot that focuses on Monroe's rear end and her swaying gait as she moves away from the camera? Aspiring actress Ellen Burstyn admired Monroe's commanding walk across the screen, a visual embodiment of self-possession. On the wide screen, Marilyn Monroe became the picture, so to speak, available to everyone and yet elusive. As critic Graham McCann remarked, "She was like the movies: we can all see her,

Niagara (1953)

there, but no one can keep her." Other films would develop other aspects of her screen presence, to be sure, but *Niagara* initiates the many "Marilyns" to come—a point Andy Warhol grasped brilliantly in his many portraits of "Marilyns," all of which derive from the image of her singing "Kiss" in *Niagara*. She has to be understood, Warhol implies, in the plural. The basis of her appeal is her ability to be reproduced; the public wants to see that walk over and over again, and film—unlike any other medium—is equipped to replicate the sequence indefinitely. Unfortunately for Monroe, the lurid color in which she is framed resembles that used in the boxed strips of comic books. Like the parodic sexual siren of cartoons—say, Betty Boop—Monroe's character, Rose Loomis, is the target of quips and innuendoes. When the nice, neat, and clean young honeymooning husband (Casey Adams) kiddingly asks his bride (Jean Peters) why she doesn't wear tight-fitting dresses like the ones Rose wears, the bride responds that a woman has to "start laying plans" for such a dress when she's about ten years old. Such remarks define how far Monroe's character has strayed from the conventions most women follow in presenting themselves and how deliberately she is consigned to her own peculiar realm of being.

Monroe is isolated while singing of "Kiss" dreamily, moodily, and so suggestively that the crowd of young people who have been dancing recede from her in hushed wonder. As in Monroe's most suggestive publicity photographs, she seems to be caressing herself, to have retreated into the deepest recesses of her private fantasy life. She holds her passions so far away from both men and women in this film that when a young man asks her to dance, she warns him, "better not." In this scene she seems warmed by her own sensuousness, as she sings to the record she has asked a young man to play for her, and as she embellishes the song the camera tightens on her ecstatic countenance. In close-up, in reverie, her face clearly is meant to arrest attention and to fashion Monroe as a fantasy.

The film's hackneyed plot matters very little, except in so far as it furthers the implications of "Kiss." Rose Loomis's depressed husband, tortured by his awareness that he cannot satisfy his sensual wife, and that she must be looking for other men who can gratify her, interrupts her singing of "Kiss" and breaks the record. This act foreshadows the fulfillment of his barely suppressed urge to destroy her when he learns that she has plotted with her lover to take his life. She is bound to die, evidently, because her sexual energies go beyond the bounds of what people can tolerate or the screen can show.

Niagara gave Monroe her only opportunity to portray an evil woman solely concerned with herself and willing to commit any crime to accomplish her own ends. Near the beginning of the film, her anxious husband stands over her bed softly calling her name as she pretends to sleep. There is yearning in his voice; he is half-heartedly seeking her sexual favors, although the censorship of the time and his diffidence forbid the making of an explicit request. What he wants from her is clarified later when Rose says of him to her lover, "[T]here's always a way to get around George." George's momentary relaxation and humor in a bedroom scene shortly afterwards proves her point. This venal employment of sex deeply disturbed some members of Monroe's audience, and she never attempted anything like the role of Rose Loomis again.

After *Niagara*, Hathaway wanted to cast Monroe in other dramatic roles, but Zanuck would not allow it. Unquestionably, he mishandled Monroe's career, which accounts, in part, for the enmity she would express against Twentieth Century-Fox. She had a right to distrust Zanuck's judgment. Hathaway noted that "Zanuck was never smart about women. Look what he did—while he had people like Marilyn, he signed up people like Bella Darvi," one of several mistresses that the studio head failed to turn into stars. An angry Hathaway believed Monroe, a frustrated great artist, never got over the missed opportunities to play serious roles: "You don't have to hold an inquest to find out who killed Marilyn Monroe. Those bastards in the big executive chairs killed her."

Publicity for *Niagara* demanded that its female star engage in crude exploitation of her sexuality, and Monroe obliged by appearing at public gatherings in skin-tight costumes from her movie wardrobe. DiMaggio refused to accompany her on such occasions and bitterly protested the show she was making of herself. Hollywood columnists played up her exhibitionism, and soon newspapers and fan magazines were receiving letters criticizing her vulgar behavior. Monroe created such a sensation at a *Photoplay* awards dinner that Joan Crawford publicly condemned her for conduct unbecoming an actress and a lady. Besides adopting her familiar guise of injured innocence, shortly after the release of *Niagara* Monroe wrote a public letter to columnist Dorothy Kilgallen that drew a distinction between the actress and the women she played. In *The Asphalt Jungle*, she noted, "I played a vacuous, rich man's darling attempting to carry herself in a sophisticated manner in keeping with her plush surroundings. I saw her as walking with a rather self-conscious slither and played it accordingly." Her succinct summing-up of her characters—"[I]n All About Eve, I was an untalanted [*sic*] show girl walking with deliberate exactness"—emphasizes the intelligence and clarity of her professional work, especially in her attention to the small physical details that indicate a character's mental state. She was articulating what Chekhov taught her.

As for *Niagara*, "[T]he girl I played in that was an amoral type whose plot to kill her husband was attempted with no apparent cost to her conscience. She had been picked out of a beer parlor, she entirely lacked the social graces and she was overdressed, overly made-up, and completely wanton. The uninhibited deportment in the motel room and the walk seemed normal facets of such a character's portrayal. I honestly believe such a girl would behave in that manner."

Monroe believed her acting ability entitled her to try more challenging roles—Gretchen, in *Faust*, for example. She had impressed Chekhov with her Cordelia in acting class, and she had pleaded with her unsympathetic studio to test her for serious roles. If Henry Hathaway had won his point, he would have cast her as Grushenka in *The Brothers Karamazov*. Monroe's employers were content with her popularity as evidenced in box office receipts, in fan mail, and in two awards she received in March of 1953: "Best Young Box Office Personality" (*Redbook* magazine) and "Fastest Rising Star of 1952" (*Photoplay*).

In the spring of 1953, with Monroe's concern over craft mounting, she enrolled in mime classes at Lotte Goslar's Turnabout Theater, a small repertory house in Hollywood, where Monroe had been impressed by a production of one of Anton Chekhov's plays. She wanted to work alone with Goslar, but the teacher convinced her she would benefit most by interacting with an exciting class of ten other pupils studying dance, mime, movement, and acting. Although reserved at first, she eventually grew comfortable with the group, and Goslar was struck by her serious and modest appearance and her exceptional talent. This talent manifested itself in an ambitious project that called for each student to develop a character from infancy to old age. In every phase—childhood, youth, maturity—the actor had to be convincing as the same person. The class was moved by Monroe's mastery of this difficult exercise in creating the full range of human behavior. In these moments of intense creativity, Monroe asserted control over her own person and filled in the gaps in her own development. Goslar's exercises complemented Chekhov's and the ideas of Mabel Elsworth Todd, whose book Chekhov recommended as essential to the completion of an actor's training. *The Thinking Body* emphasizes that all of human life is involved in a struggle for balance, and that human beings can consciously promote and control the forces that motivate sensations and physical activity. Monroe had dramatized her life precisely as a struggle to achieve harmony.

Hadn't the actress's own experience, at least since adolescence, confirmed Todd's initial pronouncement? "Living, the whole body carries its meaning and tells its own story, standing, sitting, walking, awake or asleep. It pulls all the life up into the face of the philosopher, and sends it all down the legs of the dancer." Here was a holistic view of human activity Monroe could identify with and practice, a teaching that could turn her toward therapeutic inspection of herself and away from Hollywood's mechanical magnification and distortion of what were supposed to be her better parts. Like Chekhov's approach, Todd's is integrative: "Mechanically, physiologically and psychologically, the human body is compelled to struggle for a state of equilibrium." Through a better understanding of the body's structures and functions, Todd concludes, man could better preserve his unity and cope with the world. Monroe needed to believe that the greatest source of her strength came from within, that she projected her power through a camera and onto the screen rather than the reverse, in which the camera produced and then stripped away some personal, unreplenishable essence. Todd taught that the proper treatment of the body stimulated and rekindled its energies. Thus Monroe's constant study of *The Thinking Body* may have been one of her primary ways of fighting the fear that films not only enhanced her self-image, but also robbed her of a more fundamental existence.

Todd develops a series of exercises (with appropriate illustrations) designed to demonstrate the body's intrinsic balance and the way that balance can be consciously managed. Rather than simply describing what she means, Todd has the reader participate in thinking about the body, so that her prose often resembles the language of acting manuals. For example, after a passage on the spine, in which she carefully describes how human weight is balanced by the pelvis, thigh joints, and femora, she shifts to a concrete, imagistic passage that puts this knowledge about how weight is economically distributed into practice:

Think down the back and up the front. Let the spine drag. Picture it extended like the dinosaur's tail, but keep the front wall of the body up. The spine travels the whole length of the back, while the whole front of the body is suspended from the spine and head, directly and indirectly, through connecting bone, muscle and soft tissues. Thinking "up the front" of the body without lifting any of its bony parts will establish proper traction in the connecting muscles to keep the ends of all bones in the front of the body-wall at proper levels for a balance of weight at their spinal attachments. Thus tensile members at the front balance compression members at the back.

Monroe confessed that she found Todd difficult reading, but she was grateful to know what to look for, and Todd's thinking up and down the body neatly paralleled Chekhov's exercises on the opening and closing of the self. Both teachers required Monroe to act, to discover for herself her own unity. Several years later, when Ralph Roberts met and became Monroe's friend, he found they shared an enthusiasm for Todd's book, from which the actress had adapted her own set of physical exercises. Acting is a matter of finding a concrete, functional way of interpreting character, of developing the right psychological gesture, Chekhov counsels. And Todd says much the same thing about "learning consciously to employ the motivating picture to create the conditions for appropriate movement responses." One has to know "three things: exact location, direction and desire to move. When conditions are right, movement takes place."

But moviemaking rarely offered the right conditions. Howard Hawks persuaded Darryl Zanuck that Monroe had been miscast in *Don't Bother to Knock*. Her gift, Hawks assured the studio head, was for light comedy of the kind the director had in mind for his next film, *Gentlemen Prefer Blondes* (August 1953): "Darryl, you're making realism with a very unreal girl. She's a completely storybook character. And you're trying to make real movies." When the adamant Hawks told a skeptical Zanuck that Monroe could sing (the director heard her singing to the radio), Zanuck relented, in a fateful decision that virtually ensured the actress would never again be offered a dramatic role in a Twentieth Century-Fox film.

Howard Hawks and his screenwriter, Charles Lederer, grasped the evolution of Monroe's style: She was becoming self-referential. She played characters like Rose Loomis, who had no past, who needed no past; they just had to be. Hawks and his crew helped Monroe to transform herself into a self-generating phenomenon, a *perpetuum mobile* of desire. The allure of *Blondes* is the way it stands apart from, is divisible from reality— just as Hawks intended. The movie begins with Lorelei (Monroe) and Dorothy (Jane Russell) singing "We're Just Two Little Girls from Little Rock," although no attempt is made to make them look or sound like two little girls from Little Rock. On the contrary, we get the distinct impression that Monroe and Russell are entertainers playing roles and setting scenes; we are not to take them seriously. They are on stage, backstage,

At Grauman's Chinese Theatre (1953)

or off stage; almost everything they do is defined by the stage setting. As soon as they begin singing or dancing, their world becomes a stage, a series of scenes. When Lorelei sings to her fiancé in the ship's cabin, when Dorothy sings for the US Olympic team around a swimming pool, and when both women sing "When Love Goes Wrong Nothin' Goes Right" in a French café, crowds gather as audiences and private emotions are transformed into public performances. Dorothy, however, is allowed to slip out of her role as performer so that she can function as a person who often advises Lorelei against acting. At the very end of the film, Dorothy's differentiation from Lorelei is apparent. At their double wedding ceremony she says, "Remember, it's all right now to say yes." Her comment implies that Lorelei may not be clear about the limits of her role, that she might just go on playing it because the role is not a means to an end (marriage), but just a means, a way of being (a women in pursuit of a rich husband) in which she has fully invested herself.

More is under consideration in such a scene than Lorelei's dumbness. She is distinguished by her ability to hold on to a role, to retain nothing of herself for other times, other settings. What Lorelei is as a person is forever elusive. Sometimes she seems just plain dumb, as when she does not know the difference between a tiara and a necklace. But then she confounds her future father-in-law (Taylor Holmes) by getting the better of him in argument by frankly admitting that she can be smart when she wants to, "but most men don't like it." The line was added by Monroe herself, as a script assistant's notes record. The actress wanted her audience to know that her character, like herself, was role-playing. Just how much does Lorelei know about her dumbness? On occasion she is dumb with Dorothy. Has her role overtaken her? Somewhere apart from her role Monroe is having fun with her audience, she is parodying her own glamour girl style. But where exactly is that parody located? Billy Wilder later exploited this ambiguous aspect of Monroe as put-on in *The Seven Year Itch*.

Throughout *Gentlemen Prefer Blondes* Lorelei polishes her role, not her person. Dorothy, on the other hand, asks, "[I]s there anyone here for love?" She chafes against the restraints of role playing; she wants to be herself and to be loved as herself, although she enjoys impersonating Lorelei in one scene, and sees nothing wrong with scheming and staging scenes for her own protection. She can dissemble, but her identity is intact, mature, even motherly in the way she guides Lorelei, whose babyish voice implies an identity that is undeveloped, despite her shrewd understanding of how to play her role.

The justly famous "Diamonds Are a Girl's Best Friend" musical number elevates and consecrates the glamorous child-woman myth that envelopes Lorelei-Monroe throughout the film. She appears in a fetching satin dress and glossy makeup reminiscent of her most lurid publicity photographs, but there is an elegance in her long gloves and in the men in tuxedos who attend her. At the same time, the gentle way these men

Gentlemen Prefer Blondes (1953)

carry her through the number, and the conspicuous way her dress trails what almost looks like a chick's tail feathers when she hops, indicate an infantile, unconscious nature (first glimpsed in *Love Happy*) that belies her cynical song about how women lose their charms (looks), but rocks (diamonds) don't lose their shape. As in her nude calendar, heavy use of red throughout most of this number is obviously intended to evoke the heat of passion, and the glare of diamonds is the brilliant reward for shrewd application of that passion. In this complex mix of contradictory implications (all myths have this affinity for blending conflicting impressions, in this case cute naïveté and adult seductiveness), the reds recede and a single beam—Truffaut calls it "a kind of dim church light"—isolates Monroe with her arms straight above her head and her fingers outspread as she smiles and luxuriates in self-love and in the adoration of her gentlemen, who are on their knees with faces and arms uplifted. Notice how she places her hands on her chest and shakes her breasts and how many of her gestures are self-referential, even as she plays to a worshipful audience. If *Niagara* first defined the visual angles of Monroe's appeal, then *Gentlemen Prefer Blondes* explores audience reaction to that appeal, so that the sound track includes a long admiring chorus

"Diamonds Are a Girl's Best Friend" (publicity still, 1953)

of "ooh-ooh" timed to coincide with her exaggeratedly slow side-to-side hip movements. While "Diamonds Are a Girl's Best Friend" burlesques Monroe as sex symbol, the number's extravagance is more than humorous, for it heightens her symbolic status. Such a lavish production goes well beyond anything required to embellish Lorelei's personality. The setting, the costumes, the jewelry, the makeup, and Monroe herself are designed to be thoroughly dazzling. Every move she makes sparkles and glitters; her voice and the accompanying music are amplified and modulated to project both the raucous response of unrepressed sexuality and her soft, mellow, caressing tones. "Diamonds" is a scene that in every possible way has been arranged for Monroe, so that by the end of the number she has moved in every direction and filled in every corner of the movie frame. As a result, the frame is transformed into her vehicle of self-incorporation.

After *Gentlemen Prefer Blondes*, every film would be more or less written to play off against the person and the symbol that was Marilyn Monroe. In true Hollywood spirit, *How To Marry A Millionaire* (November 1953) expanded on its predecessor's formula. Since pairing Monroe with Russell worked so well, Fox supplied a bigger ensemble—this time with Monroe, Betty Grable, and Lauren Bacall all involved in catching wealthy husbands. Nunnally Johnson wrote the part of Pola with Monroe in mind. He wanted to treat comically and compassionately what he saw as her insensitivity—her way of cutting off the world—and her self-absorption. He created a myopic Pola, who refuses to wear her glasses because she fears that she will not be able to attract the rich millionaire she is seeking. The contradictions of Pola's plight are amusing, for how can she find her rich consort without seeing him?

Johnson seems to have identified a crucial aspect of Monroe's personality. She was certainly self-involved, especially during the making of this film. Lauren Bacall recalled that Monroe "just had to concentrate on herself and the people who were there only for her." At the same time, she had to reach out; she would persistently try to overcome her self-absorption because it made her vulnerable, shutting her off from others and causing misunderstandings, as it did with Johnson, who thought she was stupid. So as she had done with Jane Russell, Monroe inquired about Bacall's children, her home life, her happiness. Monroe "seemed envious of that aspect of my life—wistful—hoping to have it herself one day," Bacall observed. In one of the most acute synopses of Monroe's character, Bacall concluded that Monroe was "afraid to trust . . . She made no effort for others and yet she was nice. I think she did trust me and like me as well as she could anyone whose life must have seemed to her so secure, so solved."

Like Pola without her glasses, Monroe could not perceive people as they were; they had to be within her myopic range. She had to feel that others were with her; if a given individual was not a sympathetic soul, she sensed an enemy. Jean Negulesco, her director on *Millionaire*, noted that "it is difficult to come close to her. She becomes vague. She puts up a curtain between herself and people." In his autobiography he recalls the sudden appearance of the hooded expression that disturbed Natasha Lytess: "With a soft-spoken voice, helpless as a sharp knife, her eyes at half mast like a cobra watching its prey, she was a cruel child tearing off butterfly wings—gay, mean, proud, and inscrutable." Negulesco was willing to cultivate her, to explain carefully the necessity of wearing glasses—she was afraid she would be made too unattractive—by mixing personal and professional relations in the course of having several dinners with her. He made a point of his interest in her as a person, and like Karger, Lytess, and Chekhov, he discussed art and literature to establish a rapport with her. He even painted her portrait, pointing out various artistic techniques. She was intrigued by his discussion of post-impressionist artists and asked "sensible" questions about them. She was slow to absorb his direction and hated script changes, yet her stamina over very long work hours and her total concentration impressed him. Several years later he remembered how "she had such a right sense of knowing the character she was playing—the way to enter a scene, to hold singular attention as the scene developed, the way to end a scene—so that no other actor existed around her."

There were times, however, when it seemed virtually impossible to mediate between Monroe's self-absorption and the corporate film world of cast and crew. During one trying afternoon on the set of *Millionaire*, Monroe kept "blowing one take after another, fluffing her lines, or forgetting them." Everyone was tired and tense in the late afternoon, and Johnson—sensing growing resentment and feeling sorry for Monroe—prepared to console her as she compulsively consulted a mirror to adjust her makeup. He told her she was doing well. There was nothing to worry about. She looked up from the mirror and seemed puzzled, for, according to Johnson, it was clear that she let him and Negulesco "do the worrying." All she cared about was her own part.

A publicity still from *Millionaire* elaborates on Monroe's tendency to pose for herself. The mirror shot has her in a typical position, with her right arm parallel to her face and her forearm bent backward as if to suggest, once again, a self-caress. The four-part mirror reflects four different angles of the same pose, with each angle gradually turning the star's face from distant profile to a three-quarter open view. The photograph en-

As Pola in *How to Marry a Millionaire* (1953)

closes Monroe within the panels of her own appeal. Her images revolve around her person, or is it the person—who is smiling dreamily—revolving around the images? With the aid of a mirror, one pose begets four different images; this is precisely the sort of self-amplification that Monroe seems to be enjoying in the photograph.

In the film, however, the scene in which this mirror appears is quite brief, and Pola only uses the mirror to check that everything is in the right place. *Millionaire* does not explore Monroe's interesting polarities of self-commitment and self-to-world involvement. Pola is too naïve, too limited in experience, and cannot approach Monroe's complexity. Or, stated another way, Monroe's psychological myopia is played for laughs by giving Pola a physical disability and various sight gags. Pola runs into walls and takes the wrong airplane, and Monroe is very skillful and funny performing the physical business of her role. It was characteristic of her to call on Chekhov to help with the timing of her comic scenes. Because Pola moves blindly through the world, she cannot see herself, a point that is vividly made during her encounter with Freddie Denmark (David Wayne), who wears glasses. Sitting next to her on a plane, he observes her reading a book upside down. "Why don't you wear glasses?" he asks. At first she denies her need for them, then hesitantly admits to her blindness when Denmark freely confesses his own reluctance to wear glasses until the day he said hello to three different men to whom he owed money. Denmark is forthright and obviously comfortable wearing glasses. He encourages Pola to wear hers and confides that he thinks with or without glasses she is "quite a strudel."

Monroe plays Pola's reactions perfectly. Waves of panic move across Pola's face as she tentatively puts her glasses on. Denmark's response is immediate, positive, and decisive. He tells her the glasses give her a "certain difference or distinction," and Pola glows with a happy sense of importance she has never felt before. She is directed to a sense of self-worth, just as Monroe sometimes depended on the sensitive guidance of others for belief in her own strength. But while Pola's salvation is accidental, Monroe sought and perceived ways of building a better self. Pola is passive; Monroe, who could retard her progress through inertia and timidity, was nevertheless dynamic and inventive in working out her own career.

Part of Monroe's problem was that many of her directors and the studios that hired them expected her to play a persona. This was the Howard Hawks approach. Capitalize on Monroe's physical features and mental quirks. Let her play those. Questions about "motivation" just got in the way and sounded pretentious to professionals concerned with the "big picture." That she could be so serious about her comedies was a contradiction in terms. Yet Monroe's demand that her parts yield more than her directors expected is precisely why her work survives. She endowed her performances with a subtlety that is apparent mainly in retrospect, when so much more is known about her preparations for the camera. So much of what an audience could see of her depended on the cultural climate. "The times being what they were," critic Molly Haskell suggests in *From Reverence to Rape: The Treatment of Women in the Movies,* "if she hadn't existed we would have had to invent her, and we did, in a way. She was the fifties' fiction, the lie that a woman has no sexual needs, that she is there to cater to, or enhance, a man's needs."

Marilyn Monroe ended the year 1953 at number five in the top ten list of box office stars. Both Lauren Bacall and Betty Grable had been gracious about the younger actress's star power, the latter saying to her, "Honey, I've had it. Go get yours. It's your turn now." Not in Howard Hawks's class as a director, Negulesco produced an inferior but popular film that proved Monroe could perform basically the same character again and again, no matter who directed her. If this knowledge was comforting to the studio, it was disturbing to Monroe. If she paid even less attention to most directors in her future roles, she did so, in part, because she believed that she was the only one looking out for her talent.

And yet in Monroe's public appearances, she seemed all too ready to rely on male directors of her life. She called on decisive Joe DiMaggio for support when she confronted the tyrannical Otto Preminger during the filming of *River of No Return* (May 1954). She had torn a knee ligament while struggling to meet the demanding director's schedule. DiMaggio arrived with a doctor to shore up both Monroe's mental and physical defenses, which were crumbling rapidly. Or were they? According to Shelley Winters, Monroe may have staged her accident to scare Preminger and her studio and to create sympathy for herself. After her accident, Preminger became amenable and DiMaggio ardent. She and DiMaggio had a lovers' quarrel before the start of the film, but sometime during filming they decided to marry.

In *River of No Return,* Monroe plays a dancehall girl, a "whore with a heart of gold," as Joan Mellen puts it. It is a poorly conceived movie, as Monroe knew, but that does not excuse her stilted, mannered speech, which is completely out of character, and which Preminger blamed on Natasha Lytess's emphasis on enunciation. Monroe is persuasive in her dancehall songs (Lotte Goslar helped her with them) and even compelling when she sings to a young boy (Tommy Rettig). In such scenes she

River of No Return (1954)

appears utterly at ease, charming, and at one with the western setting and her role. But her character, Kay, is passive. She has been mishandled by disreputable men and collaborated in their shady dealings. With her poor background, she has had few opportunities to be as good as she should be—although she does evolve emotionally and exhibits some feistiness when she makes Matt Calder (Robert Mitchum) abandon his "preconceived notions" about her dancehall career and acknowledge that she is capable of change. She seems less than the "real woman" Molly Haskell professes to see, however, and at the end of the film Calder literally carries her off to become his wife and the mother of his young son. All she needed, the film implies, was one good, clean, hardy, honest man to set her straight.

Monroe dismissed *River of No Return* as a "z western." Preminger seems too entranced with exploiting the widescreen possibilities of cinemascope, filming stirring scenes with Mitchum and Monroe on a raft in the rapids, so that spectacle overwhelms the drama and character development. Preminger and Monroe fought over Natasha Lytess's presence on the set, but Monroe appealed to Zanuck, who now felt he had to make certain concessions to a major star and took her side.

On January 14, 1954, shortly after the completion of *River of No Return*, Monroe did indeed marry a good, clean, hardy, trustworthy hero, Joe DiMaggio, the Yankee Clipper. The marriage was a sensational event. The couple found themselves on the covers of magazines, in the headlines of newspapers, and at the top of gossip columns all over the world. Monroe's studio had suspended her for refusing to do *Pink Tights*, which she regarded as a Betty Grable retread, but then it revoked the suspension and send congratulations to the honeymooning couple in Japan. "Joltin' Joe" was her slugger, Monroe told the press. Their marriage was another chapter in the American dream. Two of the beloved national pastimes, sports and movies, had been conjoined—"the merger of two worlds," *Life* (January 25) called it.

When they were en route to Japan, an army officer invited Monroe to entertain the troops in Korea. Without DiMaggio's endorsement, Monroe headed off to respond in person to the headlines, which elevated her in the public consciousness to a level she had never imagined possible. She had to improvise an act quickly, since she had not come to Japan with performing in mind, but she had no great problem with this change of plans. She took a few songs from her films and choreographed a personal triumph. One soldier, writing home to his mother on February 25, 1954, described Monroe's appearance in a "low cut, sheathe dress of purple glittery sort of material. She is certainly beautiful!!! When she appeared on the stage, there was just a sort of gasp from the audience—a single gasp multiplied by the 12,000 soldiers present was quite a gasp." The poor sound system did not matter. All that mattered was that she was *there*, the soldier emphasized: "[U]nlike lesser entertainers, after the show she autographed, chatted, and posed for pictures. Then thru all the trucks and jeeps she rode perched on top of the seat of her jeep, smiling and

Korea (1954)

waving. I think it was pretty wonderful that she came to Korea at all, and doubly so that she came to the divisions that have been so long on the line, and by-passed the easy duty in Seoul, Inchon, and the southern cities." Altogether she entertained approximately one hundred thousand troops over ten performances. Pictures of her singing and dancing in sub-zero temperatures were published all over the world. By all accounts she put on a remarkably poised and witty act—quite a feat for an actress who was not used to live audiences.

Monroe returned to DiMaggio in Japan suffering from pneumonia, but the cheers she had evoked warmed her immeasurably, even if this kind of fame could not fulfill her permanently. In *My Story*, she recalls that backstage before her first performance she could hear "music playing and a roar of voices trying to drown it out." An excited officer told her that she would have to "go on ahead of schedule . . . I don't think we can hold them any longer. They're throwing rocks on the stage." The repeated roar of her name demonstrated that her identity had an echo and an impact. She told Sidney Skolsky, "I felt I belonged. . . . For the first time in my life I had the feeling that the people seeing me were accepting me and liking me. This is what I've always wanted, I guess. That's why, without realizing the full meaning of what I was saying, I told Joe that for the first time I felt like a movie star."

At her last performance, Monroe told an audience of cheering soldiers that they made her feel for the first time in her life completely accepted. It had always been what she wanted. But now she wanted "to start a family. A family comes before a career." That was certainly what Joe DiMaggio wanted to hear and perhaps even what Monroe—free for the moment from the pressures of filmmaking—believed at the time.

Monroe was speaking of course to men who taped pictures of her in their lockers and who read *Stars and Stripes*, the military newspaper that frequently published photographs of her. She was, as Lois Banner notes, a Cold War symbol of American freedom and the "major pinup of the War (1950–1953)." Much of her fan mail came from servicemen who would be returning home to resume the family life she imagined for herself. These men were thrilled to see her, which perhaps accounts for the way she formulated her pleasure at "the feeling that people seeing me were accepting me and liking me." Without the apparatus of a studio, without the troubling setups, directors, coaches, cast and crew, and with no worries about her lines or the need to hide in her dressing room, she had made a success of herself. In Korea, Monroe was able to fuse herself with her film and photographic image, to be exactly what her audience had supposed her to be. In Korea, she became one with the imprint of her fame.

CHAPTER SIX

Half-Life (April–
November 1954)

Who is she—who does she think she is,
Marilyn Monroe?

L ike professional athletes, most stars have short careers. The exception is the actor—a Gary Cooper or Cary Grant—who can surmount the limitations of formulaic films. And Holly-wood has been especially tough on women. Even legends like Joan Crawford, Katharine Hepburn, and Bette Davis have succumbed to "box office poison" periods and have had to stage comebacks. Exceptions aside, stars could "malfunction," to use Janine Basinger's word in *The Star Machine.* Like a piece of equipment, the star could wear out, failing to perform at peak levels. "If some of the malfunctions had been assigned better roles or better advisers, or had come along in a different decade, or not been compared unfavorably to already established stars, or hadn't run away from it, bungled it, or even died, what might have happened?" Basinger asks. Her book is replete with examples of actresses who almost made it, who had gifts similar to Monroe's, but never found their niche—their piece of the Hollywood market. It was a fraught business, keeping oneself in proper condition. June DiMaggio noticed that Monroe was always worrying about her weight.

Monroe also had to watch out for studio missteps. As she learned the "business," she also learned to distrust Fox executives and directors who might not be able to use her the right way. Approaching her mid-twenties, Monroe also knew that at best she could continue as "the blonde" for perhaps another five to ten years before Hollywood would find a replacement. Leading men like Clark Gable and Jimmy Stewart could continue to play romantic parts into their early sixties, but Hollywood did not believe audiences would accept an older woman as the main love interest. In the 1950s, the trajectory for women on screen and off began with a brief career and ended in marriage. Certainly this was the scenario that Joe DiMaggio counted on and that Grace Kelly, Monroe's contemporary, achieved in her fairy tale marriage to Monaco's Prince Rainier, rumored to have been interested in Monroe before he settled on Kelly.

This era of the "feminine mystique" posited a world in which careers, higher education, and the professions were open to women but also quickly sealed off even for female college graduates, who anticipated working for only a few years at most before marrying and starting families. As Betty Friedan put it in her highly influential book, "The feminine mystique says that the highest value and the only commitment for women is the fulfillment of their own femininity." Women made a mistake when they tried to compete like men. They were going against their natures. Women could do the job, to be sure, but at great cost to the nurturing, maternal aspects of their nature. Even a highly ambitious poet like Sylvia Plath did not want to be known as a "career girl."

Monroe, devoted to her career, was nevertheless susceptible to this basically Freudian depiction of the unfulfilled woman. She believed in psychotherapy and participated in some form of analysis for most of her life. Although much has been written about the childhood traumas that contributed to her mental upsets, cultural determinants played a significant role in how she thought about herself as a woman and an actress. She never relinquished her commitment to acting as key to developing a sound identity, and yet marriage and childbearing remained just as crucial to her well-being. Her culture told her so.

Monroe performed in a patriarchal system, with Darryl Zanuck exercising the privileges of an authority figure, and Joe DiMaggio stamping her with his brand. To be sure, Monroe resisted this model of male domination—hence her fights with both Zanuck and DiMaggio—but she had very few female role models to suggest how she would establish her own authority, a point that Gloria Steinem, Donald Spoto, and Lois Banner explore in their biographies of Monroe.

Friedan had Monroe in mind when she wrote that the actress was the one type of career woman that women's magazines endorsed. But their role model was not the female star of the 1930s and 1940s, both comely and competitive—a Rosalind Russell or a Barbara Stanwyck—but instead a docile and rather dense figure like those Monroe and her imitators (Jayne Mansfield and Mamie Van Doren, for example) impersonated.

So long as women's magazines and Hollywood defined women solely in terms of their sexuality, their desire to do more with their lives and careers seemed oddly misplaced. Thus articles ridiculing or at the very least doubting Monroe's commitment to acting and her quest for serious roles were not seen as demeaning, but as part of mainstream thinking about Monroe's place in the culture.

When Betty Friedan questioned the Smith College graduates of 1959, she found many of them conflicted about their futures. Many were engaged and seemed relieved to have marriage solve the dilemma of what to do next, but they also seemed vaguely resentful that they would not be putting to use what they had learned at Smith, even though there was much unconvincing talk about continuing "work" by becoming involved in neighborhood and community activities. Those graduates who were not engaged to be married seemed equally at sea, not sure what they might do in terms of careers and somewhat envious of their engaged contemporaries, who seemed to have solved the problem of what to do with their lives. In truth, Friedan suggests, neither group of graduates seemed content with its choices—although they were less than candid about their feelings when talking together with Friedan. One of them took the author aside to say that what Friedan had been told publicly masked the anxiety these women felt about their limited options. In this regard, Marilyn Monroe, for all her fame and success, confronted the same narrow field of prospects—as would become apparent in due course when she began to protest the career her studio projected for her.

In one sense, no one understood Marilyn Monroe's plight better than Joe DiMaggio, a world-class athlete who hobbled into his thirties with a foot injury that shortened his career, although like Monroe he continued to perform at the highest levels. Up to 1953, DiMaggio had put up with the demands of Monroe's career, realizing how badly she wanted to succeed. But by the end of 1953, she had proved her point—or so it seemed to him. He did not believe that Hollywood would give her the opportunity to perform in a breakout role, one that would shatter the dumb blonde image. And he had no respect for Hollywood per se, regarding it as an industry full of phonies. The best she could do was swing a few big deals and then get out. He had never liked the publicity that came with becoming a star—not for himself, and certainly not for the woman he wanted to marry.

DiMaggio, very much a man of his era, believed that a home and family would be the best solution to Monroe's desire to fulfill herself as a woman. In this regard, he seemed no different from Freud himself. As Friedan points out in *The Feminine Mystique*, Freud implored his future wife to "withdraw from the strife" of unmarried life and seek refuge in the "calm uncompetitive activity of my home." He married his "adored darling" expecting her to have no identity other than "loved wife." A patient DiMaggio thought that Monroe would eventually tire of the studio grind. Making films is an arduous process, demanding long hours on movie sets, waiting and waiting and waiting for camera setups, sound checks, makeup, lighting—an incredible concatenation of machinery and technicians that requires enormous physical and mental concentration. When he visited her on movie lots, he noticed how tired and upset she would become. Was it really worth all this pain and struggle? he asked her. For all her stardom, she was still a contract player, which meant she had to take the roles assigned to her, no matter what she thought of them, and virtually punch a clock like any low-level employee.

DiMaggio's sense of dignity deeply appealed to Monroe. She wanted as much for herself. To him, her subservient roles both on screen and in relation to the studio were degrading. By and large most biographers have focused on the tensions between this couple because of DiMaggio's insistence that Monroe quit her career, but a corollary factor in their mutual attraction was his keen understanding of what she was due as a moneymaker for the studio. A hard bargainer himself, and no stranger to contract disputes, he counseled Monroe not to sell herself short. The couple continued to quarrel about her career, but even so she drew on DiMaggio's strength and his demands that she stand up for what she deserved. They understood one another as products of the Depression, both coming from poor families and yet fulfilling the grandest of American dreams.

DiMaggio's fame, especially at this juncture in Monroe's career, was crucial. "Sitting next to Mr. DiMaggio," Monroe said after their first date, "was like sitting next to a peacock with its tail spread, that's how noticeable you were." The media attention helped to establish her iconic status as the consort of the national pastime's heralded hero. A mystique had built up around the taciturn DiMaggio, making him the perfect foil for Monroe—the flamboyant actress who could act the demure date with him, a role movie studios loved because it allowed them to present their stars as being not so different from their fans. Marilyn Monroe wanted, it turned out, just what every other young woman wanted in America: a husband to take care of her. If her films projected an image of a woman who was seemingly available to every man, in "real life" this availability could be balanced by showing that she belonged, like most women in America, to one man. Such mixed messages were the very stuff of Hollywood's appeal to millions of moviegoers, beginning in the late 1920s with the establishment of fan magazines and gossip columns about Hollywood stars that paradoxically promoted both the stars' glamorous and yet supposedly conventional, morally acceptable, lives.

DiMaggio had a reserve so deep, and so profound a desire to be untouched by the world's interest in him, that he fascinated Monroe, who could be needy and demanding. How relaxing to be in the company of a man so self-contained. And yet he wanted Marilyn Monroe. This need gave him poignancy. Journalist Jimmy Cannon, who became a DiMaggio confidant (in so far as anyone could actually serve in such a role) called him the loneliest man he had ever met. That such a man should crave Monroe's company when he found it so difficult to share himself with others made him especially appealing to her. Unlike nearly every other man she met, this was one who could not possibly want to exploit her. Indeed, he promised to do just the opposite, to take her away from a world that overexposed her. And yet without that public recognition and acclaim Monroe seemed restless, anxious, and committed to resuming her film career.

In the spring of 1954, just after their honeymoon trip to Japan, Monroe and DiMaggio began quarreling. They were in San Francisco, his home town, where he apparently took up a "semi–bachelor" routine, while she waited impatiently to resume her career in *There's No Business Like Show Business*—a hackneyed musical she agreed to do only because in return she was promised the role of The Girl in *The Seven Year Itch*, a film adaptation of a hit Broadway play directed by Billy Wilder, one of Hollywood's greatest talents. Monroe also anticipated a new contract that would significantly raise her pay to the one hundred thousand dollars per picture that her agent Charles Feldman demanded from Fox. That she still had no creative control over her work dismayed her—and so did DiMaggio's reaction, because he thought she should be content with a raise. He never did appreciate her devotion to the art of acting, and his skepticism about her abilities became a factor in the rapid disintegration of their marriage.

Although DiMaggio grudgingly moved to Hollywood, he was not on the movie set to give Monroe support, as he had been for part of *River of No Return*. She, in turn, devoted little time to home life and conferred continually with Natasha Lytess, whom DiMaggio detested. Indeed, dur-

There's No Business Like Show Business (publicity still, 1954)

ing *Show Business* Monroe began to encircle herself with an entourage that would cater to her on subsequent movie sets. DiMaggio, no doubt, felt excluded from this group of followers, as did some of Monroe's co-workers, who came to deplore her menagerie of helpers, preferring to believe that she would have been better off relying on her own strengths rather than using others to shore up her weaknesses.

In *Show Business*, Monroe plays Vicky, a hatcheck girl who aspires to be an actress. Like Monroe's, Vicky's lowly beginnings provoke people—like Tim Donahue (Donald O'Connor), who will become her boyfriend—to scoff at her pretensions. She is pictured in front of a mirror,

There's No Business Like Show Business (1954)

posing for herself, rocking her head, and her lack of inflection, her way of pronouncing every word with equal emphasis—as in her line, "This gentleman was just leaving"—make her a wooden, uninspired copy of Monroe's earlier film characters. It is as if one of the well-worn pages of her studio biography had simply been inserted into the film. Her first musical number, "After You Get What You Want You Don't Want It," is an embarrassingly bad imitation of "Diamonds Are a Girl's Best Friend." Although she sings the number well, so that the song's wry sensibility is sophisticatedly poised in her warm, delicate phrasing, she is forced to throw herself at the various couples seated at nightclub tables, while she eyes men and turns her body at various angles to make her legs or her breasts more prominent. She also uses a familiar gesture from "Diamonds," placing her hands on her chest and shaking her breasts, but the scene as a whole fails to sustain the rapport between her person and her audience that the earlier film establishes. There is something very static and remote about this scene, even though Monroe is maneuvered into filling the movie frame in ways similar to those employed in *Gentlemen Prefer Blondes*. In a still often reproduced from this scene, she is captured with her arms extended upward and with her hands bent at the

On the set of *Show Business* (1954)

wrists and turned toward each other over her head, so that once again she frames herself in her own appeal, emphasizing her smiling, open-mouthed self-intoxication. Unlike her avatar, Lorelei Lee, Vicky is slightly freakish, a bizarrely angled bird with too much plumage, too much frippery that turns her into a prop, a thing on which to attach items of sexual provocation. Note the studio's description of the costume Monroe wears in this still: a "high necked, long-sleeved, slit-long-skirted evening gown of white illusion net over flesh crepe, with white-beaded lace appliques embroidered in strategic places."

Monroe's Vicky is essentially a character to gawk at, as she is in the other big production number, "Heat Wave," where her repertory of gestures is severely limited and the camera often concentrates on her crotch and other body parts. The film never attempts to integrate the vulgarian of these musical scenes with the poor naïve Vicky who is seen in short episodes with her boyfriend Tim. Somehow, more or less like Monroe, Vicky has become a rising star after having been on her own since she was fifteen. This cheap use of Monroe's by then already well known biography does nothing to enhance the characterization of Vicky, but it does demonstrate how Monroe was forced into dull formulaic work. It is difficult to appreciate her presence in this terrible film; her role is negligible, and overshadowed by such musical comedy stars as Ethel Merman and Dan Dailey. Monroe was ill throughout the making of Show Business, suffering from ailments variously reported as anemia, a low-grade virus, and just sheer physical exhaustion.

Rose Steinberg Wapner remembered Monroe on the set going over the same scene again and again until Wapner could see physical weakness in her eyes. It is the only film in which she observed this kind of weariness and dissipation of creative energy in Monroe. Reports of Monroe's excessive drinking, addiction to sleeping pills and amphetamines, and her need to consult a psychiatrist first surfaced during the making of this film. Not all of these reports are verifiable, yet it is apparent that she was under more stress than in any previous picture or period of her life. Her dress designer, Billy Travilla, remembered Monroe crying and expressing fears about losing her mind. "My brains are leaving me. I think I'm going crazy," she told him.

DiMaggio was extremely jealous and, according to some of Monroe's friends, physically abusive, although his niece, June DiMaggio, insists he expressed his anger by giving Monroe and others the "silent treatment." He suspected she was having an affair with her voice coach, Hal Schaefer, who later admitted as much. Like Fred Karger, Schaefer did not allow his feelings for her to interfere with the cultivation of her talent, and the intimacy between him and Monroe did not develop until several months after their film work ceased. Their affair, in fact, was an ordeal for him and contributed to a suicide attempt he barely survived.

Monroe's faltering marriage made work difficult, as Susan Strasberg observed on a visit: "Marilyn was perspiring heavily and kept falling out of step. Joe DiMaggio was on the set that day, so she was under additional tension. He hated the film and appeared on the set only this one time, refusing to be photographed with his wife and hurting her feelings when he agreed to posing in a two-shot with Ethel Merman. Monroe slipped in the middle of a complicated step and fell soundly on her backside. Taking a break she came over to us, still embarrassed from her fall." On the set of *Show Business* Monroe seemed to flounder. "She didn't appear to have any guidelines," Wapner remarked. In retrospect, it seems as though a phase of the actress's career was over, and that she would have to find some way to avoid these base imitations of herself.

Monroe had already begun to consider alternatives to Hollywood. In September of 1953 she had met the photographer Milton Greene, who began to encourage her to join him in the formation of her own film production company. And she had probably heard from Elia Kazan and others about the Actors Studio in New York, so when on the set of *Show Business* she finally met Paula Strasberg, the wife of the Studio's eminent head, Monroe declared: "I've heard so much about your husband, I think he's wonderful.... I've always dreamed of studying acting with Mr. Strasberg." In sum, Monroe had already made tentative contacts that made her move to the East less abrupt and less arbitrary than it appeared to the press who reported on it in her day.

When Monroe went to New York on September 9, 1954, to do location shooting for *The Seven Year Itch*, she resumed meeting with Greene and began confiding in him and his wife, Amy, about her career and her troubles with her husband. She was also keeping in touch with Arthur Miller by telephone, writing a few letters to him, and occasionally visiting Brooklyn, where he lived. She particularly enjoyed the heterogeneous life of urban streets and spoke to reporters about retiring to Brooklyn. Apparently, Monroe was meditating on a break with Hollywood long before she actually took up permanent residence in New York.

The Seven Year Itch may have represented a kind of culmination for her, one that made a break easier to contemplate, for her role in the film epitomizes the screen persona that had first been fully manifested in *Gentlemen Prefer Blondes*. Her character in *Itch*, The Girl, is given no name until near the end of the film, when her would-be lover, Richard

The Seven Year Itch (1955)

Sherman (Tom Ewell), says in swaggering fashion to another male that maybe The Girl is Marilyn Monroe. Audiences still explode with laughter at this in-joke, just as audiences roared their approval in 1955.

In *Itch*, Monroe plays at being herself, parodying the screen persona she has become. Many of The Girl's lines are similar to Lorelei Lee's. For instance, Lorelei could easily have spoken The Girl's line about knowing how to identify a piece of classical music: "[T]here is no vocal." When The Girl does her commercial for Dazzle-dent toothpaste, she couches her words and her figure in the simpering attitudes of Monroe's early publicity photographs. Better than any movie up to this point, *Itch* exemplifies the range of Monroe's appeal. In *Gentlemen Prefer Blondes*, she is paired at various times with a precocious young boy possessed of a mature voice; a wimpy young man with an adolescent outlook; and an old man with some sexual vigor left in him. In *Show Business*, an ordinary looking song-and-dance man charms her. In *Itch*, she fills in the middle ground of her democratic attractiveness by becoming the object of a middle-aged, middle-class male's sexual fantasies.

Sherman works for a publishing house capitalizing on the advent of mass-market paperbacks, just then becoming a staple of the book trade.

Even classics like *The Scarlet Letter* are given lurid covers that previously had been the province of pornography. Sherman's firm is about to publish an academic psychological study of the seven year itch in the middle-aged male with a sensationalized cover. Of course, the film exaggerates this trend toward the sexualization of everything, but Hollywood, the cosmetics industry, and the entire business of beautification burgeoned in the 1950s, as women gave themselves home permanents, and bought padded bras that brought their figures in line with the likes of Monroe, Jane Russell, and Jane Mansfield. The complaint that one woman might make about a rival flaunting her sexuality—"Who does she think she is? Marilyn Monroe?"—was common enough by the mid-1950s.

Monroe arrives as The Girl everyone can enjoy. She is no longer someone else's mistress (*The Asphalt Jungle, All About Eve*), someone else's secretary (*As Young as You Feel, Monkey Business*), or someone else's wife or girlfriend (*We're Not Married, Niagara, Show Business*). Indeed, The Girl has no boyfriends or bosses, and she does not see herself in competition with other women. She is readily available to even the most passive male. Sherman, like the moviegoer, only has to dream about her in order for her to appear. She remains accessible even after Sherman blunders badly in his seduction of her; she is, in short, the perfect plaything—a living doll, as one of the characters in the film keeps insisting. "You're just elegant," The Girl tells Sherman at a strategic moment when he is feeling particularly inept and unattractive, and she earnestly hopes that his wife will value him more highly. She constantly strokes his middle-aged ego. She tells him he has powerful thumbs as he pops the champagne cork, which is clearly a not so covert allusion to his wanting to pop her, a girl who is as effervescent as the champagne she loves to dip her potato chips in. Similarly, his twitching thumb is a barely disguised token of what is no doubt—the audience is invited to imagine—his other pulsating member, the strong sexual drive he tries to suppress in loyalty to his marriage of seven years. The Girl delivers puns on phallic penetration without a flicker of self-consciousness, and she is oblivious to Sherman's "grownup" leer about her "interesting point of view." She seems infinitely innocent and willing to follow every turn of Sherman's erratic stop-and-go romancing.

The celebrated skirt-blowing scene is, of course, the finest instance of a Monroe character's ability to suggest simultaneously both child-like pleasure and sexual delight. Photographs of Monroe straddling a subway grating with her dress forced high above her thighs by the rush of air coming from below appeared in magazines and newspapers around the world. It seemed that she was caught in a spontaneous moment of joy and relief on a hot city summer night, and that moment was suspended above ground and defined from nearly every conceivable angle. She was shot in profile, straight on, with her head tilted backward, forward, or turned three-quarters of the way toward the camera. In one pose she is holding her dress, so that it fans out in front of her, revealing her panties, and fans out behind her, as she twists her neck in ecstasy. In another pose her whole body surges forward with one of her fingers seemingly shooting in the direction of the camera that is shooting her. The self-reflexiveness of such shots does not carry over into the filmed scene. On the contrary, it seems subdued and understated after one has become accustomed to the plethora of poses available in the photographs. In the film, the forced air lifts her dress rather sedately above her knees, although in a second shot the camera fastens on and moves along the surface of the subway grating as if tracking the gust of air shooting up from a speeding train, and simulating the rush of feeling exemplified in The Girl's lifted spirits and skirt.

Monroe is something else besides an object of male fantasy, or an airy symbol of a nature goddess almost able to raise herself in her magical skirt above the grimy subway grating to fly as high as her soaring orgasm of delight. She also plays The Girl as a woman who is herself; that is to say, there is a matter-of-factness about her, a down-to-earth directness reminiscent of Clara Bow. This aspect of the The Girl disconcerts Sherman. She is kind to him, but she makes it clear that his air conditioner, in this hot city summer, is one of his main attractions. She is less impressed by his efforts to be suave than she is by his genuine modesty and self-effacement. What he excites most in her is compassion and sincere respect for his homely strengths. She clearly indicates that she rebuffs good-looking, conceited young men who try to overwhelm her with their high opinions of themselves. Although one could interpret her preference for Sherman as another one of his middle-aged projections, there is a solidity to The Girl, a sureness that surprises him and makes it unlikely that she is just his fantasy. In fact, her lack of embarrassment about her motives, and her charming way of conveying them to him, make her seem—at least in this respect—not at all dumb, but instead more mature than Sherman.

Take, for example, the scene in which she discovers that by simply pulling up a few nails she can open a trap door that leads immediately to a set of stairs that descend from her apartment into his. As she reaches the landing, she pauses with a hammer poised delicately in one hand and a toothbrush in the other and sweetly announces, "You know what? We can do this all summer." The camera holds on her wide-eyed child's face as she subtly shifts to a narrow-eyed, adult concentration conveying an unmistakable sexual innuendo—to which audiences respond with both laughter and the verbal asides that one expects in connection with double entendre. Such minutely perceptible modulations in the way Monroe plays The Girl—and the camera's facility in fastening on her long enough to suggest that more is there than the initial impression of naïveté—has the audience, rather than the actors, doing double–takes. Monroe's character is as infinitely suggestive as she is innocent.

As usual, the publicity surrounding this Monroe film virtually obliterated any consideration of her talent. Instead, primarily because of the skirt-blowing scene, she was treated as having shown more of herself than ever before. The filming of this celebrated scene at 2:30 a.m. on September 10, 1954, in New York City, attracted a crowd variously estimated to have been between one thousand and four thousand people, who watched Monroe's skirt fly up fifteen times as the scene was rehearsed. DiMaggio had arrived two days earlier and drew the attention of some fans and the press. Amid shouts of "higher" and "hurrah" as the wind-blowing machine puffed his wife's skirt over her head, DiMaggio retreated in silent anger. Monroe herself seemed taken aback at the spectacle Billy Wilder had made of her. She is reported to have asked him if he was going to show the more lurid shots to his male cronies.

Around 4:00 a.m., Monroe returned to her hotel room. DiMaggio arrived somewhat later. Evidently they quarreled over her night's work, for "some shouting and scuffling was overheard by other hotel residents nearby, followed by hysterical weeping." The next day DiMaggio departed for California, and Monroe remained heavily sedated. When she arrived on the set of *The Seven Year Itch*, her bruises had to be covered with makeup. As awful as DiMaggio's attack may seem, in the 1950s and in earlier generations wife beating was rarely reported as a crime, and many wives put up with physical abuse. Barbara Stanwyck, one of Hollywood's most stalwart stars, suffered repeated beatings from her first husband, Frank Fay. After he knocked her down in front of their son, she decided to divorce him. Like Monroe, Stanwyck had been attracted to an older man she thought of as her protector—until he asserted his male prerogative. As to why she spent years in an abusive marriage, Stanwyck explained, "Gee, it's swell . . . to have somebody to stand between you and the world." It was not unusual for Hollywood films of the 1940s and 1950s to include jokes about wife beating. Rita Hayworth, Hollywood's reigning sex symbol in the 1940s, tolerated physical cruelty in her marriage to Dick Haymes during a period when the very concept of domestic violence was unfamiliar and seldom addressed with intervention by public authorities. That Monroe responded quickly and decisively to DiMaggio's aggression suggests how determined she was to change direction. Less than a month later, on October 4, her attorney would announce the end of her marriage, and she would proceed to finish *Itch* without the breakdowns, tardiness, and falterings that now were customary on her sets.

Monroe remained adamant about her decision to dissolve the marriage and seemed just as determined to demonstrate her commitment to her career. She also seemed intent on exploiting every opportunity for publicity. Sidney Skolsky, present during the preparations for Monroe's appearance before the press to announce her divorce, recalls how Jerry Geisler, her attorney, acted like a movie director, explaining the mood he wanted. Skolsky was to offer his support, while the attorney held Monroe tightly in his grip. The newsreel footage of the announcement certainly suggests a staged, melodramatic scene in which Monroe's sorrow is made public in the way Geisler planned. She walks out of the house, faces the microphones, begins to speak, falters, and wells up with tears. As her attorney supports her, she slowly shakes her head from side to side as if to signal that she cannot trust herself to say anything.

Why did Monroe face the press and cameras in this carefully framed way? Because she learned to view her life in terms of camera set-ups. Her real distress over the break-up with DiMaggio had to be used as another scene in her script. Another eyewitness account of Monroe's preparations for the press has her "numb from emotional fatigue. New floods of tears ruined her mascara every few minutes so Marilyn was obliged to spend much of her time in front of a mirror in her second-floor bedroom." She was forced to put a face on her emotions, to repair her image in the mirror repeatedly, because that was the only way she knew how to put herself together. Monroe was living with the consequences of having become a performing self, the kind of self for which, Shelley Winters remarks, reality has to be heightened by turning one's private life inside out: "Sometimes I'll be weeping and I'll look in the mirror and I say, 'Why do I twist up my face?' I'm right in the middle of agony and I'm sort of remembering how I got to this feeling of agony. . . . I'm not sure that this is good, in fact, I think it's bad, but maybe you can't help it if you're an actor." The actor's only instrument is herself, and she has to be on view for every occasion and know how to project her life into her roles. As a result, much of her experience is filtered and stored up for public exposure. Actors conduct constant raids on their own lives. For Monroe, the accretion of photographs, films, and mirror images tended to prevent her from being direct with herself. Working with her life had come to resemble working with the paste-up she had done for *Show Business*, in which she recorded the "Heat Wave" song twenty-five times for one of her singing coaches, Ken Darby, who took "the twenty-five pieces of tape home with him and cut them up and put them together so that she had the proper phrasing in each part of the song" and could then re-create it in the studio.

Given Monroe's superb command of Hollywood publicity, it came as a shock a few months later when she announced that she was leaving Twentieth Century-Fox and moving to New York. Almost immediately, however, her move was suspected to be a publicity ploy, and few people seemed to appreciate that she had become so saturated with her own stardom that she felt stymied. Although Monroe would indulge in various kinds of publicity maneuvers for the rest of her career, never again would her life be quite as public as it has been during *The Seven Year Itch* and her divorce from DiMaggio. In her last years she was—in a way that anticipated the Beatles—in revolt against herself, or against the popular personality she had created. Like the Beatles, she had served a long apprenticeship in which she had worked much harder than others reaching for the same kind of recognition. Like John Lennon, she voiced the "infantile longing behind every star's obsession. 'Why didn't anybody notice me?'" She shared the Beatles' talent for turning everything into an event, a spectacle, and she succeeded—as they did—because on and off stage and screen she was good theater, a good ad-libber, a wit, a vivacious creator of comic cross-talk that foreshadowed the Beatles' press conferences. She regarded her appearances before the press as little comedy shows that she deftly directed. She acted out her personality in films just as the Beatles created their personalities through their music and movies. She became increasingly skilled and sophisticated in her film work, just as they became more musically ambitious and adept. Finally, like them, she mythologized herself, drawing on her past and future as, in essence, her only subject, even while withdrawing from the public and focusing more on her art than on public acclaim.

CHAPTER SEVEN

Search for Self:
The Method (November 1954–
May 1956)

*Goethe said, "Talent is developed in privacy," you
know? And it's really true. There is a need for
aloneness which I don't think most people realize for
an actor. It's almost having certain kinds of secrets
for yourself that you'll let the whole world in on only
for a moment, when you're acting.*

M onroe had been consulting with Milton Greene for over a
year about her own production company. His idea included the possibility of buying screen properties in which she
could extend her capacity as an actress. If she could manage her career through her choice of sympathetic directors and producers, then she was prepared to entertain Greene's enthusiastic belief that
she could play the roles she coveted. By the end of 1954, Marilyn Monroe
Productions had been established, with Monroe as president and Greene
as vice-president. She had become convinced that her contract with Fox
could be declared to have no legal standing, or at least that the formation
of her own company would pressure Fox executives into giving her better
roles and more control over the filmmaking process.

Greene's reputation had been made as a superb photographer, not a
producer. In his early thirties, he was very young, many people thought,
to be taking on Fox, to be supporting Monroe during what turned out
to be a year-long battle with her studio, and to be masterminding the
making of movies he promised would be far more sophisticated than her
earlier Hollywood products. Some of Monroe's friends distrusted his

motives and suspected him of exploiting her. They advised her to pick someone with more experience, with more Hollywood savvy. Undoubtedly Greene appealed to her precisely because he was not part of the Hollywood establishment. After all, what had old Hollywood hands like Charles Feldman done for her? He had secured *The Seven Year Itch*, to be sure, but at the price of her appearance in the dreadful *There's No Business Like Show Business* and making no headway at all with Fox concerning her demands for more creative control of her movies. Moreover, she had not naïvely trusted the ambitious Greenes. She did not confide unreservedly in Milton's wife, Amy, who seemed particularly keen to ingratiate herself with influential people.

Milton Greene had been introduced to Monroe by their mutual friend, Rupert Allan, and he had come to Monroe, on Allan's advice, with his portfolio in hand. Greene was brash and youthful looking. "He appeared to be about eighteen years old in those days," Allan recalled. "You're just a boy," Monroe exclaimed. "You're just a girl," Greene immediately replied. Could Greene somehow take Monroe just for what she was and work with her identity from scratch? It is hard to say which of them was more excited by that prospect, since they were nearly equal in age and hopeful that their best years, their finest accomplishments, were ahead of them.

Greene was more than just a charming talker, a young man with a quick wit remarkably like Monroe's—or a wit adaptable to her own spontaneous humor. His photographs of her capture that rare luminescence she could have in person, a brilliance even greater ("if you can imagine that," Lee Strasberg told Fred Guiles) than what appeared on the screen. Norman Mailer has captured in a sentence some of the impressive range Greene was able to capture in his photographs, which convey "a mist of glamour, tenderness, amusement, sex, and subtle sorrow." *Of Women and Their Elegance* superbly exhibits Greene's photographs of Monroe, and it reveals much not only about his relationship with her, but also about the kind of performer she was becoming as she realized her freedom from the restraints of earlier poses and positions. One black and white sequence, for example, demonstrates the evolution of a far more intriguing personality than was found in her earlier photographs. Monroe seems much older; in part, at least, the sense of age arises from the austerity of the setting. In the book's cover shot, her figure from the bust line downward is encased in a dark garment that is virtually indistinguishable from the black background. Her blonde hair, which is usually luxuriantly displayed, is barely seen and seems almost wispy at the sides and shrouded by black at the top of her head. Her long, dark eyelashes enhance the mysteriousness of her hooded expression. She is almost smiling, but her lips are not parted. Her right eye is slightly open, and the left appears to be closed.

The familiar teasing pose—half revealing, half concealing the sex symbol—is shaded here, suggesting ambiguity and perhaps a divided self, which is the insistent theme of Mailer's narrative in *Of Women and Their Elegance*. This particular photograph is suggestive of a sexuality about which more needs to be known. But that sexuality seems rooted not simply in the body, but in what could be sadness in the eyes and smile—if she is indeed smiling. This woman's complex thoughts, her conflicting emotions, are not apparent in her earlier photographs. For the first time, perhaps, Monroe's sexuality and wry wit are seriously linked—but remain almost somberly elusive. She is a figure of shadow and light, a delicately poised, dark, impenetrable body, more nearly a part of the photographic medium than she had ever been before—and at the same time defined more provocatively as a person than any photographer had been able to do before.

Like many of Monroe's other photographers, Greene pointed out that Monroe was hardly a passive subject for the camera. She almost never initiated the idea for a pose, but once he began to suggest ideas to her, she would respond immediately by adding her own distinctive touches. No photograph could work, Greene emphasized, without Monroe's full cooperation and understanding. Their fascinating collaboration reveals different attitudes toward the camera. At times, she plays up to it; occasionally, she seems aloof and keeps her distance. Then there are poses in which her awareness of being photographed seems problematic, so that it is not clear whether she is entirely caught up with herself or seeming to be so in front of the prying lens. Or is it the photographer's selection of camera angles and focus that determines the diversity of feelings encoded in the photographs? Even if Greene was at the controls, so to speak, he had to navigate by Monroe's moods and to track an intricate and evanescent personality with the mechanisms at his disposal.

However Greene's photographs are read, they offer indisputable evidence of maturation. They project Monroe's liberation from Hollywood. By the end of 1954, she was in New York City and in contact with Arthur Miller. Over several months they drew closer together. From December 1954 to February 1955 Monroe stayed in relative isolation with the Greenes in Weston, Connecticut, before coming to New York to romance with Miller, to investigate working with Lee Strasberg at the Actors Studio, and to begin her life and career anew. Soon she would be firmly under the influence of Greene, Strasberg, and Miller—the triumvirate—as she had been previously with Lytess, Karger, and Hyde. Although she retained some of her Hollywood connections—staying in close touch with the Karger family, for example—her professional relationships, particularly with Lytess, were broken. She allowed nearly a year to pass before having Lytess officially notified by telegram that she would no longer serve as Monroe's acting coach.

To this triumvirate came Margaret Hohenberg, Milton Greene's psychoanalyst, who took on Monroe as a patient. At first, this arrangement solidified the bond between Greene and Monroe, but when the actress began to doubt Greene's loyalty to her in the following year, her therapeutic regimen seemed to result in a conflict of interest—especially when Hohenberg began giving career advice to Monroe and became, in effect, part of her entourage. Even though Monroe herself constantly mingled the business and personal sides of her life, sooner or later this expanding circle of advisers seemed to constrict her. In her mind, Hohenberg would seem part of a campaign to control her both emotionally and professionally.

But in early 1955, Milton Greene's influence on Monroe was at its greatest, especially during her nearly three-month stay in his home. His wife warmly welcomed Monroe and included her in household activities. The actress avidly read Amy's books, especially biographies of Napoleon and his wife Josephine. She was attracted to powerful mistresses of historical figures like Lord Nelson and to artists like Isadora Duncan. Of particular interest to her were women who invented themselves, so to speak, and imposed their personalities upon an age. Monroe, Amy Greene recalls, had a powerful need to hear stories, encapsulations of lives even as she worked on her own. The actress kept a diary full of her observations about conversations, magazine articles, and other items that caught her interest. In the Greenes' descriptions of this period, a remarkable sense of the actress's restlessness and drive emerges. They could hear her very late at night, sometimes reading, sometimes playing the radio. Usually, sleep would come only after her regular dosage of Seconal.

Episodes of severe distress occasioned by her menstrual periods made Monroe weep over an internal ache no analgesic could assuage. Her Los Angeles physician, Dr. Lee Siegel, noted that she suffered from endometriosis, "a condition in which womb-lining tissue forms in places other than the womb, such as the ovaries or Fallopian tubes." As a result, Monroe was often in agony and felt the pain acutely in her reproductive organs, a pain which increased due to the progressive nature of her ailment.

As her then psychiatrist Ralph Greenson learned four years later during the making of *Let's Make Love*, Monroe dealt with her cycles of pain and insomnia by resorting to a wide variety of drugs: Demerol (a "narcotic analgesic similar to morphine"), Phenobarbital HMC and Amytal (barbiturates), and sodium pentathol ("a depressant of the nervous system, primarily used in anesthesia"). She impressed Greenson with her knowledge of pharmaceuticals, but she also scared him because she would mix several kinds of drugs together and was adept at getting prescriptions from several different doctors as well as from Milton Greene. According to Donald Spoto, Greene became addicted to the same kinds of drugs Monroe used and desperately resorted to them to increase his energy levels and hers. Some of these drugs—especially Demerol—she took by injection, and Greenson put a stop to that dangerous practice.

To be always "on" is very wearing for performers. Even a strong woman like Barbara Stanwyck staggered in the glare of Hollywood's klieg lights. As the actor Robert Wagner reveals in a memoir that describes his four-year affair with her, Stanwyck regularly saw a psychiatrist. Like Monroe, she had trouble sleeping. Her psychiatrist had to prescribe sodium pentothal injections to sedate her. "Like so many people in show business," Wagner observes, "she was a prisoner of her career."

Although there is no doubt about the debilitating consequences of Monroe's drug taking, previous accounts give the impression that she was immobilized and totally dependent on stimulants and sedatives, including alcohol. Yet this impression is misleading, as Greenson implied with his reluctance to term her an addict. She did not experience withdrawal symptoms when she abstained from medication. Although drugs sometimes impaired her ability to perform, "they also became a crutch and gave her the lift some performers find in cocaine." In other words, she was caught up in intense moments of creativity while battling equally intense moments of fear and pain. While she rationalized her drug use, it is also clear that doctors, including her psychiatrists, could not identify the source of her pain or alleviate the anxiety that prevented her from sleeping. She turned to quick-fix remedies in order to cope with the relentless pressures that were a part of her position as one of the premier performers of her time.

Initially, the Greenes were a calming influence. Milton remained irrepressibly upbeat about Monroe's battle with Fox to have some creative control over her career, and Amy conducted herself with an authority the actress admired. Monroe took to heart some of Amy's advice on how to dress in a less flamboyant manner and how to handle herself in a more understated fashion. Monroe husbanded her talent after years of profligacy in Hollywood. But if she became more circumspect about herself, she also knew that Milton Greene had to be a showman and needed to keep his business partner in the public eye, so she consented to ride a pink elephant in Madison Square Garden in March of 1955 as part of a charity event. On the whole, however, Monroe became part of Greene's sophisticated style, as can be seen in the manner his photographs of her closely match those of other models in *Of Women and Their Elegance*. These photographs give evidence that for all her troubles, she had attained a fair amount of mastery over herself.

In the Edward R. Murrow *Person to Person* interview broadcast live on April 8, 1955, from the Greenes' home, Monroe appears exceedingly modest, as if she is indeed under the tutelage of this couple. Many of Murrow's questions are directed to Milton and Amy, and there is an air of condescension in his queries about whether Monroe is a good houseguest. It is almost as if they are discussing a child, and Monroe's tiny voice and diffidence certainly suggest something like a child's embarrassment in front of a camera. When asked about her new production company, she speaks of wanting to make good pictures and agrees with Murrow's leading question that she got tired of playing the same roles all the time and wanted to try something different. She offers a capsule history of her career, mentioning her work with Huston, Chekhov, Lytess, and Wilder, and she attempts to make a significant comment on the importance of a director who "is with you . . . really with you every moment." There is more behind her faltering comments than she conveys, but she appears vacuous and at one point shrugs her shoulders as though she is belittling what she has just said. She sounds like a little girl when she describes what joy it was to ride on the elephant in Madison Square Garden. All the while, Amy appears to be feeding Monroe cues, and as Amy strokes the dog that is lying beside them, Monroe does the same. She seemed to be confused about how to appear, writing a note to herself after the show: "I'm not M.M.—I'm not permitted to be," and then crossing out "not" and "to be."

Monroe's confidence in the Greenes seems to have weakened after the

Murrow interview. It was one thing to learn a more subtle way of presenting herself in the privacy of their home. It was quite another to have her tentativeness exposed on television, which was more than she—or probably anyone—could bear with equanimity. Monroe made no overt effort to break with the Greenes, but her suspicions were aroused—especially since she found it difficult to cope with the ambitions of others and could not accept that inevitably their motivations would be mixed. She wanted to believe, on all counts, in their selflessness—or in a short time she would not believe in them at all. Perhaps the Greenes were to her something like temporary help in her quest to revamp her career. She could never give herself to them as wholeheartedly as she did to her acting teacher, Lee Strasberg.

At a dinner party in March, about a month before her interview with Murrow, Monroe met Cheryl Crawford, a Broadway producer and one of the co-founders of Actors Studio, the principal agency of Lee Strasberg's formidable influence on American acting. Apparently Monroe was quite candid about her ambition to act larger, more complex roles, and Crawford responded by recommending a visit to Strasberg, who would size up her talent. It is quite likely that Monroe had been angling for an appointment with this acting master, but at the same time she probably dreaded his legendary reputation for incisively evaluating the actor's method, for she had Elia Kazan accompany her on her first meeting with Strasberg. That initial encounter was nothing less than a comprehensive examination of her reactions to very personal, embarrassing questions designed to gauge her sensitivity, to ascertain how easily, quickly, and imaginatively she could react to what Strasberg termed "the stimulus." Her extraordinary responsiveness surprised him, since he would have expected such acuteness to have been killed by her Hollywood milieu. Instead, it had "remained fresh and alive . . . without really having been hurt." If anything, the sum of her experience had made her more sensitive than she had ever been before. As he described his impressions to Guiles nearly five years after Monroe's death, Strasberg's voice still carried something of a sense of wonder and a note of the incredulity that may have arisen during his first discovery of the miracle of Monroe's sensitivity. In his direct, even blunt treatment of her, and in his unshakable faith in her talent, Strasberg may well have reminded her of Michael Chekhov, a man, Strasberg observed to Guiles, who intrigued Monroe.

The change from Chekhov's to Strasberg's teaching was not disruptive. After all, both men had been schooled in the Stanislavsky approach to acting, and Strasberg professed nothing but respect for Chekhov. Thus she came to Strasberg not to learn a whole new way of acting—although newspaper accounts would make it seem so—but to work on, as Strasberg told Guiles, her conscious control of herself as an actress, on her discipline and concentration. Although Strasberg doubted that she read much of Stanislavsky and suggested it was enough for her to absorb his principles in acting classes, it seems more in character for Monroe to have read part of Stanislavsky seriously—to have attempted him just as she tackled but could not totally master Todd—and then turn to Strasberg for further inspiration. Like Chekhov, he was a scholar of the theater, and he responded to her out of his deep immersion in theatrical history, comparing her favorably to the finest stage performers, like Jeanne Eagels in *Rain*, an actress who haunted his imagination.

Strasberg took Monroe out of the vacuum of her search for self and method, out of those necessary but now superannuated three months of quiet study at the Greenes. He urged a fundamental recovery of her roots as a person and a basic reassessment of her techniques as an actress, so that the sources of her creativity could be revealed and channeled into finer performances. He saw that she was already an accomplished actress—especially in *The Seven Year Itch*—but he also saw her uncertainties. Even though audiences had been satisfied with her performances thus far, the actress acknowledged the futility of not knowing how to achieve her best work.

For both personal and professional reasons, Monroe worked privately with Strasberg. He explained to Guiles that "it was too difficult for her to subject herself to public scrutiny. Work at the Studio is done before members who then take what you've done apart." Edward Easty, a fellow student at the Studio, found Monroe's reluctance to act in public unusual, but Strasberg stressed that she was terrified of a live performance because all of her professional work had been done on film. Moreover, she was braving an intimidating situation that many actors and actresses—even those who had gone through the trials of opening on Broadway—would not countenance. James Dean, for example, walked out of a Studio class that he felt was sterilizing him with severe criticism. Stella Adler, one of Strasberg's Group Theater associates, attacked him for having stripped actors of their personalities by encouraging what is commonly known as the Method, an intense concern with how the actor's private life informs his acting roles.

Monroe's use of the Method remains controversial, and opinions of her directors, casts, and crews on the sets of her final films, from *Bus Stop* to *The Misfits*, remain deeply divided about its usefulness. Even Strasberg's supporters do not deny that the Method makes actors vulnerable. Ellen Burstyn points out that the increased sensitivity produced by the Method might threaten the equilibrium of the self, might make life more painful. But actors require that excruciating sensitivity, she believes, and they have to be willing to risk themselves for their art. It is an art, Helen Hayes suggests, that by its very nature makes actors "volatile" and "overly emotional because we are so aware of our own pain and doubts and fears in life, just as we are aware of those of everyone around us. And when you are in on those inner secrets of people's hearts and souls, you can't just become as wonderfully detached and cool-headed as a surgeon or a legal mind."

Some of Monroe's friends opposed her use of the Method because they believed it fractured her ego by having her recall traumatic past experiences. Arthur Miller, always wary of the Strasbergs, contended that the Method imprisons actors in their subjectivity and turns the social life of the theater too far inward, so that the reciprocal relationship between characters and their audience is ruined. In film, on the other hand, the Method is more acceptable, he conceded, because it is adaptable to the camera's proximity to private emotions. Miller may have been thinking of film's singular ability to suggest inner feelings by focusing so precisely on an actor's features and gestures. Monroe claimed that before her film career began her feelings were not reckoned; they simply vanished unrecorded and unheeded by others. It is easy to understand why she would find the Method attractive, for it makes acting excruciatingly intimate, close-up to the actor's person, thereby fusing—or at least bridging—the break between private and performing selves. Strasberg was responding to both sides of her, and she found it necessary to center her career hopes on his efforts to unite her disjointed identity. Or as he put it to Maurice Zolotow, "[W]hat was going on inside was not what was going on outside, and that always means there may be something there to work with." Strasberg would serve, in many ways, as the integrating force in her life and would earn the gratitude and respect of many of her professional associates. John Springer, who would work as Monroe's East Coast publicist during the final three years of her life, had ample opportunity to witness the positive difference Strasberg made in his client's life. Indeed, to listen to Springer describe Monroe's deep involvement with Strasberg and the Actors Studio is to realize how close she came, under Strasberg's guidance, to making acting and her life all of a piece.

With Michael Chekhov's death in September of 1955, Strasberg became the sole focus of Monroe's highest aspirations as an actress. On first hearing of her work with Strasberg, Billy Wilder suggested that it would spoil Monroe's natural instincts; she would become self-conscious and lose her audience. He subscribed to a rather common belief that she was a "natural." But he was ignoring much of her deliberate preparation for earlier films. He regarded her as an essentially passive actor, which meant that Strasberg was doing something to her; strenuous acting exercises would burden her with extraneous techniques. Yet for all of Wilder's difficulties with her later on their film, *Some Like It Hot*, he had to admit that, if anything, her acting had improved. As John Huston put it to Fred Guiles, she acted from "the inside out," allowing the camera to record emotions as they arose to the surface of her whole visible self. Like many other accomplished screen actors, she learned to let the camera trigger her feelings and target her attention. Both Strasberg and Joshua Logan, her director on *Bus Stop*, suggested as much.

Strasberg realized that the Method was the actor's means of collaborating with the camera's pinpointing of action, and his insistence that every gesture, every movement, have its motivation made clear his affinity with psychoanalysis. He used terms like "sublimation," by which he meant the actor's ability to free his own experience, to make it available for contact with the character she is playing. With Monroe, Strasberg found it necessary, as he had with other actors, to recommend that she see a psychiatrist, so that the deeply emotional re-creations of her past in acting exercises would receive appropriate clinical treatment. If it was dangerous to evoke her childhood traumas, there is no evidence to suggest that he burdened her unduly with recollections of the past or that he emphasized them inordinately. On the contrary, his practice was to use no more of such past experience than was absolutely necessary to a part. He had little patience with self-indulgence and could abruptly dismiss a student by saying, "Don't enjoy your ability to weep."

Robert Hethmon observed Strasberg handle personal emotions "with great delicacy and tact, and with great watchfulness"—as can be seen in this tape-recorded example of his instructions on the use of "affective memory": "[Y]ou try to see the people that you saw. You try to hear the things that you heard. You try to touch now the things you touched then.

You try to remember through your senses what your mouth tasted and what you wore and the feeling of that garment against your body. The emotion you try not to remember at all." He sharply cut off any attempt to withdraw from the actuality, the objectivity of the actor's performance: "Really look at us. Don't just make believe. Really see us. Make clear to yourself that you're real and we're real. . . ." There had to be an engagement between actor and audience, not a retreat into fantasy. Instead of causing further distress by recalling what was sometimes a painful past, Strasberg found in his own practice that "the work [at the Studio] helped the [psycho]analysis, and the [psycho]analysis helped the work." Certain "very sharp or strong things" aroused in Monroe's acting could be further explored in therapy. Or certain things that were "blocked" in her psychoanalytical sessions were revived and clarified in the concrete acting exercises designed to stimulate sensory memories. Thus psychoanalysis and the Method were mutually beneficial.

Monroe herself seemed to endorse the symbiosis between the Method and psychoanalysis in a dream starring Strasberg as the "best finest surgeon" cutting her open after Dr. Hohenberg had prepared the actress for an operation that aimed to bring her back to life. But what had caused her "terrible dis-ease" baffled Monroe, whose hyphenated spelling of the word, which she underlined, signals her lack of equilibrium. Arthur Miller stood outside in this dream, "worrying and hoping" for a successful outcome "for many reasons—for myself—for his play and for himself indirectly." In retrospect, the dream seems prophetic, since it acknowledged Monroe's confusion about exactly what troubled her, even when she thought she was receiving the best of care. Miller's presence may be comforting to her, but it is also disturbing, since she senses that his success depends somehow on her own. In other words, Monroe was coming to the realization that Miller was becoming as dependent on her as she was on him. Others, such as Hedda and Norman Rosten, hover as concerned friends, without the power to do no more than check in on her, while Milton Greene is pictured "relaxed and enjoying himself even if he is very worried at the same time." The source of his worry is not identified, although in the context of the dream it would seem that Monroe's health is probably his concern. But the dream may also signify that like Miller, Greene is just as concerned with his own well being, now that it is tied to hers. The shocking denouement of the dream is that "there is absolutely nothing there"—in other words, the void is within herself. The import of the dream would later become the basis for Norman Mailer's biography of Monroe, even though he did not have access to this account of her dream A deeply disappointed Strasberg is "academically amazed" because he was so sure there would be "so much—more than he had ever dreamed possible in almost anyone." Instead only "finely cut sawdust— like out of a raggedy ann doll . . . spills all over the floor & table." Both Strasberg's "dreams & hopes for theater are fallen," and Hohenberg's "dreams and hopes for a permanent psychiatric cure is given up—Arthur is disappointed—let down."

Of all Monroe's enablers, Lee Strasberg may have seemed to her the least self-interested. The Method promised Monroe a renewed sense of authenticity. Of her struggle with her Hollywood career, he observed, "Sometimes when an actor is in her position the successful playing of the same kind of thing causes you to feel that you are getting away with something. A feeling of guilt develops." Throughout his talks at the Studio, Strasberg stressed the actor's frustration with the repetition of what Hethmon calls "essentially the same element of himself that brought him initial success." Like many other actors, Monroe regarded the Studio as a sanctuary and a laboratory where she was free to experiment, to confront openly the questions many typecast actors ask: "Can I do it again?" "Can I do anything else?" "Can I work with a different director?" "Can I play a different type?" "Do I really have talent?" On the set of *Show Business* Monroe had been terribly embarrassed when she met Susan Strasberg and her mother, Paula, because she had performed clumsily. At the Studio she heard Lee Strasberg say something like, "This is a place where you can fall flat on your face," when actors came to admit and then solve their problems. The Studio offered the only kind of institutional support—and the only kind of artistic continuity—available to Monroe, who like most American actors lacked access to something like the English repertory system, where actors are more or less constantly employed in a variety of roles. In describing how it was for even the most successful actors, Strasberg revealed why it was possible for Monroe to feel acute distress in spite of having performed well: "[T]he actual conditions of work are for the actor extremely poor. The actor works, let's say, on a movie. It takes him months. He works in a disjointed way that hardly permits his imagination to be aroused. Then he loafs around because he's glad to loaf around after getting up all those months at six o'clock in the morning and finishing at six at night. He gets pretty tired. Then he does another picture somewhere else." The disruptive routine of picture making is ex-

Actors Studio (c. 1956)

actly what Monroe had forsaken in an effort to rouse her deepest creative instincts.

She courageously left Hollywood at the height of stardom, and Strasberg responded to her risk-taking by carefully timing her transition into acting at the Studio. After about three months of private study in his home, she appeared confident enough to join one of his classes of about thirty students that met twice a week. This did not make Monroe an Actors Studio member, for that privilege could be earned only through a rigorous series of auditions. She entered the public Studio classes as an observer, like other interested parties, including Gloria Steinem, who met her briefly. A quiet Monroe rarely asked questions. Occasionally, she took notes. According to one observer, she exhibited "an avid interest in every scene performed by her fellow actors and in every word of criticism and instruction offered by Strasberg." She had difficulty understanding his classes—perhaps because of terminology like "justification" and "substitution"—and one of her fellow students helped to "translate" the teacher's words. She behaved like a neophyte, as did other actors and actresses with significant reputations who felt humbled by the experience of probing so profoundly the fundamentals of acting. This group activity encouraged a sense of equality. For the first time in her career, Monroe's dedication to herself and to acting was part of a collective enterprise.

Strasberg called upon actors to engage in what Stanislavsky called "living the part." This meant both observing and internalizing not just human emotions and actions, but also animal behavior and the function and placement of objects. As with Todd and Chekhov, Monroe was called on in Strasberg's classes to identify with principles of structure and composition, while at the same time feeling her way into the shapes and positions of things and into the gestures and rhythms of creatures other than herself. For example, she had to improvise her version of a kitten. She prepared by borrowing one, studying him intensely for two weeks, and then presented herself to the class as "a playful, lazy, stretching, scratching, purring kitten." This classic Stanislavsky exercise, with its call for acute, penetrating observation of life in all of its specificity, contributed to Monroe's ease of movement on stage, even as it sharpened her concentration and control. It is not as if she had not moved well before, of course, but now she recognized that even greater ease of movement was the product of intimate contact with nature—another cardinal goal of Stanislavsky's approach that made her achievement seem, once again, organic, an aspect of existence itself and not an external copy of it. One can readily imagine Monroe identifying with the kitten's feline grace. But more significantly, to be a kitten involves shedding adult inhibitions in order to recover a primordial spontaneity free from stereotyping, from the Hollywood manufacturing of Marilyn Monroe. Society as a whole imposes rigid codes of behavior, and theater, similarly, contributes its clichés, Stanislavsky noted. In order to enact life, to embody a character with originality, he counseled that "an actor, like an infant, must learn everything from the beginning, to look, to walk, to talk, and so on." We do these things badly in ordinary life, and our faults show on stage, he concluded. To behave like a cat is to loosen up immediately, to become aware of how we have learned to contract our muscles in conformity with social habits and public decorum. We stiffen on the stage unless we learn how to release physical tenseness.

As a new Strasberg pupil having to go through the entire regimen of the Method while stripping away layers of conventional behavior, Monroe studied everything. Fresh characterizations are obtained only through exacting training of the body and the self. She was instructed to sing a popular song without moving her body, "so that she used the inner nervousness subjectively instead of leaking it out through random, unconscious bodily tics and jerks." Strasberg echoed Stanislavsky's emphasis on "the necessity for 'gestureless' moments of immobility on the part of the actor, to concentrate on his feelings all the attention of the spectator." Various exercises were used to induce relaxation and to stimulate spontaneous expression.

Monroe progressed from acting exercises to the performance of scenes in class. With a fellow student, Phil Roth, she first chose to prepare a scene from Clifford Odets's *Golden Boy*, a drama about a young man, Joe Bonaparte, who abandons the development of his "real self," of a career in music, for the monied success of the prize ring. Harold Clurman, Odets's good friend and Group Theatre colleague, called the play a story of the artist who becomes a "thing," and noted that "Hollywood and what it represents provided the play with its inner theme, its true subject matter." Monroe had acted in *Clash by Night*, written for the screen by Odets, and the playwright had met her on a few occasions, hoping to cast her in one of his projects. Odets's own struggles with his integrity as a writer in Hollywood would obviously have interested her as a kind of subtext, and she would have quickly seen how the play defined not only the writer's dilemma but her own. Odets, like his character Bonaparte, had once been a golden boy, enticed by fame and fortune to Hollywood, abandoning the promised great work of his theatrical career. Monroe, in every way a golden girl, had to wonder if she would ever get the opportunity to fulfill her artistic ambitions.

Monroe's character, Lorna Moon, has "a certain quiet glitter . . . and if she is sometimes hard, it is more from necessity than choice. Her eyes often hold a soft, sad glance." She feels like a "tramp" because she is always the mistress, never the wife. She is looking for legitimacy and for someone to authorize her worth, just as Monroe—feeling outcast and demeaned—hoped to marry the highly principled Arthur Miller, who could confirm her probity. Lorna is very much like Monroe in finding it difficult to hope for her heart's desire, yet hoping for it nonetheless. Through Lorna, Monroe made contact with the incisive, somewhat hard-edged, working class side of her personality, the side that Richard Meryman encountered during his *Life* interview with her. Stanley Flink called this aspect of Monroe her "street smarts." Flink remembered that she was especially good at sizing up people and gauging their motivations, just as Lorna does on several occasions.

Lorna is also reminiscent of Peg, the supporting character Monroe played in *Clash By Night*. Peg expresses an uninhibited, robust physicality and a firmness of speech and gesture. "When I want you to kiss me, I'll let you know," she curtly tells her boyfriend, Joe (Keith Andes). She sticks out her tongue at him and will not be bossed. Unlike Monroe the glamour girl, she does not slur her words suggestively; instead, she is very direct and aggressive. She punches Joe when he jealously tries to deflect her interest in another man (Robert Ryan). This raw energy reflects the off-screen Monroe, who delighted in telling Stanley Flink how she would perform the physical business of her roles. Peg does not hesitate to order Joe to get her sweater or to bring coffee for visiting friends. She is ebullient, and she can be roughly affectionate—as Monroe could be when jumping off the scaffolding of a movie set into the visiting Flink's arms. Lorna Moon is a harder, more cynical version of Peg, "a conniver of the first order" who is "overwhelmed by a feeling of genuine love for the first time in her life" for the fight manager, Tom Moody, who will turn Bonaparte away from music. Edward Easty noticed Monroe's "ease of movement" as Lorna: "Gone were the strained efforts of artificial behavior and clichés. . . . She held nothing back." After the scene, Strasberg "could not resist turning full way around in his front row seat, facing the entire assemblage and asking or rather demanding, 'Well, was the scene excellent or not?' To this the answer was resoundingly unanimous in the affirmative," Easty concludes.

Monroe's triumph had come amid difficult circumstances, for many students at the Studio distrusted Strasberg's championing of her, believing themselves far superior to this Hollywood "import." Monroe had to satisfy a group of students, some of which suspected the teacher had been corrupted by recent favorable publicity and was abandoning his principles. According to Easty, the audience sat in stunned, silent appreciation of Monroe's truthful rendering of Lorna Moon. Monroe had moved slowly in her preparations for this scene, and he suggests, "[W]e might have had quite a long wait before seeing what she could really have done professionally. The sad part is that we all thought she had time." His use of "we" after carefully noting the previous division of opinion on her talent suggests the community of feeling Monroe was able to arouse and share, a solidarity of sentiment so different from the acrimony the prevailed on her movie sets.

In December of 1955, after nearly ten months of study, Strasberg judged Monroe ready to do a scene from Eugene O'Neill's *Anna Christie* for Actors Studio members. As early as the fall of that year, it had been decided that she would rehearse a scene with Strasberg's son, John, from Tennessee Williams's *A Streetcar Named Desire* for her private class as a way of practicing for her public debut, which finally occurred in early February 1956. The characters she chose to portray while at the Studio reflected her own profound feelings of orphanhood, exploitation, and alienation: Anna Christie, in search of her father and feeling abused by life, prostituted; Lorna Moon, "a lost baby" whose mother was a suicide and whose father was an alcoholic; and Blanche Dubois, caught up in dreams of a romanticized self and terrorized by fears of fading beauty. These characters reminded Monroe of the attenuated hopes of youth, of how difficult it was to achieve a mature identity. Approaching the age of thirty, Monroe knew that she had to move on to the next stage of her career, to take full possession of these roles. She chose scene 5 of *Streetcar*, in which Blanche tries to seduce the young man collecting for the *Evening Star*. The scene demands that the actress convey a sense of Blanche in all her loneliness, coquetry, sensuality, romanticism, and resignation. Blanche dreams of a better, idealized world, while acknowledging the sordid one that is partly of her own making. In playing this role, Monroe confronted her own propensity for aggrandizing reality. "Young man! Young, young man! Has anyone ever told you that you look like a young Prince out of the Arabian Nights?" Blanche asks, in a desperate attempt to hold on to this youth and her own. Strasberg believed that Monroe rendered Blanche with a "strangely poetic quality." For him, there was not only sensitivity, but grandeur in her evocation of Blanche's sadness and suffering. Monroe brought beauty to the part, he concluded. Evidently she understood that, like herself, Blanche Dubois, properly played, is a tragic, not a pathetic character.

The opening scene from *Anna Christie*, which Monroe had used for an exercise with Natasha Lytess, was much longer and more ambitious than what she had attempted in *A Streetcar Named Desire*. In Strasberg's words, Anna is supposed to be "nervous . . . sick, she comes back [to her father], she doesn't know what's going to happen." The dialogue at the beginning of the play is not of much help to the actress in conveying Anna's feelings, Strasberg observed, for at the moment of her entrance "you almost don't know who the girl is." And Anna is not ready to speak directly about her feelings. Monroe's success in adapting her "tremulousness" to suit Anna's febrile character was extraordinary. Strasberg emphasized how surprised the audience was that she could use her sensitivity so precisely. The precision had been developed during Monroe's serious study of the whole play. With Arthur Miller's help, she went over the text for a couple of hours, exploring Anna's identity, her way of thinking, her view of life. Did Anna want to die? Monroe's query derived from her perception of an exhausted, played-out character. She wanted to know exactly what accounted for Anna's fatigue, since her actions, not her words, would have to convey first her listlessness, then her growing anxiety about meeting and coping with her father. Monroe's questions cut two ways, toward the character and toward herself. Like Anna, she had set out on a quest to find her father and had on more than one occasion intimated to friends her desire for death. Like Monroe, Anna is quick to resent people she thinks are laughing at her, and she feels she has been put upon, deprived of her integrity, and exploited by her foster family. Anna implies that she was sexually violated at sixteen by a cousin on the farm. If Monroe was reaching into the innards of her own life to play this part, she was also employing questions to get at what Strasberg called the "subtext," that portion of the character's thinking that is indicated but not fully expressed. Even the character's life before she entered a scene should be considered as a way of getting at Stanislavsky's notion of "the imaginative fiction of another person." The playwright leaves certain aspects of the character unexpressed, and it is the actor's responsibility to go beyond the "scraps and bits" to create a whole person, a complete role with "comparatively unbroken lines," Stanislavsky points out. What was the unbroken line of Anna's emotional life? This is what Monroe wanted to know, so that she could establish the continuity of her performance and make Anna's life her own.

Strasberg was unequivocal in his praise for Monroe's handling of Anna Christie, and he was struck with her presence, "the unusual quality which she was able to maintain . . . to keep and somehow to create and also to transmit more on the stage even than on the screen." Was he responding to her aura, to the uniqueness of her original self? Strasberg speculated that the "self-consciousness of the screen"—the fact that everything has to be framed—blocked some of the brilliance he saw in the immediacy and exceptional control of Monroe's live performance. Evidently her concentration was perfect, and even those in the audience who were not particularly taken with her admitted that she did not blow a line and that she had at least been competent—although one male Studio member vigorously rejected the idea that Monroe was "capable of playing Anna Christie." Kim Stanley, on the other hand, remembers that despite her initial skepticism, Monroe's performance "was just wonderful. She was wonderful. We were taught never to clap at the Actors Studio—it was like we were in church—and it was the first time I'd ever heard applause there. Some of us went to her privately and apologized."

Strasberg acknowledged to Fred Guiles that doing the scene had been very difficult for Monroe, and he was not certain that she could "follow through" with a complete performance, but he persisted in his belief that she was making her way toward a stage career. Cheryl Crawford rated Monroe's acting "quite extraordinary—full of color," but she could not credit Monroe with a place in the theater: "[S]he was paralyzed with fear. It was too rough. She'd have a spasm every time she'd go on." Maureen Stapleton, Monroe's partner in the scene, tried to relieve the tension by suggesting they put a copy of the play on the table in front of them. "Lots of people do it," she reassured her earnest colleague. But Monroe treated the occasion as though it were opening night on Broadway and refused to regard her performance as informally as Stapleton suggested it was. Rehearsals were repeatedly interrupted because Monroe forgot her lines, yet her actual performance was flawless. "[T]hat exceedingly wispy voice of hers seemed to carry all right, for all her worrying about it," Stapleton recalls.

Afterwards, she accompanied Monroe to a bar on Tenth Avenue, and "celebrated having cheated death one more time." Performing well for this high-strung actress seemed tantamount to surviving as both a person and a professional. Monroe herself is said to have been distraught immediately after her Anna Christie scene. "I was terrible," she sobbed. Friends tried to console her, citing Strasberg's superlatives, but she remained unconvinced, insisting that "the only thing that was great was Maureen." Strasberg himself lauded her concentration, which "did not give way or slip once," as she recorded in a note to herself. "Marilyn, there will be very few times ever on the stage where it will be necessary to keep

Monroe interviewed (1956)

such a concentration for one half hour straight." Instead of accepting his
compliment, she wondered if her triumph had simply been accidental.
But as she recorded in her notes, Strasberg refused to stint on his praise,
suggesting, "[Y]our sensitivity would not be the same if you didn't have

the fearful misgivings." She should not ignore them, but instead handle them by growing more proficient in the "technical things" that could be used to channel her anxiety. Strasberg's own daughter, Susan, had unusual self-discipline, he told Monroe, but she had a sensitivity, "much deeper and stronger than that of Susie's." That very sensitivity left Monroe dangerously exposed and accounted for her fear of performing, which reminded him so much of the great actress Duse.

Monroe's anguish could not have been unexpected, for she had so much at stake. And it was part of her nature—as Milton Greene and Rupert Allan stressed—never to be content with her work. Susan Strasberg, on the other hand, attributes to Monroe a ploy performers often use: Criticize yourself before others get the opportunity, and you may be able to elicit sympathy and create a protective coating for yourself. Certainly Monroe had used such a strategy in her Hollywood career. About a week after she did the scene, Fred Stewart, an actor who knew Strasberg well, complimented Monroe on her Anna Christie by emphasizing the actress's strength, her way of making "the character herself." Monroe was still very unsure about her success because she had no way to measure it. Doing a scene in front of a live audience was new to her, she told Stewart. She was happy to receive his support and gradually began to believe in the power of her stage performance—so much so that she was "exhilarated" and tremendously grateful for the opportunity Strasberg had given her. Even years later, Ralph Roberts, John Springer, and other friends vividly recall how large a role her work with Strasberg played in Monroe's plans for her future.

Monroe had completed assignments on three difficult roles and was acting with renewed conviction as she made plans for *Bus Stop*, the first film she had worked on since leaving Hollywood in late 1954. In late December of 1955, prolonged negotiations with Twentieth Century–Fox culminated in a new seven-year contract, which stipulated that she would could specify a list of directors acceptable to her and be allowed to do outside productions. She would have to appear in four Fox films, for which her corporation would be paid a hundred thousand dollars per film, to be split evenly between herself and Milton Greene.

After having spent a rather quiet year on her own, Monroe left New York on February 26, 1956, for Hollywood, inspiring intense curiosity among members of the press. To one reporter she seemed somehow different—she replied almost shyly that her suit was new but otherwise she was the same person. It was a typical light-hearted, self-effacing comment that belied the new confidence and control she would soon display in her portrayal of Cherie.

Monroe's progress from Strasberg's classes to the set of *Bus Stop* is comparable to the advance in sophistication reflected in Stanislavsky's progress from *An Actor Prepares* to *Building a Character*, his classic texts on acting. In the first two chapters of the latter work, one is able to observe the actor moving beyond his exercises in *An Actor Prepares* to mastery of a whole role in a complete performance. Indeed, Monroe's creation of her character, Cherie, reads almost like a textbook case, an idealized version of the collaboration between script writer, director, and actor that the great film theorist Pudovkin called for, but regretfully did not realize in his own work. After Josh Logan completed his direction of *Bus Stop*, he said that Monroe "conceived the basic approach to Cherie." The director, of course, helped her "get it on film," but it was "her feeling about the whole story" that stimulated Logan and the screenwriter, George Axelrod, who would incorporate the actress's interpretation of her role into his rewriting of certain scenes. Only rarely have actors had the opportunity to influence a film so directly. Logan's supreme trust in Monroe, built on his belief that she was "one of the great talents of all time," has on occasion been matched by other directors but never surpassed.

Logan had not been predisposed to praise Monroe. At the first suggestion that she play Cherie, he exclaimed, "Marilyn Monroe can't bring off *Bus Stop!*" He acknowledged her box office success, but he did not believe she could act. Strasberg's belief in her greatness astounded Logan. How could the "smug and pedantic" acting teacher take Monroe seriously? But for the first time, Logan had heard Marilyn "praised by someone in the theatre." He decided to risk working with her and changed his mind about her during their first meeting. She talked persuasively about *Bus Stop*'s story, had carefully observed Kim Stanley's portrayal of Cherie on the New York stage, and demonstrated how easily she could catch her character's Southern accent. Then Logan had one of those perceptions that seemingly join the realms of film and reality: "[O]f course she was the perfect girl to play the part. Kim Stanley had had to readjust her looks, her height, her weight, and everything else to appear as this girl, but Marilyn was Cherie, presto in the flesh." Monroe had her character's childlike enthusiasm and dreaminess, but she was much more lucid and perceptive than her counterpart—as Logan indicated. "[S]he struck me as being a much brighter person than I had ever imagined," one whose

Bus Stop (1956)

"accurate reactions to each well-made point" filled the director with a wonderful sense of promise about the whole production.

It is likely that Monroe was following Stanislavsky's injunction about "living the part" and sought to show Logan her mastery quickly. As they worked together, Logan recalled, "[S]he wanted to know all about my studying with him in Moscow. She wanted to know all about the way actors lived and acted there. How Stanislavsky talked to them and they talked to him—intimate details." She used Freudian terminology somewhat clumsily and self-consciously, but Logan was certain that Strasberg "had opened a locked part of her head, given her confidence in herself, in her brainpower, in her ability to think out and create a character." The acting teacher had provided Monroe with "an outline, a kind of map" to consult en route to her role, Susan Strasberg explained. Strasberg's mother, Paula, was the "great technician" who helped Monroe explore "the streets, the towns, the rivers," the fine details of a role. Like Natasha Lytess, Paula Strasberg was put in an uncomfortable position every time Monroe insisted that she be present on the movie set. Strasberg would be suspected of usurping the director's responsibility for guiding the actress during her performance. Few directors—not even the sympathetic Josh Logan—were in a position to witness the way Paula and Monroe worked on scenes together, such as in the "Old Black Magic" sequence, which called for the subtlest execution of a bad performance. Overdoing the song would coarsen Monroe's character; underplaying it would diminish her character's vitality. Interpreting the number's every note engrossed the actress and her coach and irritated others, who were intolerant of Paula's claim on Monroe's time. Even Logan, the most generous of Monroe's directors, did not recognize the style Paula helped to develop.

Why did Monroe, who had such good instincts in her reading of a role, need a coach at all? She often spoke poetically, in similes and metaphors that someone had to help her unravel and interpret. Hers was not a logical way, Lee Strasberg explained to Fred Guiles. Rather, she would make comparisons—"[I]sn't this like or so on"—and she would be completely right about a part while still needing to locate the precise terms that writers and directors commonly deal in. She could seem very "kooky" to a professional who did not have the patience to follow her. "What do you mean the character should be burning as if she's sitting on a stove?" is Strasberg's example of a frustrated response to Monroe's figurative language. "She would become clearer as she went on," he remembered. "[S]he would always see the character; she would always see what the real event was, not just what the people were saying." She was so good at evaluating scripts that Paula Strasberg planned to publish Monroe's marginal notations after the actress's death.

Monroe attacked her part with a dynamism that still invigorated Logan's prose when he recalled her taking charge. When the costume designer delivered a set of clothes that were "too grand, too movie star—not pitiful, comic, and humorous enough for Cherie," Monroe laughingly told Logan that they were going to "shred it up, pull out part of the fringe, poke holes in the fishnet stockings, then have 'em darned with big, sprawling darns. Oh, it's gonna be so sorry and pitiful and it'll make

Cherie and Bo (1956)

you cry." She then proceeded to rummage through the costume department to find "the oldest, the most worn, the saddest" bits of clothing
that would still somehow express the spirit of a character whose reach
would exceed her grasp. Similarly, Milton Greene eschewed using Monroe's usual "honey-colored" makeup in favor of a "light opalescent color,

very thin and white." It was a daring experiment that the actress and her co-workers enthusiastically accepted as appropriate "for a little nightclub singer who always went to bed at five or six in the morning after drinks, and woke up way past noon to a breakfast of black coffee and aspirin—a girl who never really saw the sun," Logan remarked. Although her studio bosses vehemently protested the risks Monroe and her collaborators were taking with the film, Logan insisted on artistic control, and Monroe had her way—with Logan's consent—on most of the major decisions in the production. As a result, she exuberantly put herself into the whole film, even suggesting ways of staging certain scenes and setting up cameras.

Only twice did Monroe exhibit the temperament that bedeviled her earlier, less sensitive directors: when Logan caught her still looking at herself in her dressing room mirror hours after she was due on the set, and when she lost her composure with her co-star, Don Murray, and raked him across the face with her sequined costume, scratching the corner of his eye. Murray dismissed her aggression as that of a "childlike personality." She operated from "a very self-centered viewpoint. She wasn't deliberately mean." But she did show a surprising lack of empathy. When Murray balked at mounting a horse because he had not yet had a riding lesson, she said, "Just do it." It was his first film, and her lack of professional skill surprised him. She came to the set late, could not remember her lines, and often did as many as twenty takes of a single scene. She kept missing her marks, the positions actors have to "hit" in order to be properly lit and recorded. Word also got out that she was annoyed with Murray because he seemed far more interested in Hope Lange (he married her), who played Elma Duckworth, a young girl Cherie confides in.

Murray's testimony demonstrates the stress Monroe's self-absorption put on cast and crew. In other contexts, however, she exhibited a special talent for taking people on their own terms. Rupert Allan remembers the way she would "work a party," making sure that she met as many people as possible, sitting down with them and really taking an interest in their lives, while remaining accessible. Logan observed that "she was always . . . the most fun to talk to, to listen to—warm, witty," and enthusiastic. Her training in the Method enhanced this outgoing quality. Part of Stanislavsky's legacy—first adumbrated for her by Michael Chekhov—was the directive to urge actors to take in "everything," to "adopt a broad point of view . . . to interpret the life of human souls from all over the world." Strasberg speculated that the painfulness of Monroe's own past and her wounded sensitivity created an "avidness for life," a "reaching out that she had when she would listen to you . . . her eyes were all wide, and I don't think she was just acting . . . she really took in whatever it was that she was interested in." Similarly, Rupert Allan recollects Monroe relishing the *New York Times*, the excited interest she would exhibit in speaking of world affairs, in one specific instance calling him to make a shrewd comparison between front-page stories in the New York newspaper and the *Los Angeles Times*. Her correspondence about politics with Lester Markel, then Sunday editor of the *New York Times*, corroborates Allan's memories of Monroe's keen engagement with current events.

In "dressing" her character, to use Stanislavsky's term, Monroe was employing everything she knew about self and society and turning away from her the image she had developed in previous films, in which she had been encouraged to act from the outside in, taking care to have her look like the part before she felt the part. As a result, both her self and her roles were somewhat specious. Now she proceeded in the opposite direction, delving within herself to authenticate both her person and her character, Cherie. Since Monroe could not think of Cherie as simply a role given to her, she had to come up with a Cherie of her own. Like the actor in *Building a Character*, she found there is no quick route to rapport with a role. The actor begins in uncertainty not only about his character but about himself: "I was not I, in the sense of my usual consciousness of myself. Or, to be more precise, I was not alone but with someone whom I sought in myself and could not find." It is as if the actor abnegates himself, holds himself in suspension, in order to create room for the role to emerge: "I existed, I went on with my usual life, yet something inhibited me from giving myself up to it fully; something was disturbing my usual existence. I seemed divided in two." The actor becomes aware of a "secret subconscious life," a second life, after confronting the "question of whom I was to play." Looking into the mirror does not aid the actor in discovering his identity, because he has not yet found the source of it within himself. He begins to feel himself in character as he alters his conventional theatrical makeup, his costume, and selects the props for a character he still cannot properly name. Nevertheless, he seems compelled to apply himself to a characterization that is slowly rising from inside of him until, glancing once again in the mirror, he does not recognize himself. He has, in fact, used himself as an instrument to transform himself. Every step he has taken in the creation of his character is his own, yet the result is that he is not entirely himself. He has created something new, original, fresh—

much as Monroe, according to Strasberg, "took in" the feelings of others and had an extraordinary ability "to see something in a fresh way that was completely her own and to draw attention to it with a kind of directness," a precision "which couldn't be said or seen for that matter in any other way."

Now Monroe had a role that was not just bits and pieces of film, but a role that had grown organically and that might survive the edited process. This was certainly not the first time she had come to a movie set with her character well worked out, but it was the first instance of her total immersion in a character, speaking in that character's accents even when filming had stopped, as other Method actors like James Dean had done. Monroe still found the actual process of filming discontinuous and profoundly disturbing. Sometimes she would hold onto a crewmember's arm and pace around the edges of the sound stage. Occasionally she would retreat in total isolation from cast and crew. She interrupted scenes and requested time to think off to the side of the action. Logan remembers her "feverish concentration," and how in her effort to perform well she would "stop and wrinkle her face as though in pain before she could continue." Interruptions in filming would throw off her concentration, and it could take several minutes before she was able to resume her character's mood.

Logan decided to keep his cameras going in order to overcome Monroe's halting performances. Instead of crying cut after each take, he simply put her into the position appropriate for the beginning of the scene, or handed her the first prop in the scene, or had the script supervisor give her the first line, so that she and the camera kept moving. Logan had come to perceive that "the moment the camera started turning, Marilyn 'turned on' with it." This unusual and expensive way of filmmaking yielded several interesting takes of individual scenes, none of them "dull or routine," and he therefore had "a chance to piece bits and pieces of brilliance together until the final scene shone." Although her acting was mediated by film technology and the director's art, Logan was, in effect, inducing a live performance from Monroe by partially eliminating the stop-and-go element of filmmaking for her. The director suspected his star was "inherently" a stage performer, and he treated her as one by also recording her "Old Black Magic" number live in order to capture the spontaneity that would be lacking if she sang the song "to a playback" and then again for the camera by lip-synching. "She could never memorize exactly the way she had sung it, breathed it, performed it, and still make it sound spontaneous," Logan concluded.

Film conventions disconcerted the actress, Maurice Zolotow reported, corroborating Don Murray's observations: "[S]he had to keep fixed positions, marked out on the set." A "spontaneous reflex of emotion" might move her out of the designated position, so that the carefully set up camera framing would be destroyed. On the other hand, she delighted in the one-to-one relationship it was possible to have with cameras. Logan remembers the day she "was dancing around like a child in anticipation of having a big head close-up as Garbo had had." All the features of her face would be enlarged, for the lens could concentrate on "every vein, every tiny bit of facial fuzz, the watery depths of her eyes, the detail of her skin, her nostrils." Even when the close-up revealed a string of saliva as Monroe moved her head from the hand it had been resting upon, she agreed with Logan that the delicate moment "showed great emotion" and ought not to be edited out of the film.

Logan put Monroe's performance in an intricate series of frames that had the effect of concentrating more attention on the impact of her character's personality, an effect not attempted by previous directors. At the beginning of *Bus Stop*, she is viewed in the frames of two windows. The first sight of Cherie is self-consciously cinematic and virtually voyeuristic in revealing the interior of her life. As Virgil (Arthur O'Connell) watches from his window in the boarding house, Cherie is already positioned on the ledge of her dressing room window with her right knee bent and her high-heeled shoe extended so that the pointed toe touches the side of the window frame. She is hot and weary, fanning herself; she seems almost ready to drop as her hand falls downward in a limp gesture. She is looking down disconsolately as cowboys crowd into her private moment, petitioning her for a dance. The camera cuts from Virgil watching her, to Bo (Don Murray) admiring himself in all his freshness in the mirror of the boarding house room he shares with Virgil, to Cherie sitting again on the window ledge—this time harassed by her boss, who asks her why she is not inside "where you belong." He shakes her and tells her to go to work, throwing her onto a chair. As Virgil enters the saloon, she is pictured in front of the mirror crying and complaining about the boss who has called her an ignorant hillbilly. Her hand is cupped to the left side of her face, as she looks down and then up to her friend, Vera (Eileen Heckart). Cherie scratches the back of her head, then hides her face in her hands, and then scratches the back of her head again as she explains to Vera how she has been "trying to be somebody." Then she puts her face in her hands again, places her hand to the right side of her face, and completes the repetitive cycle of hand and head and face gestures begun on her left side, a chronic cycle that she maintains with delicate consistency throughout the movie. Monroe's constant repositioning of her hand and head and face—and Logan's relentless reframing techniques—complement each other brilliantly in defining Cherie's fatiguing searching for an identity.

When Cherie talks about River Gulch, "the little town where I was born," she puts a finger to her lips, foreshadowing the lifted spirits that result from when she fingers the map that traces "the history of my life." Her eyes open wide as she speaks of her dream of reaching Hollywood and Vine, and she dresses herself in her dreams as she picks up her saloon costume—the one she will wear when she sings "That Old Black Magic"—and dilates on the magical impact of the movies that gave her a "direction" in life. In these brief moments of getting ready for the saloon crowd, Monroe is able to move her character deftly through memories of childhood, adolescence, and adulthood—many of them reflected in her changing expressions in the dressing room mirror. As Cherie gets into her dress, she conveys the feeling that she is getting into her life—which she almost seemed to have relinquished in the first shots of her.

Joan Mellen has pointed out the obvious connections between Cherie and Monroe's biography, but of special importance is Cherie's dreaminess and her exact plotting of her journey to movie stardom, which parallels Monroe's calculating and determined route to her career. Although Cherie desperately wants to escape from Bo, her cowboy lover who believes he has found his "angel," she hesitates momentarily when she learns that a *Life* photographer will be present at her dreaded marriage. As it did for Monroe, the camera has almost a perverse fascination for Cherie, fixing itself in her consciousness even at a time when her appearance before it will cause her pain. As beguiling as these comparisons between the actress and her role are ("[Y]ou cannot possibly tell where to draw the line between you and your part," Stanislavsky insists), it is not fair to say the actress was playing herself. Cherie shows none of the hostility Monroe could exhibit towards Murray, a newcomer like Bo, who treated Monroe respectfully, putting up with her sulks and refusal to apologize for scratching his eye. Cherie shares none of Monroe's informed commitment to her art or her talent and is unsophisticated when compared to the thirty-year-old woman who played her. At best, Cherie might have represented a former self to Monroe, the one who was a star-struck young girl, already a kind of cliché to Stanley Flink when she walked into the office of *Life* magazine in 1950 and presented her portfolio to him.

Even at her worst, however, Monroe could never have given a performance as poorly delivered as Cherie's pathetic "Old Black Magic" number. Monroe maintains just the right balance between Cherie's meager skills and her naïve certainty. This balance is best illustrated when Cherie achieves her own lighting effect during her song. She confidently yet awkwardly kicks a switch on stage that puts a spotlight on her, emphasizing the shabby gaudiness of her costume. She sings a song in a bad imitation of Hildegarde, and has tailored her figure out of parts taken from other performers—the scraps sewn together from a very limited theatrical wardrobe. She is hopelessly off key and seemingly oblivious of the cowboys who ignore her as they continue their rowdy conversations. Several light bulbs suspended over the small band that accompanies her accentuate the tackiness of the scene. Yet in her own light, Cherie shines. Somehow she has managed to enclose herself in her own world, and her features are animated by her conviction that she has delivered a good performance—so much so that it is believable when Bo, the young cowboy on his first big trip off the ranch, is captivated by her angelic luminosity. She is the living embodiment of his obsession with the ideal. Indeed, the romantic, yearning theme song from *Laura* graces his entrance into the saloon—as Cherie commands the stage with her presence, performing above the darkened noisy crowd that Bo does not notice until he has trouble hearing her song and whistles, warning the cowboys to be quiet. Her singing is dreadfully embarrassing, but there is a crazy zest in the way she spoils the rhythms of the song lyrics, and an endearing warmth in her Ozark drawl, as she makes do with drooping long black gloves and swings her scarf, sweeping Bo up in the emotions of his discovery.

Bo's tribute to her reinforces Cherie's stilted, extroverted gestures as the cowboy crowd quiets. She winks at him, absolutely delighted and mischievously smiling like a kid who has been allowed to continue mimicking adult behavior. She tugs at her long sleeves, trying to keep them up, like a child struggling with an improvised costume. All of her gestures are elaborately staged. "I hear your name" and "only your kiss can put out the fire," she sings, as she cups her hand to her ear and puts her fingers to her lips. There also seems to be a momentary reference to Monroe's own cheesecake days when she half closes her lips and eyes in comic sultriness, as though she were finally shedding all of the silliness of her former selves. Cherie is not just another one of Monroe's dumb blondes. There is a difference in the writing and the performing of this character—as there would be in her successors. Like Elsie Marina, Sugar Kane, Amanda Dell, and Roslyn Taber—the women Monroe plays in her last four films—Cherie has suffered disappointments in her effort to defy the world's intractability. Cherie has dreams of Hollywood stardom, but she seems much older, sadder—if not wiser—than Bo. She is certainly cautious, and skeptical of the promises made to her. She has lived the romantic yet melancholy music of *Laura*. She is more a whole person and less an unblemished character, not unreal like The Girl or Pola or Lorelei Lee. She will not have the world on Bo's masculine terms and will not be cowed by "all that lovin' stuff" that other men have handed her. Bo ropes her not because she is innately helpless, but because she has been quite literally knocked out by her nightclub life, by defeats that Bo has yet to suffer. His untested energy is what overwhelms her. So much is apparent when he tries to rouse her from bed; physically she is incapable of competing with him, but she never gives in to him completely. Instead, she uses the ploy of the physically weak: She tries to escape or to distract him.

At the same time, Cherie has avoided the crudity of backstage life. She betrays none of the bitterness Monroe expressed on movie sets. Cherie has not cultivated the cynicism that would arm her against a rapacious world. Her face often registers bewilderment and the vague pain of confusion, as does her characteristic gesture of putting her hand to the side of her face as if to search for the source of her distress or to soothe her delicate nerves. In Bo's clutches she sometimes behaves like a startled animal. There is something very fresh in Monroe's acting in these scenes, for Cherie's emotions are primary, unguarded—and Monroe plays them with great finesse.

In his review of *Bus Stop*, Arthur Knight comments that there is no evidence in the film of "the calendar girl." Indeed, in some scenes Monroe and her director deliberately diminished her physical presence to give Cherie what one reviewer calls "a little girl lost quality." For example, in the roadside diner, Cherie is photographed in her chilling uncertainty against a large, vertical black stove that stands imposingly behind her, its pipe running up to the ceiling. She has just come in from the cold to escape from Bo, who is sleeping on the bus, and for warmth and comfort she clutches the front of her flimsy monkey fur coat with her left hand

and with her right hand holds the collar close to her neck. She is near panic and is baffled by Bo's stolid pursuit of her. She is trying to hold herself together, and she looks waif-like and abandoned and caught in a moment of frightful transience emphasized by the stands of cheap paperbacks and postcards that flank her. How is it possible to believe that Cherie is an "angel" after so many shots of her wasted appearance? Oddly enough, her skimpy, ragged clothing invest her with an irresistible genuineness; divested of resplendent costumery, Monroe makes Cherie's pale countenance ethereal—"incandescent," as Knight puts it.

After Bo has been beaten by the bus driver, Carl (Robert Bray), who defends Cherie's right to resist Bo's advances, the camera moves in on Monroe's character in the close-up that so excited her. After his humiliation, Bo has softened, has seen how roughly he has trodden upon Cherie's feelings, and meekly begs her pardon. His humble apology awakens her tender emotions, which were stirred once before when he first declared his love for her. In tight close-up, she declares to Bo with the whole force of her being, "I'd go anywhere in the world with you." She throws away her map, abandoning her illusions about Hollywood. Bo has relinquished his about her as well, for he finally accepts her confession that she is not an "angel," not the virginal figure he had made of her. Paradoxically, at this point, with their illusions destroyed, Cherie looks most like Bo's vision of an angel. His gaze into her face is swallowed up by the white depth of her skin. Her face covers the screen, and suddenly the rare sensitivity that has made Cherie so vulnerable and yet inviolable is fully revealed. Bo will take her back to his ranch just as she is, because she still speaks to his sense of beauty and perfection.

Bus Stop has a sentimental ending, to be sure, but it avoids having Monroe lapse into the passivity of her earlier roles. It is clear to Virgil, the old friend who has guided Bo to manhood, that Cherie will take care of Bo as much as he will her. In the final scene, she emerges as Virgil's equal when she insists that Bo allow him to go his own way: "If he don't want to come, you can't make him." Cherie's words are moving, but the authenticity of Monroe's whole characterization is what makes the conclusion. Notice how sensitively Cherie's hands hold the ring box Bo has given her, and how her hand is tentatively laid on his shoulder, indicating her nervous realization of her attachment to him. Behind her diffidence is a lifetime of disappointment because her simple human gestures have been disregarded. Monroe makes palpable the risk Cherie feels she takes off with Bo. When he first offers her his coat, she looks at it in a surprised and uncertain manner, and then she leans back against him and smiles securely, her head tilted back and her eyes opening in recognition of what she has won. She enjoys enveloping herself in the big coat, in its warmth and softness, easing herself into this new relationship. Then she completes the gesture by turning her head to the right side of the coat with her mouth open and her eyes closed, just as she did with the left side. Bo draws the coat closer around her, and she brings her hand to her neck, also tightening the coat around her in a firm gesture radically different from her scared hunching inside her flimsy costume coat in the bus stop. She draws Bo's hand to her and around her, and then, after closing her eyes and luxuriating once more in the coat, she ties her scarf around his neck, for now they are truly united. Monroe's gestures, like the whole film, are organic. Superb acting, the full creation of a character, make the corny conclusion convincing.

Monroe's effort on *Bus Stop* was, as Logan affirmed, "some kind of peak in her emotional as well as intellectual life." It was as if she made the movie set into a disciplined, innovative Actors Studio, and as if Logan helped her make good on Strasberg's ennobling and liberating advice to another actress: "Be your own Stanislavski." "I was twenty-five before I really understood what the whole creative process of acting was," Anne Bancroft remarked. Now, at thirty, Monroe might have said the same.

CHAPTER EIGHT

The Poet of Her Aspirations (December 1950–July 1956)

After all I have come up from way down.

When exactly did Marilyn Monroe become aware of Arthur Miller and of the special relevance of his writing for her? She had read his novel *Focus* (1945) before their first meeting on a movie set in December of 1950, and she seemed prepared that same week to engage him during their second encounter at a Hollywood party. After that evening of considerable conversation and silent rapport, she told Natasha Lytess, "It was like running into a tree! You know—like a cool drink when you've got a fever. You see my toe—this toe? Well he sat and held my toe and we just looked into each other's eyes almost all evening." Miller talked about his next play. They shared their admiration for Lincoln, and later Miller recommended Monroe read Carl Sandburg's Lincoln biography. She hinted at her need for a hero and observed that she never even had a father to admire. Had Miller, coming to her just after Johnny Hyde's death, played the father for her, touching only her toe while he seemed absorbed in the tale of her whole life?

Miller behaved like a secret sharer of Monroe's dilemma, and in a long letter written shortly after their second meeting he urged her to keep her own counsel: "Bewitch them [the public] with this image they ask for, but I hope and almost pray you won't be hurt in this game, nor ever change. . . ." Perhaps she was attracted to his seemingly selfless identification with her problem; here was a man who was not after her sexually and who did not dispute her integrity. He had seen her whole, objectively, and she responded to his quiet, soothing presence—very much like Maggie in Miller's *After The Fall*, who commends her husband Quentin for hav-

Monroe and Miller (1956)

ing once looked at her "out of your self." In other words, Miller had not responded to her as a stereotype, a projection of his fantasies, but instead had accepted her on her own terms. He seemed fully aware of the stereotyping that could destroy her (he had already created Itzik, the character in *Focus* who "should never have allowed himself to accept the role that was not his").

Miller became one of the guiding lights of Monroe's life, as they continued to correspond over the next year. One of her friends recalled that on visiting Monroe's apartment in late 1951, she recognized, to Monroe's surprise, a snapshot of the playwright hanging over the actress's bed.

Monroe conveyed the impression that she and Miller were greatly attracted to each other. Similarly, Natasha Lytess and Sidney Skolsky reported that the actress committed herself to someday pursuing the playwright. He was "the kind of man she could love," Monroe excitedly told Lytess.

It is easy to see why Miller, the person and the playwright, so attracted Monroe. Shortly after their marriage, James T. Farrell called Miller "the poet of the frustrated, the poet, therefore, of her own aspirations." She may have empathized with the hero of Miller's only novel, *Focus*, who insisted that he "was not what his face meant to people, he simply was not." In the novel, Lawrence Newman is typed as a Jew because his glasses somehow link him with the image his society has of Jews. Like Newman, Monroe came to see herself as an outcast desperately seeking the approval of the majority culture—appealing to its sense of melodrama in the Shirley Temple, Little Orphan Annie, versions of her life, while rebelling, as Newman eventually does, against its appropriation of her figure.

Miller's renowned drama, *Death of a Salesman* (1949), spoke directly to Monroe's own desperate search for a satisfactory identity. Like Willy Loman, she had to sell herself. She shared his obsession with personal attractiveness, with being "well liked," which came out of his terrible uncertainty: "I still feel—kind of temporary about myself." Like him, she wondered about her own authenticity, accusing herself—as he did—of being a "fake" with no "character." She could easily see herself in this small, immature man who never quite grew up. Willy was self-centered, a dreamer who wanted to "add up to something." He saw himself as singular and was both ludicrous and grand in his attempt to invent himself. As Lee Strasberg observed, "Marilyn Monroe was a dream of Marilyn Monroe." Her faith that "anything's possible, almost"—expressed in her *Life* interview—is echoed in Willy's exclamation that "the greatest things can happen," that the world can be conquered through force of personality. And when that idea of stardom was diminished for him, he found a way of displacing his disappointment in himself by putting the burden of success on his son, Biff, who was "going to be magnificent!. . . Yes, outstanding, with twenty thousand behind him." Similarly, in her years with Miller, Monroe would shift back and forth between her dreams of personal success and mass appeal to a hope for her progeny, who were part of what Clifford Odets termed her desire "to make herself more humanly productive." Resembling a character emerging out of Miller's own imagination, she demonstrated to him "the potential for greatness," and Miller sought to protect and nurture her talent after having been struck by her dedicated attack on the role of Anna Christie. "She had a real tragic sense of what that girl was like," Miller told Guiles. In other words, he realized that like one of his major characters, she was unwilling to accept complacently society's characterization of her.

Monroe found in Miller much more than the somber, taciturn personage who rarely smiled in public—who preferred, like Joe DiMaggio, to look stonily at the cameras, conceding none of the attractive facets of personality observable in the private man. She admitted to Alan Levy that at first she had something of a "pupil-teacher" relationship with Miller, and it is tempting to imagine her giving birth to herself under the playwright's direction. She would be literally trying to live by Stanislavsky's declaration that "in the creative process there is the father, the author of the play; the mother, the actor pregnant with the part; and the child, the role to be born." In her marriage to Miller, the professional and personal sides of herself would coincide. New roles would be conceived for her, including motherhood. She had become her own Stanislavsky.

While working on a scene from *Of Mice and Men* with her close friend Ralph Roberts, Monroe remarked that developing a role to full expression was like carrying a child to term. Acting was a way of articulating her continuity with life itself, with the desire to further it, to enrich it, just as Stanislavsky had pointed out: "Our type of creativeness is the conception and birth of a new being—the person in the part. It is a natural act similar to the birth of a human being." To marry Miller amounted to nothing less than an organic imperative. By all accounts, Monroe was deeply in love with him, not marrying him simply because he provided the theme by which she could live and work. He had a boyish charm about him for all his august reputation in the theater. He spoke simply, directly, and without condescension. He had a love of nature and of vigorous outdoor life that made him similar to Monroe's previous husbands. Although he was often withdrawn and shy—rather like DiMaggio—he could also be demonstrative and was not afraid to show his affection for her in front of close friends like Norman and Hedda Rosten, who warmly welcomed Monroe into their home during the early days of her life in New York. Miller was unaffected and equally at ease with all kinds of work, from writing plays to repairing machinery. For a woman who felt herself of the people, Miller had the right sort of demotic temperament; he was a Lincoln to whom she could relate on many different levels.

In the same way, Miller appears to have been captured by Monroe's many-sidedness, her sincerity, honesty, and earthiness. He enjoyed her "enormous sense of play, inventiveness—and unexpectedness—not only as a wife but as an actress." He had taken her for a "serious actress" and "adroit comedienne" even before he met her, but it was the person—not the actress with potential for playing tragedy—he loved. Miller had come to his generous estimate of Monroe cautiously, making sure that his first marriage could not be saved before he began to court her discreetly. By early 1956, Mary Slattery Miller had separated from her husband in acknowledgment of an estrangement that had begun several years earlier. He had been seeing Monroe in the homes of friends since her arrival in New York in late 1954. He was a hesitant lover, judging by her delicate, patient pursuit of him. She put no overt pressure on her reluctant suitor at a time when, she realized, he was struggling not only with his personal life, but also with an impasse in his work.

By late February 1956, as Monroe departed New York to work on *Bus Stop*, the ebullient Miller acted like a "kid in love," as one of his friends put it. The lovers managed discreet trysts at the Chateau Marmont in Hollywood during the making of *Bus Stop*. In late May or early June, Monroe returned to New York from Hollywood. Miller, in Nevada near Pyramid Lake awaiting his divorce decree, called her to discuss the possibility of marriage. By the middle of June, a divorced Miller introduced Monroe to his parents, but the couple continued to deny rumors of their romance. Not only were they trying to preserve their private lives, there is every indication that until his public announcement, surprising Monroe, Miller was not certain he would marry, in spite of her willingness to become his wife.

Miller's controversial politics complicated their decision. He had been denied a passport in March of 1954 because of his alleged communist sympathies. When the House UnAmerican Activities Committee (HUAC) summoned him to testify in late June, he agreed to discuss his political history, but he refused to identify others who participated in his political activities. Unlike most other witnesses HUAC interrogated, Miller did not invoke the Fifth Amendment. Invoking the Fifth Amendment is an American citizen's right, and doing so is not supposed to imply that the person relying on it is guilty of a crime. But in practice, HUAC witnesses who invoked their constitutional rights were deemed guilty and called "Fifth Amendment communists." They avoided the contempt of Congress convictions that sent the Hollywood Ten (a group of screenwriters and a director) to prison, but they also lost their jobs when

Hollywood studios decided not to employ anyone who declined to cooperate with HUAC.

When called to testify in July 1956, Miller adopted the very tactic that resulted in prison sentences for the Hollywood Ten. He invoked his First Amendment right to freedom of speech and association. While he endured his share of criticism in the press for his refusal to collaborate with HUAC's insistence on public naming of communists and communist sympathizers, he also became a kind of folk hero. He was the playwright who had protested the persecution of subversives by writing *The Crucible*—ostensibly about the seventeenth-century Salem witch trials, but read as an allegory about the frenzied hunt for communist spies and "fellow travelers."

Marilyn Monroe, something of an institution herself, embraced Miller in public, shyly clinging to him and in her devotion reinforcing the powerful ideal of a just man opposing governmental forces that threatened free speech. Her pronounced deference to Miller in public also made her and the playwright seem quite conventional—just a couple who wanted to be happy. But this union with Miller, like the one with DiMaggio, served to magnify Monroe's iconic status. Monroe gave no political speeches, only expressing her faith in Miller. She did not have to say more. It was enough to be there with him, radiating her approval.

During his testimony, Miller adverted to his impending marriage to Monroe. This announcement came as a shock to her, since he had never actually proposed. She felt rushed. Like her decision to marry DiMaggio, her choice of Miller seemed somewhat forced. Whatever his intentions, Miller had, in effect, made her part of a political ploy. Threatened with contempt of Congress, he was liable to serve a year in prison and pay a $1,000 fine.

Monroe continued to stand by Miller even though her studio suggested her career could be ruined if she did not persuade him to be cooperative with the congressional committee. In *Timebends*, Miller describes the personal visit that Spyros Skouras, president of Twentieth Century-Fox, made to the couple, promising he could arrange a private session with HUAC for Miller, provided that the playwright cooperate with his congressional inquisitors. Monroe, visibly moved by Skouras's apparently genuine concern for her, nevertheless supported Miller's decision to testify only about himself. She steadfastly refused to be intimidated, explaining to Alan Levy after her divorce from Miller that the playwright "introduced me to the importance of political freedom in our society."

Monroe identified with Miller's stand against an establishment that could crush the individual, and no doubt she quickly made the connection to what she considered to be the unwarranted authority of the studio. In many ways, she was an instinctive critic of society and recognized herself in Miller's dissent. Like him, she had a healthy skepticism about government, a distrust that Rupert Allan vividly remembered when he related her reaction to a *New York Times* article reporting the downing of an American plane over the Soviet Union. Allan was inclined to accept the US government's explanation that the plane had not been on a spy mission. "Oh, I don't know," Monroe countered. "I don't trust us."

The press portrayed Miller and Monroe's plight as a human-interest story. Editorials in England and France protested the abusive treatment of one of America's most distinguished writers. Shortly after this public outcry, the State Department quietly issued Miller a passport so he could accompany his bride to England to make *The Prince and the Showgirl* and to observe the production of his new play, *A View From The Bridge*. In newsreel footage taken just before their wedding, the two appear charmingly at one with each other. Monroe is shy and Miller is quietly confident. Neither of them has much to say for the cameras, as if they have reluctantly vouchsafed a fleeting glimpse of happiness they would rather keep private. Indeed, Monroe rarely faces the camera and seems ready to slip into the intimacy of their passion, for she has eyes only for Miller. She constantly looks up at him, nuzzling her head into his neck and holding on to his arm. She is very physical with him in an unconscious, dreamy way that is briefly interrupted when her eyes widen to take in the question the interviewer has asked her. She has put herself alongside Miller in every sense of the word—that seems to be the logic of her movements, in sync with him, who is as solid-looking as the tree he once reminded her of. He cannot easily forget he is being filmed, as she seems to— although she almost makes him do so during those split-seconds he spends away from the camera, gazing down at her in the utter ease of their mutuality. As during Monroe's marriage to DiMaggio, the world clamored for pictures, and the press pestered Miller about the details of the wedding. Like DiMaggio, he compromised with his sense of privacy and promised press conferences in order to preserve a modicum of peace, but the couple managed to elude reporters, quickly marrying in a courthouse and then again on July 1 in a Jewish ceremony held at the country home of Miller's agent and friend, Kay Brown.

Norman Rosten, an old friend of Miller's from their University of

Michigan undergraduate days and, along with his wife Hedda, one of Monroe's closest confidants, puzzled over Monroe's conversion to Judaism. Conversion seemed so unnecessary. Miller was not Orthodox, not even particularly religious. His parents put no pressure on her to convert. Rosten, who was at the ceremony, observed that "she participated with touching seriousness. Those who had secretly laughed at or mocked her desire to adopt the Jewish faith were moved to silence." Yet he could not help wondering at the "unreality of her conversion. Was it another game for her? A psychic toy?" As Rosten knew, she wanted to be an intimate member of Miller's family. She wanted to share his traditions, just as she had shared his trouble, staying with Miller and his parents after his HUAC testimony. Biographer Edwin Hoyt points out that Monroe took an avid interest in DiMaggio's Catholic faith and family, although Catholicism does not seem to have been as compelling for her as Judaism. Without denigrating her sincerity, it is inviting to adopt Rosten's notion that her conversion amounted to trying on another role—not in the superficial sense of seeking a diversion, but as a solemn way of tying herself to a religion that might strengthen her sense of belonging. Many of her successful friends—Skolsky, the Strasbergs, Milton Greene, Norman Rosten—were Jews. She may have associated her feelings of persecution with the history of a suffering people, a minority that had survived.

Milton Greene's photographs of the Jewish wedding appeared in the July 16 issue of *Life* with a brief description of the ceremony and of the couple's plans to spend a brief period in Roxbury, Connecticut, before Monroe's trip to England with Miller to begin work on *The Prince and the Showgirl*. Shots of a veiled Monroe smiling, of Miller grinning, kissing, and embracing his bride, of some of his friends and family, all in a casual, folksy, outdoors setting, suggest much warmth and genuineness all round. Rosten remembered it as "a giddy, delirious day," with Monroe saying "I do" in "a clear if shaky voice" and receiving "dozens of kisses from some twenty-five friends, relatives, and a few reporters." If she had last minute qualms, as Donald Spoto reports, she overcame them to give a brilliant performance.

A clarity in Monroe's demeanor, an openness and freshness dominated the days of her betrothal to Miller. Friends found that she had made an abrupt break with her past, set aside the defenses and the wisdom she had acquired. She strove, in Guiles's words, for a "purified state," which some feared might leave her vulnerable. Paula Strasberg interpreted Monroe's crystalline sensibility much more positively: "She's beginning to have new experiences, good ones. It's part of growing up, and perhaps the first time she's allowed things to happen to her. She's like a clear vessel—whatever you pour into her will show up." In spite of Strasberg's confidence, in retrospect her metaphor indicates something exceedingly fragile, indicative of a brittle Monroe whose composure could be easily shattered. Reflecting on his marriage, Miller remarked in 1969 on how even routine matters could "offend or undermine her." In certain moods "she was like a smashed vase. It is a beautiful thing when it is intact, but the broken pieces can cut you." It is striking that in trying to concretize Monroe's fragility Miller should create a metaphor favored by R. D. Laing to describe the schizophrenic, who "may say that he is made of glass, of such transparency that a look directed at him splinters him to bits and penetrates straight through him."

In July of 1956, Monroe gave no sign of going to pieces. On the contrary, she embodied the lifted spirits of the moment; she was, in Rosten's view, "more beautiful than ever, in a way more unreal." She was "more ethereal, more poignant." She was "really ecstatic. She gave off luminosity like the Rodin marble; she was the girl in 'The Hand of God.' It was the culmination of a dream and carried with it the danger of all dreams." Rosten may have written these last words with the benefit of hindsight. The wedding ceremony itself, he thought, "It was a fairy tale come true. The Prince had appeared, the Princess was saved."

The Prince and the Showgirl (January–October 1956)

[Y]ou know when you get grown up you can get kind of sour, I mean that's the way it can go . . .

Sir Laurence Olivier arrived in America in February of 1956 to join Monroe at the press conference announcing their plans to co-star in the film adaptation of Terrence Rattigan's play, *The Sleeping Prince*. Olivier, perhaps the greatest actor of the time, was greeted as visiting royalty. Monroe was much less certain of her reception:

> Some people have been unkind. If I say I want to grow as an actress, they look at my figure. If I say I want to develop, to learn my craft, they laugh. Somehow they don't expect me to be serious about my work. I'm more serious about that than anything. But people persist in thinking I've pretensions of turning into a Bernhardt or a Duse—that I want to play Lady Macbeth. And what they'll say when I work with Sir Laurence, I don't know.

She had met Olivier briefly about four years earlier. Would he remember her? She bore special responsibility for this project, since her production company had purchased the play and selected Rattigan to write and Olivier to direct the screen version. For some members of the press and the public, surrounding herself with such conspicuous talent seemed pretentious.

At the end of January, when reports began to appear about the forthcoming film production, the press's flippant tone made Monroe's effort to be taken seriously all the more difficult. For example, on January 30, *Time* quoted Olivier on his eagerness to make the picture with her: "I regard her as an actress and a comedienne of the first order . . ." *Time's* punch line, however, inferred that he was more interested in being seduced: "Who would resist an approach from Miss Monroe?" To her, sexuality emanated from her intelligence and craft, but press summaries of her performances rarely recognized her artistry.

Even before Olivier's appearance in New York City, Monroe had misgivings about the course Milton Greene set for the film. In January, immediately after learning of Strasberg's mild expression of approval, Greene asked Sir Laurence to direct the picture. Anxious to secure this distinguished actor, Greene acted hurriedly without thoroughly consulting her. She had lost the possibility of meeting her co-star on equal terms now that he possessed still another title to lord over her on the movie set.

Olivier recalls in his memoirs that Monroe kept him and Rattigan waiting for an anxious hour before their first meeting, but that on her appearance "she had us all on the floor at her feet in a second." He was deeply impressed, as though he were the one visiting royalty. He echoes Josh Logan's praise of Monroe when he avers that "she was so adorable, so witty, such incredible fun and more physically attractive than anyone I could have imagined apart from herself on the screen." Evidently she made every effort to please him, even if she had doubts about their collaboration. They appeared together at the press conference and seemed to do everything possible to help each other. Olivier, elegantly dressed in a dark suit, white shirt, and dark tie was complemented by Monroe, who wore a black silk dress and black silken cape, which she removed to reveal two slender straps on her naked shoulders. The expected "ohs" and "ahs" followed, and twenty minutes of picture taking ensued while reporters asked questions. According to one eyewitness, three-quarters of the questions "were fired at Marilyn," but Olivier began to play his role as director. Commanding the microphone, he slowly and deliberately rephrased the reporters' questions so that Monroe could craft her responses carefully. Several times he replied for her, until she gradually began to answer for herself with considerable wit and aplomb. Presumably one part of Monroe drew sustenance from following Olivier's lead, but another part of her may already have been storing up resentment at his pre-emption. He was gallant in his protection of her, but she was capable of twisting his gentlemanly behavior into the schizoid's dread of being disrupted and divided from others. Olivier uses this psychological term in his recollections about her personality, and it is a term Greene also favored in summing up his view of her behavior. She could not compete with this Englishman's profound self-assurance and may well have come to feel he was using it against her all along.

By the middle of July, when Monroe departed with her new husband for the making of *The Prince and the Showgirl* in England, she was capturing the same kind of public enthusiasm and international press coverage that had attended her marriage to DiMaggio and their trip to Japan. But with an uncomfortable Miller at her side and with an important movie about to be made, she seemed somewhat subdued—at least by the ebullient standards she had set for herself in earlier years. British reporters sensed sourness in her reserve, not guarded maturity. After all, she was known for her eagerness to please. Since she was not cheerfully forthcoming, the press grilled and ridiculed her about her intellectual interests, her fondness for Beethoven and Dostoevsky. She humored reporters with self-deprecatory repartee:

REPORTER. Are you really studying acting?
MONROE. Yes. I'm serious about it.
REPORTER. What inspired you to study acting?
MONROE. Seeing my own pictures [smiling gaily].

In a quieter, private moment, she had a different kind of conversation with a British reporter, Tom Hutchinson. He remembered her perceptive comments about Franz Kafka's *The Trial*, in which Josef K. is arrested for a crime against the state that is never explained to him: "It's like we all feel, this sense of guilt. I know they say it's the Jewish thing with Kafka—that's what Arthur (Miller) says anyway—but it goes beyond that. It's about all men and women. This sense that we have fallen or something. I suppose that's what they mean by Original Sin." Reading Kafka confirmed her sense of strangeness, of foreignness, of breaking rules she did not know existed. She was uneasy in Olivier's charge, for he was on home ground and working with a cast and crew he could address as old friends. Monroe, in Norman Rosten's view, was the outsider, the one needing to prove herself. She would have to "get accustomed to their way of doing things," Olivier remarked. His manners were impeccable, yet his "slight smile" and change in tone when addressing her were annoying. With others, he was a fellow professional; with Monroe, he was careful and

Poster: *The Prince and the Showgirl* (1957)

elementary, thus emphasizing her status as neophyte. Olivier's behavior seemed patronizing and her guard went up, Rosten concluded.

The Strasbergs, the Greenes, and Miller—all of whom respected Olivier enormously—corroborate Rosten's impression that Monroe felt demeaned. Each of them would make mistakes in handling Olivier that would contribute to her disaffection. The Greenes and Miller were too deferential to the director, a mortal sin in Monroe's view. Increasingly isolated and bitter, she depended on the Strasbergs for moral and artistic support. The Strasbergs conceded Olivier's genius but undermined his authority by calling his performance artificial and by catering to Monroe's worries. In Olivier's view she had far too many helpers, so that he had to run through considerable interference to get to her. For all of them the film became an ordeal to finish, as Monroe's distrust of her director grew and her health deteriorated.

Much has been made of Monroe's outraged reaction to Olivier's direction, "Be sexy." She called Lee Strasberg at his London hotel to express her resentment. She was no sex machine, and Olivier was ignoring her sensibilities as an actress. He had almost no interest in her method of making contact with her role. Indeed, on many occasions he voiced criticism of Strasberg's teachings, since he conceived them to be "deliberately antitechnical." The Method dictated "an all-consuming passion for reality, and if you did not feel attuned to exactly the right images that would make you believe that you were actually it and it was actually going on, you might as well forget about the scene altogether." For Olivier, acting was pretending. Many directors shared his belief, including Alfred Hitchcock, who told Ingrid Bergman to "fake it" when she complained that she could not feel her character's motivation. In the many accounts of the Monroe-Olivier duel, scant attention has been paid to just how old school Sir Laurence was. In "Stanislawski Was Racked by Self-Doubt" (the *Guardian*, March 16, 2013), Simon Callow notes Olivier's conspicuous absence from the roster of great British actors—such as John Gielgud, Michael Redgrave, and Paul Scofield—who had absorbed Stanislavsky in the two-decade fervor, stretching from the mid-1950s to the late 1970s, that had actors exploring the psychological truth of their roles. Even as Olivier decried Monroe's self-indulgent concern about her connection to her character, he realized that something was wrong with his own approach, which yielded only a stillborn performance—passable and even accomplished but without the sparkle and ease that Monroe worked so hard to achieve not in spite of her self-doubt, but because of it. Stanislavsky himself had been tormented by his self-consciousness and found relief from it only when he began to analyze those moments when he felt most relaxed and performed well, which were also moments when he identified aspects of his own experience that he shared with the characters he portrayed.

In retrospect, Olivier conceded that Monroe had a point. Indeed, he had no choice, since after *The Prince and the Showgirl*, he turned to a contemporary play, *The Entertainer*, a drama of raw realism, in which his portrayal of a performer called for an intense search for the psychological truth of his own performance. In his autobiography, he concedes the usefulness of Stanislavsky's principles, and he later admitted he had not worked "terribly hard to get on" with Monroe. Failures of perception were fatal for her, since she was quick to read the nuances in all of Olivier's behavior one way. He found her strangely lacking in humor, perhaps because she was unwilling to joke about the one thing she took most seriously: her acting. He may have been joshing her when he said "be sexy," or merely stupidly insensitive as to how she would take such a comment. Either way, she could not forgive him.

Olivier was apparently unaware that Monroe's closest friends were critical of her behavior. Hedda Rosten, who accompanied Monroe on the trip to England, remembered that she was dubious about the application of the Method to the light, comic part Monroe played; her devotion to character motivation seemed fussy and excessive to Rosten. Paula Strasberg, according to her daughter, agonized over Monroe's unprofessional behavior and shouldered much of the blame for it. Milton Greene angered Monroe by trying to dilute the amount of gin she requested with her tea at 9:00 a.m. before appearing on the movie set. "I would have to feed her the uppers she wanted. They came in a different color in London, and she'd think I was faking, changing the pills." Miller, like Greene, seemed to act as Olivier's conscientious surrogate, trying to get his wife to the studio on time and generally urging her to fulfill her commitment to the film. These acts she came to interpret as her husband's betrayal— especially after she discovered his misgivings about her, recorded in a journal he thoughtlessly left open on a table.

Monroe had driven Miller to desperation with her insomnia, incessant pill taking, and sluggish, drugged days and nights of worry and inactivity. In his journal he let his disillusionment show, and she was crushed. She went weeping to the Strasbergs, and rather incoherently tried to convey how devastated she felt about Miller's loss of confidence in her. There is considerable dispute about what he actually wrote—and Miller does not clarify the matter in his memoirs—but Norman Rosten did not doubt that by the end of 1956 "a change was discernible in Marilyn. The tone of the marriage had changed." Close friends sensed something "new and mysterious" between husband and wife, Rosten recalled. In her own notebook, Monroe speculated that she had always been "deeply terrified" at the thought of being a wife, since she knew from experience that "one cannot love another, ever, really." In a later entry she spoke of seeking joy, only to find it "clothed with pain."

The measure of Monroe's distress can be gauged in her decision to consult Anna Freud in London. The psychiatrist wrote about their encounter, "Adult patient. Emotional instability, exaggerated impulsiveness, constant need for external approval, inability to be alone, tendency to depression in case of rejection, paranoia with schizophrenic elements." Toward the end of her life, Monroe would speak of her loneliness, by which she meant, it seems, her inability to rely on her own inner resources. It was this aspect of her plight that Anna Freud identified. In her will, a grateful Monroe left a bequest to Anna Freud's London institute for the treatment of children.

However disappointing Miller might seem, Monroe still turned to him for support and guidance. She keenly appreciated her husband's professional appraisal of her talent and began in England to ask him to judge photographs, a task more suited to Greene. Miller also began to question the propriety of Greene's handling of his wife's business affairs and pointed to instances where Greene acted precipitously. For Greene, the worst of it came when Miller tried to rewrite certain scenes in the film and kept Monroe away from the set reading British reviews of his new play, *A View From the Bridge*. Finally, an exasperated Greene urged Miller to "Be a husband!" and stop interfering with the production. Miller responded by losing patience with Greene. Midway through the film, Monroe's business partner realized that he had been effectively compromised by her husband. Miller probably did not anticipate that in cutting Greene off from Monroe, he would cause his wife to shift more of her frustrations to him—and then lose some of her admiration for him because he had tied himself so closely to her career. Donald Spoto notes that Miller had ignored the advice of his agent, Kay Brown, when he decided to pool his income with Monroe's—in effect trying to make it less conspicuous that his earnings were dwindling, even as he was obligated to pay his ex-wife sixteen thousand dollars a year in alimony. As in so many of Monroe's relationships, she began to suspect that he had become her servant only to satisfy himself.

Olivier, with his equivocal temperament, exacerbated the difficult conditions in which Monroe struggled to create her screen characters. On the one hand, he went out of his way to consult Josh Logan and Billy Wilder on the best way to handle Monroe, but on the other, he was not willing to take their advice that he simply put up with her vagaries. He either ignored or forgot Josh Logan's suggestion that he work closely with Paula Strasberg, but bar her from the movie set. Olivier preferred complaining to Greene or Miller to forthrightly addressing his co-star. When he grumbled to Logan that Monroe was rude to him—that she walked away when he tried to instruct her in how to read a line—Logan replied that he had never had that problem because he had never attempted to tell Monroe how to say her lines. In short, Logan and Olivier were fundamentally different directors, with the latter having almost no confidence in the integrity to which the former deferred.

Accounts of Olivier's treatment of Monroe during the shooting of the film differ. Some observers always found him gentlemanly, while others reported some nasty scenes with Monroe. But it seems indisputable that he was determined not to coddle her, not to go against certain principles that were his pride as a director and actor. As he put it to one member of the cast, "There are one or two things I will have right." One eyewitness account of Monroe has her "too dumb and uncultured and obsessed with herself" to be able to cooperate with Olivier. Similar to Nunnally Johnson's earlier characterization of her work in *We're Not Married*, this criticism is nonetheless hard to credit in the main, given her alert preparations for *Bus Stop* and Hedda Rosten's observation of Monroe working on *The Prince and the Showgirl* with great concern as to how her role fit into the entire production. Conflicting versions of her awareness and intelligence stem in part, it seems, from her traumatic approach to the camera that sometimes made her close up and fumble even the simplest lines and actions. To Olivier, one observer attributed her failure to follow through to a "quite unconscious but basic resistance to acting." At any rate, it seems that, she was "practically paralyzed with nerves." This extreme nervousness, which Lee Strasberg tried to assure her was characteristic of many actors, sometimes made her seem inept, withdrawn, and resistant to direction.

None of Monroe's tentativeness showed up on screen, which came as a surprise to Dame Sybil Thorndyke, who at first felt Monroe was small and understated, but who came to call her the perfect film actress, since she came alive on celluloid in a way unrivaled by her fellow actors. The economy and celerity of Monroe's performance is noticeable when compared with her busy, fretful portrayal of Cherie, a portrayal that is a precise measurement of that character's frustrations. Elsie Marina, in contrast, is able to speak and move freely without seeming knotted up and fatigued. Monroe embodies the character's spiritedness by minimizing cramping gestures to the head and the body, which were so appropriate for the introverted Cherie. Instead, almost all of Elsie's movements are outward—sometimes lateral—so that she glides effortlessly from side to side, continually foregrounded for the viewer. In such moments, Elsie is elegant and graceful, more aware of her surroundings than previous Monroe characters, who hug themselves in displays of a cruder exhibitionism.

Although *The Prince and the Showgirl* is faithful to Rattigan's play, it seems that he was taken with Monroe's personality and shaped the film's structure around it. She, in turn, was able to use her role to provide perspective on her earlier characters. For example, as in *Bus Stop*, Monroe's character is quickly defined by mirror shots, by her self-examination in a mirror and her dressing up to meet the Grand Duke (Olivier), who is coming backstage after the performance of a play in which she has a very small part. Mirror scenes occur in *Don't Bother to Knock*, *Gentlemen Prefer Blondes*, and *The Misfits*, all of which relate to a groping, wayward, sometimes delighted dressing of herself for others. Elsie Marina, like Roslyn Taber in *The Misfits*, is characterized by her tardiness. *The Prince and the Showgirl* copies an incident that occurred at the Monroe-Olivier press conference in New York by having Elsie's shoulder strap break as she meets the Grand Duke. Thus the impression of a somewhat disheveled personality is created.

Elsie does not, however, lack confidence. It is true that she is surprised by the Grand Duke's interest in her and that she uncertainly fusses over what to wear at their meeting—as Monroe did in preparing to meet Olivier in New York—but she is quite sure of her values and represents them robustly. Because her role in the play the Grand Duke has seen is small, Elsie is surprised that she has excited his attention. Nevertheless, she is not intimidated by his rank or flattered by his attentions, for she has a strong sense of self-worth, which comes to the fore when she lectures him on democracy and family feeling. She lacks exposure to a larger world, and she is working class and ignorant in many ways, but the film never condescends to her or makes sport of her simplicity. On the contrary, as Foster Hirsch observes, Elsie is shown to have great dignity.

Elsie has been invited to what she thinks is a party given by the Grand Duke, when in fact he has planned a private assignation. Her befuddlement as to his intentions, and her slow acclimation to the royal chamber and its furnishings, are humorously acted out in her awkward but successful efforts to avoid colliding with the serving men who bring in supper. She sidesteps, darts forward and backward, and swerves around them in maneuvers that are a warm-up for her circumvention of the Grand Duke's amorous advances. Her limberness contrasts starkly with his stiff, hardened opinions and bearing. As soon as she realizes that she will be the evening's sole entertainment, she determines she will leave, telling the English foreign service officer who has arranged the meeting that she knows only too well the outcome of such seductive suppers for two. Like Cherie before her and Sugar Kane after her, Elsie has been disappointed by men and is determined to avoid their sexual gambits. She stays only when the Englishman promises to extricate her immediately after she finishes dining with the Grand Duke.

Elsie seems constitutionally incapable of calling the Grand Duke by the appropriate royal title and finally gives up, saying, "the hell with it." She is riled by his dismissive comments on democracy and speaks up for the popular will in just the way Monroe herself would (although in this case Rattigan was not influenced by Monroe, since the Elsie Marina character in *The Sleeping Prince*, named Mary Dagenham, had already been conceived with this populist bias). Monroe fit the role because she represented a certain kind of American sensitivity to the individual, which in its extreme form provokes Elsie to worry about the fate of an imprisoned politician, Wolffstein—just as Monroe pestered Miller and Rosten to offer Indonesian prime minister Sukarno refuge when she learned he was in danger of being deposed.

The inattentive Grand Duke, more concerned with concluding some business of state by phone than dining with Elsie, is subjected to her astute mimicking of his European brusqueness as she begins to eat and drink for both of them. As she loses her inhibitions, she mocks the conventions of royalty—at one point ridiculing the way everyone backs out of the room in deference to the Grand Duke. Sinuously, she retreats through the door, only to pop back into the room again to invite his admiration of her exit: "Pretty good, huh?" Even after he decides it is time to seduce her, she handles the Grand Duke expertly, noting that his performance is clichéd and his romancing pedestrian. In the play, Mary Dagenham brushes off the Grand Duke's pass by jabbing him hard in the stomach with her elbow and jumping out of the chair provided for her. In the movie, Monroe's Elsie is more forceful and funnier, as she uses an arm to sweep him aside and against a wall. This is a gesture of immense strength and is indicative of Elsie's unwillingness to adopt the genteel manner of deflecting a pass. Instead, she automatically accepts the Grand Duke's gambit for what it is—much to his chagrin—and good naturedly responds, "And better luck next time."

This honest directness, a part of the Monroe persona in many films, amiably enhances the way Rattigan conceived the American girl in his play. All of the physical business of her role, which endows her with great spontaneity and hardiness, also makes it difficult for the Grand Duke to dominate her. Although he succeeds in awakening her romantic interest, and in stimulating her to banish and perplex the Englishman who tries to make good on his promise to interrupt the tête-à-tête, she stresses that she has made a conscious choice to fall in love with the Grand Duke, a choice she demonstrates by vigorously aligning his face with hers in order to kiss him. There is a hint of melancholy in Elsie's voice, however, a latent vulnerability in her warning the Grand Duke to "watch out," because she is going to fall in love with him. She means that she will loosen her guard, and she knows that such a full expression of her emotions will exhilarate but ultimately sadden—perhaps even sour—her. Owing to past experience, she realizes that the love they share will be transitory. Comically, Elsie does "fall" for the Grand Duke, passing out from drinking too much vodka before he can have his way with her. But she remains lovely, undefiled—like The Girl—and intact in her peaceful, innocent repose, which serves as a transition to the film's consecration of her inviolability in the coronation scenes that follow.

This day, which marks the crowning in London of George V in 1911, is Elsie's dream day and Monroe's apotheosis. At the heart of the film, Olivier exposes the figure of the actress and her character in extreme close-ups that are bathed in light in much the same way as Logan caught the shimmer of Monroe's soft, ethereal face. In notes on the film's final cut, Monroe indicated she thought these scenes would please British audiences but bore Americans. But they succeed in magnifying her aura. During the coronation procession, the Grand Duke's severe demeanor begins to give way into a smile, as he allows himself to react to Elsie's freshness and vitality. In the cathedral, she gazes upward in awe and is herself portrayed as a fit object of adoration, her face framed in a stained-glass window so that she appears angelic, as even holy. Monroe's popularity is here transformed into veneration. She is presented as an icon, a focus of worship—as Ken Russell realized in *Tommy* in the cathedral scene that includes Monroe acolytes.

Logan waited until late in *Bus Stop* to attempt such a daring elevation of Monroe's person, so that his close-ups summon all the details of her performance and all the allusions to her as an angel. After the opening long shots of her through two window frames and later scenes of her running from Bo's smothering embraces, the final close-ups, tenderly played, are beautiful resolutions of the contradictions of her character, of all her human and ideal qualities. In *The Prince and the Showgirl*, Olivier makes the strategic error of elevating Elsie too soon, so that Monroe is forced to play her character for several more scenes after her sanctification. Monroe's performance does not slacken, but she is working against the film's logic. Similarly, Olivier has waited too long to have his Grand Duke fall in love with the showgirl—even though he is wonderfully adept at showing how his character giddily throws off the formal constraints of his position.

The rest of the film has difficulty sustaining interest, despite some wonderful scenes in which Elsie takes charge of the Grand Duke and eventually has him patch up his quarrel with his son, the heir to the throne of Carpathia. In a foreshadowing of *Some Like It Hot*, the ultimate seduction scene in *The Prince and the Showgirl* shows Monroe in command, looking her partner over, gazing at him below her, as she feeds him the same lines and adopts the same ploys he has used in his effort to manipulate her. Indeed, Monroe's Elsie takes on the roles of diplomat, politician, and power broker as she goes back and forth, bargaining between father and son. This reversal of expectations—what was once a momentary jest in *Gentlemen Prefer Blondes*, where "dumb" Lorelei gets the better of her future father-in-law in an argument—is carefully built into the structure of this film. Monroe's mischievous wit is shown to full advantage in Elsie's strategy, while the man—even a superbly polished Grand Duke—can seem as clumsy as the nebbishy Richard Sherman in *The Seven Year Itch*.

The poignant ending of *The Prince and the Showgirl* has captivated some critics. The Grand Duke finally confesses that he loves Elsie, and she takes him in her arms. He has made arrangements for her to follow him to Carpathia, where he must rule another year and a half before his son assumes the throne, but she declines his invitations, preferring to wait until he can leave his country to join her. It seems unlikely that the couple will be reunited, in spite of their depth of feeling for each other, and Elsie may be responding to the unreality of a match between a prince and a showgirl. The camera shows the Grand Duke exiting through the doorway of the embassy as Elsie stands to one side watching him depart through the door she entered at the beginning of the film. With the camera trained on her as she stands at the door of the drawing room with her eyes closed, she slowly backs away as she surveys the scene of their mutual seduction. Then a long shot of Monroe's back filmed from the vantage point of the drawing room, looking outward to the entrance, depicts her in solitude framed by two doorways, walking out into the world. The focus, as Joan Mellen notes, is not really on Monroe's behind, but on her sad feelings. She is isolated in the double frame, but is not as disconsolate as Cherie in the double framing Logan employs near the beginning of *Bus Stop*.

When she became soured on her screen roles, Milton Greene used to cheer up Monroe by invoking the possibility of working with Chaplin. Janice Welsch observes that, like Chaplin's Tramp, Monroe "functions in a world between comedy and tragedy and stimulates her audience to both laughter and pity." Similarly, both characters enter relationships and bring love into others' lives, but ultimately remain solitary. They set the world afire with their exuberance and yet end up with something less than whole lives. They are in constant search of some final fulfillment. At the time of *The Prince and the Showgirl*'s release, reviewers did not see any similarity between Chaplin and Monroe, and did not see the film as a development in Monroe's career. Although it received some good reviews, most of them were mixed or negative, and it has never been a popular or critical success. Bosley Crowther noted that Rattigan "has not let his story do much more than go around and around and then come [to] a sad end. . . . Furthermore—and this is disappointing—his characters do not have enough to do to allow a diverting demonstration of their elaborate acting skills." Foster Hirsch suggests that *The Sleeping Prince* remains good light comedy with sparkling dialogue, but the movie, "with its confined drawing-room setting and its artificial storyline, looks unmistakably like a theater piece transported uncomfortably to an alien and resistant medium." He concludes, "[T]he material never quite manages to move comfortably within the film frame." Even so, Hirsch rightly notes that Olivier and Monroe "play beautifully together, and the obvious difference in their styles of performance enhances the thin material," as they carry on a duet between the rigid, masked Grand Duke and the pliable, unreserved Elsie. "Significantly, Olivier is dressed up for his part while Monroe wears a simple white dress that reveals every curve and bulge in her figure." Olivier masterfully keeps everything to himself, while Monroe just as skillfully gives everything of herself away. *The Prince and the Showgirl* is not a cinematic success, in part because it seems uncomfortably suspended between stage and screen conventions that the two performers, for all their superb acting, cannot surmount. But nonetheless, the movie serves as a crucial transition between *Bus Stop* and *Some Like It Hot*, the two films that most fully bring out the comic aspect of Monroe's persona.

It is doubtful, however, that the actress felt a sense of completion. As she was leaving England in November, Monroe apologized to cast and crew, blaming her bad behavior on ill health. Olivier suspected he was not as effective as Logan and Wilder in stimulating her talent, although in his autobiography his estimation of her acting and of the film is somewhat gentler and more generous.

When Josh Logan visited Olivier and Monroe during the making of the film, he found them both feeling betrayed. Olivier blamed Logan for not giving him sufficient warning of Monroe's intractability. For her part, Monroe mistakenly believed Logan was responsible for cutting one of her most movingly acted scenes in *Bus Stop*, one that she proudly wanted to show Miller. The loss of the scene was too painful for her to bear, Logan concluded. *The Prince and the Showgirl* was to have been a film, like *Bus Stop*, in which she could express more of her real self— and her talent—than ever before. How could she trust Olivier, when Logan, who seemed to understand her so well, had sabotaged her performance? She told Logan, "I was never so angry in my entire life, and I'm just as angry now as I was then!" and banged the door of her dressing room in his face.

Through all of her trials, Monroe clung to Miller, who stayed the course with her, even if he was not quite as strong or as loyal as she hoped. Back in the United States, they would try to take their marriage in another direction, toward family and semi–retirement for Monroe until the right role was available. They had rushed from their romance and marriage to the stresses of her complicated working lives. It was time to recover their harmony as lovers and to find the habits of living that would allow them to hold one another in comfortable regard. It was time to have the home life Monroe had never really had. But neither wife nor husband was prepared to reckon with the new kind of sex symbol she had become.

CHAPTER TEN

Home Life (October 1956– August 1958)

*I was never used to being happy, so that wasn't
something I ever took for granted. I did sort of think,
you know, marriage did that. You see, I was brought
up differently from the average American child
because the average child is brought up expecting to
be happy—that's it, successful, happy, and on time.*

By the time Marilyn Monroe married Arthur Miller in the summer of 1956, a good deal had changed since she had signed her first contract with Twentieth Century-Fox a decade earlier. As a starlet, she joined an industry that attracted eighty million people to the movies weekly. Profits were at an all-time high of $1.7 billion. More than three fourths of every dollar spent on entertainment went to Hollywood. Only eight thousand families owned television sets in 1946. By 1956, over thirty-five million television sets were in American homes, as movie attendance dropped to less than half of what it had been right after the World War II.

In 1946, Monroe was only one of a myriad of beautiful young women hoping to become a star. It is not surprising that studio heads like Darryl Zanuck and Harry Cohn felt no urgency to promote her to the top of her class during her apprenticeship years (1946–52). Only gradually, as postwar America changed and the studios realized that scripts and their stars would have to provide new sorts of entertainment, did Marilyn Monroe become a major part of their plans to hold on to their diminishing audience. Bigger screens, cinemascope, and Technicolor heralded Hollywood as an alternative to the convenient and cozy appeal of television. Wide-angle lenses also facilitated the presentation of a panoramic

Marilyn Monroe doing her shambling walk on a cobblestone street in *Niagara*, and clinging to Robert Mitchum on a raft adrift on raging waters in *River of No Return*.

More than any other movie star, Marilyn Monroe had become a spectacle. Even the realism of *Bus Stop* had a fable-like aura, coruscating Monroe in her close-ups. No one in Hollywood in 1946 had predicted such a future for her. As critic Graham McCann points out, the role of the "dumb blonde"—never meant to be more than a sixty-second sexy walk-on in the Marx Brothers picture *Love Happy*, or a diverting sideshow as the alluring dim-witted secretary in *Monkey Business*—had become, by 1956, the main event.

As a new kind of sex symbol, Marilyn Monroe had to show more of herself and to make a fetish of her body in ways not demanded of predecessors such as Greta Garbo and Jean Harlow. Neither Garbo's breasts nor Harlow's bottom received the same sort of cinematic scrutiny that Monroe's body parts attracted in the Carman Miranda parody in *There's No Business Like Show Business* and the skirt-blowing scene in *The Seven Year Itch*. At the same time, Fox minimized public protests about the exploitation of Monroe's sexuality by crafting roles that carefully maintained her child-like demeanor and deference to moral conventions. On screen, she was never going to break up a marriage or, after *Niagara*, employ her sexuality as a weapon against men or other women. Above all, this new kind of sex symbol had to be the embodiment of harmless fun, devoid of Harlow's edgy toughness and Garbo's moody mystique.

From 1953 to 1956, Fox worked out a modus operandi for Monroe that the conservative studio was reluctant to modify. Any departure—such as Monroe's insistence on pale makeup and shabby costumes for Cherie—caused the cautious studio heads grave concern. In a shrinking industry (RKO, for example, went bankrupt and was bought out by television stars Desi Arnez and Lucille Ball) any fiddling with the formula meant risking profits. Monroe hated to be treated like a factory product. She resisted pressures to replay the same role, and yet in Hollywood financing depended on producing pictures that were certain to please the public. Why take a chance on casting a star like Monroe in a drama—or in any role, really, that deviated from a well-established persona? Other actresses, such as Mary Pickford and Shirley Temple—both child stars— had floundered when they tried to "grow up" on screen. Milton Greene's photographs, and later Bern Stern's, showed a more sophisticated Monroe than appeared on the screen, but those pictures were the products of one-on-one sessions, extraordinary experiments with Monroe's image that Fox dared not venture its budgets on.

Monroe wanted to continue her career, to be sure—but not by diminishing her self-respect and development as an actress. And she had put off having a family of her own in favor of a stardom that now seemed terribly limiting in both professional and personal terms. Other female stars who had wanted to break out of confining roles turned to motherhood as the Hollywood pressure to remain unchanged mounted, but without finding fulfillment. Bette Davis and Joan Crawford had children but could not seem to find an equilibrium between their on- and off- screen lives, although their publicity tried to suggest otherwise. Christina Crawford eventually produced a devastating portrait in *Mommy Dearest*, and Davis did little better with her daughter. Barbara Stanwyck lived alone, having disowned her only son. And Garbo had not only retreated into herself, she forsook movie making altogether.

None of these precedents boded well for a Marilyn Monroe still wondering how far she could take her talent and at the same time lead anything like a normal, conventional life. Initially, it seemed as though Arthur Miller might prove to be her salvation, since he professed enormous respect for her genius and honored her desire to have a child. But on the set of *The Prince and the Showgirl* he had manifestly acted like a man caught in the middle—neither loving enough as a husband, nor powerful enough to act as a go-between when Monroe wanted leverage over Olivier. Miller was not a deal maker like Doris Day's husband or a producer like Rosalind Russell's spouse. Without a clearly defined role, the flummoxed Miller retreated, warily watching Monroe, who did not want her Arthur to be directly involved in her business and yet depended on him when her career was in crisis.

Marilyn Monroe was in a category all her own. How could this postwar icon—whose identity was predicated on her very public sexual appeal—join the ranks of millions of women retreating from the workaday world? During this period most women married early and abbreviated their careers to avoid precisely the kinds of conflicts between career and marriage that Monroe tried to sort out. Betty Friedan, who graduated from Smith College in the 1940s—a time when it seemed feasible that women could both work and raise families—was astonished in the mid-1950s to see just how many young women would not even consider a career. A 1956 survey of Vassar College students reported that overwhelming numbers of these young women rejected the idea of pursuing science, the arts, and literature. Few sought the fame that Vassar graduate Edna St. Vincent Millay had achieved as a poet from the 1920s to the 1940s.

The irony for Marilyn Monroe was palpable: No character she played came close to demonstrating the determination and ambition that contributed to the creation of her icon. Cherie, in the end, had to marry her Bo and learn to delight in the major appliance he promised to buy her. The proper place for her was as a wife and mother on a ranch. No acting role prepared Monroe to become the wife and mother she now wanted to be. In short, the Marilyn Monroe character was a dead-end. Like Friedan's definition of the feminine mystique, "Marilyn Monroe" resisted "intellectual development, self-development, in favor of being 'feminine', not too brainy, not too interested, not too different from the other girls."

Yet Monroe off screen was just the opposite. She read constantly, recited Rilke, wrote poetry, drew—and craved the very intellectual stimulation that many psychologists in the 1950s warned against, because it would make women discontented with their lot. Their part consisted of buoying men up, mothering them, and managing homes that husbands could return to after a day's difficult employment in business, industry, the shop, and the store. Why should Marilyn Monroe, of all women, care about ideas? the press wondered. And very few people realized that Monroe understood just how crazy were the mad men who held sway over Madison Avenue and Hollywood. Instead, she was seen as the crazy one.

At least one woman realized the nature of Monroe's discontent and her desire to combine the sensual and the intellectual—to be, in short, a whole person. An ambitious Smith College graduate, the poet Sylvia Plath, who aspired not merely to be a great writer, but to be famous for her work, felt the powerful pull of Monroe's example. No matter how the earnest, diligent, ambitious Plath differed from most of her female contemporaries, she yearned to combine her work with the role of wife and mother precisely as Monroe was attempting to do. In her journal, Plath reports a dream about the actress that sums up the complex appeal of this new kind of sex symbol:

> Marilyn Monroe appeared to me last night in a dream as a kind
> of fairy godmother. An occasion of "chatting" with audience
> much as the occasion with [T. S.] Eliot will turn out, I suppose.
> I spoke, almost in tears, of how much she and Arthur Miller

meant to us [Plath and her husband, the poet Ted Hughes], although they could, of course, not know us at all. She gave me an expert manicure. I had not washed my hair, and asked her about hairdressers, saying no matter where I went, they always imposed a horrid cut on me. She invited me to visit during the Christmas holidays, promising a new, flowering life.

Plath imagines Marilyn Monroe as a healer and source of inspiration at a time when most women regarded the actress as little more than the embodiment of a male fantasy. As a maternal fairy godmother Monroe is comforting and encouraging. Marilyn Monroe, accessible and available, "chats" with Sylvia Plath. The sex goddess girl-talks Sylvia. This blending of high and low culture transitions into Plath's reference to T. S. Eliot, the epitome of high culture, whom Plath and Hughes would meet shortly.

Like Monroe, Plath wanted to play the "good wife" of the 1950s, even as she chose a husband in the Arthur Miller mode—a man who respected his wife's work and expected her to continue her career. Like Monroe, Plath initially adored her husband; in Plath's case, this meant not only typing his manuscripts, but also cooking for him and cleaning. As *Fragments* reveals, Monroe, too, enjoyed homemaking, designing inventive recipes and exhibiting a considerable talent for home decoration. Monroe's quest to become a whole person is part of what transformed her into an icon, not merely a symbol of a particular period, but a harbinger of women's changing attitudes in the next few decades—attitudes that would meet with varying degrees of scorn, incomprehension, and grudging acceptance. "What do women want?" Freud famously asked, baffled that his own wife seemed to have an independent streak and was not content with serving as an adjunct to his ambitions. It is not surprising, then, that in the Freudian fifties, when Freud's ideas saturated American thought and his books became a part of the American canon (as well as of Monroe's own library) she became the object of snide criticism because she was attempting to become something more than her limited roles allowed.

Miller understood Monroe's desire to break free, but like millions of other men he had been enamored with her image. He had married the icon, not the woman, and said so in that journal entry Monroe found in their London flat during the making of *The Prince and the Showgirl*. In fact, like Bo in *Bus Stop*, Miller had thought of his beloved as an angel and was unprepared to deal with a woman angered that she could not reveal all of herself. Her full humanity included a dark side, a monstrous ambition that accounted in large part for her duels with Olivier. Miller was dismayed to realize that she expected nothing less than his unwavering support, since she had also idealized him as her knight in shining armor obliged to come to her rescue. Instead, he reacted as though she were engulfing him. According to Colin Clark, an assistant director on the set of *Showgirl*, Miller told Olivier that Monroe was devouring him.

Returning home from England the couple worked hard at rebuilding a relationship already suffering from lack of trust. Other than the Strasbergs, Monroe had no one to rely on except Miller. She had broken with Milton Greene, blaming him for the business deal with Olivier that had left her feeling powerless, even though Marilyn Monroe Productions was ostensibly in charge. However hurt she had been by Miller's disappointment in her, she seemed ready to repair the damage as he worked on a screenplay of his short story "The Misfits," which would have a good part for her.

Monroe continued to take lessons with the Strasbergs. But she rid herself of Dr. Hohenberg, whose connection to Greene now seemed suspect. Anna Freud recommended Dr. Marianne Kris, whose father had been a Freud confidant. Kris, a friend of Anna's as well, would remain close to Monroe even after they terminated their therapeutic relationship. The literary critic Diana Trilling, another of Kris's patients, explained the psychiatrist's appeal: "She was . . . warmhearted, large-minded, sensitive, imaginative, a great unraveler of emotional knots. She looked wise and she was wise. Her very calm was therapeutic."

In classic Freudian fashion, the actress sought explanations for her insecurity by probing her troubled childhood. Much has been written that is critical of Monroe's resort to psychiatry, as if dwelling on her traumatic past only exacerbated her shaky state of mind. But it is difficult to see how not talking about her anxieties would have been better— especially for someone whose business as an actress involved understanding human motivation and the conditions that would foster her ability to perform. Her resort to psychiatry can be regarded as symptomatic of her distress, but hardly the cause of it.

In the spring of 1957, Monroe's conflicted feelings about her husband and career momentarily abated while she spent several busy months in a new home on a 200-acre farm near Roxbury, Connecticut. She was elated with the news that she was pregnant. She put everything else aside, although her doctor told her about his concern that her fertilized ovum might be developing outside her uterus (an ectopic pregnancy). The fetus would not be able to survive outside the womb. This diagnosis stemmed from her endometriosis, in which the cells lining the uterus (the endometrium) migrate to other parts of the body, causing inflammation and bleeding. Because endometriosis is a progressive disease, waiting until her thirties to have children put her and her pregnancies at greater risk than would have been the case were she ten years younger. But Monroe's desire to have children overrode all other considerations. She believed that a baby would fill a void in her life, made even more stressful because of her husband's troubles with HUAC and with a dogged writing regimen that resulted in very little completed work.

Monroe and Miller spent the summer of 1957 in a cottage in Amagansett on Long Island. Even during her happiest periods, Monroe had fundamental fears about the nature of existence and her place in it. And yet her exuberance and sensitivity inspired Miller to write with her in mind. He wanted to convey what might be called a metaphoric expression of his experience of Monroe. He was not writing her biography, but extending his awareness of her mythic possibilities that had been adumbrated by her movies. He proceeded cautiously and was disrupted by many false starts and by several projects, including plays, which he could not complete. Perhaps in desperation, he even proposed to write an adaptation of *The Brothers Karamazov*, one of his favorite novels, so that Monroe could play Grushenka. But photographer Sam Shaw, who remained close to Monroe, insisted that an original work from Miller would be a more fitting tribute. The care Miller took of Monroe certainly occupied much of his time, but it also seems he was struggling for a new point of view and unsure of how it would emerge. It did so later in both fiction and drama connected to her character.

Miller's short story, "Please Don't Kill Anything," (1960), centers on a character readily identifiable as Marilyn Monroe and derives its inspiration from his many months of happiness with her in Amagansett, when they were free to concentrate fully on each other and to indulge each other's vagaries. The tenor of their relationship is suggested by a wonderfully whimsical photograph of them on the beach taken in the summer of 1958. They are caught up in what looks like gales of laughter, leaning against each other, shoulder-to-shoulder, mutually supportive. The first third of Miller's story renders nearly all of its seashore scenes from an unnamed woman's viewpoint; always, what is important is what she sees, what shocks her. She makes others follow her line of sight, her waves of emotion. The woman is startled by fish struggling in a net hauled on shore by fishermen. She is virtually immobilized watching the helpless fish, but she insists on witnessing the reality of their demise. "I'll watch it. I'm watching it," she says in obvious dread. Sam, her companion and Miller's fictional surrogate, tries to placate her by throwing several of the fish rejected by the fishermen back into the sea.

Miller beautifully dramatizes Monroe's compulsion to make the world whole again, so as to compensate for her own rejection. As Norman Rosten said of her, "the survival of an unprotected shrub on a windy hillside, through rain and frost, is to her a source of trembling joy. She knew her own battle to survive and could appreciate the triumph in nature." One of the fisherman is actually embarrassed by the woman's pointed questions, and he lies when he assures her that he puts the rejected fish back into the sea.

This closeness to nature while feeling estranged from the ordered world of human affairs typified Monroe and partially accounts for her hostility to predatory authority, to anything that regimented and trapped human beings, denaturing them. She much preferred to rely on her intuitive faculties and fellow feeling than to be guided by rational explanations that regulated and, in her view, stifled creativity and ultimately life itself. In the story, Sam senses his woman's desire to reintegrate the world: "[A]s he threw the slimy fish in one by one he saw each fish separately, each straining for its quart of sea, and he was no longer ashamed." Sam is forced to see the world as a succession of individual cases, not as a single mass, undifferentiated and therefore unsalvageable. The woman is undeterred by his sensible point that all life feeds on life, one fish on another, because "she had in her head a clock which was telling her that every second counted." Similarly, Monroe was not persuaded by Miller's or Rosten's assurances that Sukarno could look after himself, that they had no connection with his political problems. She saw Sukarno as an individual who needed help, not logical explanations for inaction. She was moved by fervent sentiments similar to those expressed by Alexei Karamazov: "[E]very one of us is answerable for everyone else, but we don't know it; if we did, we would at once have heaven on earth!" Monroe ended her last recorded interview pleading for what she considered to be most important: the cause of world peace. "My nightmare is the H Bomb," she told another interviewer in what was not only a refusal to talk about her personal life, but a profound fear of the world's destructiveness.

Near the sea Monroe seems to have felt particularly close to other creatures. In her early days at Amagansett, she slept more easily at night and could almost bring her chronic insomnia under control, although she would eventually tire of the seashore and the country, unable to sustain her oneness with nature. She hankered for urban interludes that liberated her in other ways. Monroe and Miller's alternation between the country and the city—it was to become a regular rhythm for them in the two years following their departure from England—was like her oscillation between the unmatched halves of her character. If "Please Don't Kill Anything" reveals her enormous investment in the perpetuation of life, it also reflects, as Guiles notes, Miller's discovery that she was "becoming obsessively concerned with death and things dying." So much sensitivity to life held within it a terror of dissolution.

Having a child would increase her sense of a place in the world. Motherhood might provide stability and a promise of continuity. She yearned to be a mother even if that meant, in Rosten's words, "temporarily putting films aside. She desperately wanted fulfillment." She also had the conventional feeling of many parents, who compensate for their aggrieved memories of childhood by planning to give their own children a happier, more secure upbringing. Yet her pregnancy was troubled by at least one period of depression, and Rosten recalls she was subject to her usual "sudden shifts in mood. When she's high, a sweet chime of music surrounds her; when she's low, she moves to another plane, withdrawn, private." One evening during a party, Rosten found her on a porch swing sobbing. She would not tell him what was bothering her. She cautioned him to "make believe I was just out here powdering my nose or something," so that her husband—against whom she apparently harbored no quarrel—would not get upset.

Several weeks later, on August 1, 1957, she suffered a miscarriage and was rushed by ambulance to a hospital. She acted cheerful when Rosten visited her, but he was certain of her disappointment. "The love goddess, the woman supreme," could not have a baby. She was devastated. "There was something wrong with her, inside her, a defect, an evil," he surmised. Mailer and Summers give a literal emphasis to Rosten's speculation about Monroe's state of mind, passing on reports that she had several—perhaps more than a dozen—abortions that ruined her insides and made her unfit for childbearing. But as Donald Spoto points out, none of these claims has been verified, and her hospitalizations for various unspecified gynecological procedures were more likely due to her endometriosis. At any rate, life had suddenly stopped in her, and she may have felt at fault because she had postponed motherhood so long, had not wanted children earlier, and had been preoccupied solely with herself.

Motherhood had represented an alternative to the strain experienced by a woman competing in a man's world. Motherhood had its privileges and its beguiling qualities, which Monroe had never experienced or even witnessed in her own mother's behavior. In the 1950s, she wanted to join a generation of women like Betty Friedan, who recalled in *The Feminine Mystique*, "All of us went back into the warm brightness of the home, the way it was when we were children and slept peacefully upstairs while our parents read, or played bridge in the living room, or rocked on the front porch in the summer evening in our home towns." This soothing notion of family life permeated the airwaves of 1950s radio and television. "Sexual love and motherhood had to become all of life," Friedan continues, "had to use up, dispose of, women's creative energies." In Monroe, motherhood could displace that chronic desire to be a great actress. She could sublimate her ambition in a role that all of society honored.

Friedan's linking of "sexual love and motherhood" also suggests another dimension to Monroe's depression: She would be less desirable to her husband because she had not given birth to his baby. "Baby"—this term of endearment that is so prevalent in American love songs—expresses the male desire for love and children. Women are beautiful babes, prized not only for their looks but their ability to conceive—or so the mantra of popular song suggests. How could Monroe, that living doll who had to appear in public all dolled up, possibly please her husband now?

If there is no evidence that Miller—who already had children by his first marriage—wanted a child as badly as Monroe did, it seems nevertheless the case that she projected the imperative of childbearing onto their relationship. Now she suspected that Miller would love her less because she had not given birth. She loved herself less because she could not give him what a woman should be capable of giving. A child was the natural outcome of a loving relationship, a validation of the new kind of sex symbol Monroe wanted to embody. *River of No Return* ended with her character about to marry the hero and become a stepmother, and *Bus Stop*, of course, concluded by subordinating Cherie's ambitions and her sexuality to family life with Bo.

Miller attempted to cheer his wife with the announcement that he was going forward with plans to write the screenplay of *The Misfits*, which would feature a female character, Roslyn, who would be perfect for Monroe. This news, however heartening, did little to relieve her depression. Unable to sleep, she steadily increased her daily dosage of Nembutal, which gave her brief respites, but was going to kill her, Miller feared. She was having difficulty breathing and was slowly suffocating herself with one pill too many. He would have to witness several of these episodes, when her depression became so deep that there was nothing he could do to rouse her. On more than one occasion, he was forced to call a crew from a nearby clinic to revive her.

Was Monroe trying to kill herself? In addition to Natasha Lytess's report of a suicide attempt, there is Norman Rosten's recollection of a dialogue with Monroe at 3:00 a.m. in her New York apartment after she had her stomach pumped of its pill overdose (Miller was not present):

It's all quiet; private doctor, no publicity.
My wife enters the room. After a moment I follow in the dim light. I hear someone sobbing quietly. I whisper, leaning over the bed, "It's me, Norman. How are you dear?"
"Alive. Bad luck." Her voice is rasping, drugged. "Cruel, all of them, all bastards. Oh Jesus. . . ."
She doesn't say who. She has tried this before and will try it again.

Rosten made a pact with Monroe stipulating that if either of them "was about to jump, or take the gas, or the rope, or pills, he or she would phone the other." He was joking, but he took the agreement seriously nevertheless and expected to get a call from her one day.

Monroe's poetry, published in *Fragments*—and some of which Rosten included in his memoir—dramatizes the tension of a life suspended precariously and stubbornly between its dichotomies:

Life—
I am of both your directions
Existing more with the cold frost
Strong as a cobweb in the wind
Hanging downward the most
Somehow remaining
those beaded rays have the colors
I've seen in paintings—ah life
they have cheated you

Another version of the same poem emphasizes both life's fierce upward pull on her like "leaping hot fires," and its pull downward to what Rosten supposes is death. Her incomplete poem precisely replicates her idea of herself as a fragment of life; she is as unfinished and as unpolished as her verse. "Strong as a cobweb in the wind" is suggestive of both her delicacy and her stamina, which "somehow" endure, remaining as projections of nature. The image of beaded rays is elusive; indeed the last three lines are enigmatic, and Rosten offers no help with them, perhaps because they reflect Monroe's private symbolism or parts of poems she did not deign to develop. It may be significant, however, that the referent of "they" in the last line is ambiguous, so that—as in her vague cursing after her pill overdose—it is impossible to know how it is that life has been cheated. In other words, both her destructive and creative actions are truncated.

The origins of Monroe's abortive poetry can only be guessed at, but the themes of forlorn anguish and the duality of all her experience are unmistakable. The same themes pervade her drawings done on Fire Island in the summer of 1955, two of which Susan Strasberg saved: "In one, with quick, round lines, depicting a feline, sexual grace and movement, she had done a self-portrait. The other was of a little Negro girl in a sad-looking dress, one sock falling down abut her ankles. I thought that was a self-portrait, too, of Marilyn's hidden self."

Norman Rosten owned four of Monroe's drawings that elaborate on her introverted and extroverted sides: (1) a lonely-looking little girl with a tiny face and a flowing gown; (2) a simple sketch of a figure hunched, over perhaps in pain, with the caption "I'd die if I could"; (3) a singer with prominent breasts and behind; (4) an old woman studying her hand. Faces are almost never prominent or even clearly drawn. Figures count for almost all of the artist's interest, and they are rendered with great energy. Monroe's self-portrait in Sam Shaw's book is drawn in flamboyant, broad strokes, with breasts, hips, arms, and legs swinging out in wide curves that suggest a flaunting of her body. It is much harder to read the little face, since the eyes and lips are dark blots dominated by a mass of hair that stands up vigorously from her small head. The caption for the self-portrait—"What the Hell, that's life!"—may be Monroe's way of shrugging off disappointment and expressing her vitality.

On the one hand, Monroe could look and feel like the personification of health. On the other, she could have that down-in-the-mouth hopelessness that made everyone want to help her. In her drawings, she pictured herself as both the victim of her doubts and the vanquisher of her troubles. This kind of paradoxical appeal is perhaps what prompted one psychiatrist to write to her in this humorously contradictory fashion: "I am sure there is NOTHING wrong with you. Please let me know whether I can be of assistance."

Monroe's drawings, her acting, her movies, her public appearances were all extensions of a self and perhaps, for a time, retarded that inner contraction of character that made her feel so tiny, so inconsequential and abused—like the little Negro girl she drew, and so old, or at least aging, like the insular old woman preoccupied with her hand. The bushels of fan mail she showed Rosten were a way of reaffirming she had a self to exhibit—at least one she could dress up and enlarge like her drawing of the little girl with the tiny face and flowing gown.

Between the extremes depicted in her poems and drawings the actress sought equilibrium. Several of her friends remember the autumn of 1957 as having been a particularly joyful period. Monroe and Miller spent weekdays in the city and weekends at the farm in Connecticut. Sam Shaw's New York City photographs published in the October 1, 1957, issue of *Look* include scenes of Monroe and Miller preparing for a ride in their convertible, driving through the financial district, stopping for a snack at Battery Park, stretching their legs beside East River Drive, absorbed in each other's eyes against the background of a bridge and expressway, and walking together hand-in-hand on the sidewalk. Other photographs show Monroe by an elevator at Tiffany's, surrounded by a crowd on the sidewalk, reading a newspaper next to a couple seemingly oblivious of her presence, rowing a boat in Central Park, and eating hot dogs at an outdoor restaurant on 112th Street, a street where Miller had lived when young. The photographs create the impression that Monroe has given herself over to him, as he points out interesting landmarks and gazes outward on the city. They have achieved balance and equality in their lives—and a measure of serenity.

The city was also the place where Monroe could play at being other selves, where she could disguise or reveal herself at will. Norman Rosten recalled that neither he nor his wife recognized Monroe when the photographer Sam Shaw first introduced her to them. With "no makeup, hair short and careless and wet" she looked like a "pretty high school kid," and he told her she would not be recognized at a party they were to attend a few hours later. Sure enough, no one believed that this woman could be a film star, and Rosten then wondered if she had stepped "into the reality of her true self." Certainly Monroe was attractive to the partygoers, but he could not tell exactly what drew them most to her, whether it was "her voice, the half-shy, half-curious way she looked at people, her sudden warmth, that quick infectious laugh?" She enjoyed herself and did not seem at all displeased by what Rosten called her anonymity in Brooklyn. She could have fun with herself and with others when it came to trying to divine her identity. She made a game of teasing the crowd, practiced elaborate rituals of self-disguise, picked outlandish clothing to wear, and hired huge limousines with shades that invited curiosity. In effect, she was challenging strangers to say "I know who you are!" speculated Rosten.

The actress had an oscillating notion of identity, so that she would do things, so to speak, by halves. She had a fluid, even volatile, idea of herself. She was molded to the moment in the same way as Dmitry Karamazov, Dostoevsky's supreme example of the manic-depressive personality, whose histrionic sense of himself fluctuates above and below the normal ego's more or less stable lines of behavior. The mirrors that lined several walls of Monroe's Manhattan apartment repeatedly reflected the joy and despair she took in her selves. She viewed herself, as in her drawing, as a figure dressing or undressing in endless, isolated permutations. As in Truman Capote's remembrance of her, she sometimes seems to identify with the mirror image, and sometimes is able to measure off a distance between herself and her reflection. "Can I really be as good as [the Strasbergs] say?" she questions herself, staring in the mirror. "What are you doing?" Capote asks Monroe as she confronts a dimly lit mirror. "Looking at Her," is Monroe's reply. Unfortunately, she was rarely able to bring her multiple personalities together to produce a single, complex state of consciousness, a fullness of self that she perhaps felt only while acting.

Yet it was not enough for Monroe to go from classes at the Actors Studio, to sessions with her psychoanalyst, and back to her apartment, where she would play—over and over again—her favorite Frank Sinatra records, dance and dress in front of her mirrors, and nurse her sense of self-pity and abandonment with songs like "Every Day I Have the Blues." She found solace in the songs and in her social life with the Strasbergs and the Rostens. With these people—especially in their kitchens—she could indulge in homely pleasures, feel neighborly, and surround herself with a small community of friends. "Kitchen Notes," a chapter in *Fragments*, reveals her domestic side, her interest in decorating, entertaining, and cooking.

But Monroe had trouble making herself happy apart from her husband, her friends, and her roles. She could not please herself, for she lacked "a firm core of ontological security," to use R. D. Laing's terminology. Her behavior resembled Laing's view of the schizoid's lack of "an over-riding sense of personal consistency or cohesiveness," and therefore she spent most of her time simply trying to keep herself intact. Or, as Laing puts it, "[T]he ontologically insecure person is preoccupied with preserving rather than gratifying himself: the ordinary circumstances of living threaten his low threshold of security." Monroe's life with Miller was as solid and dependable as any she ever had, and yet the very matter-of-factness of it upset her, drove her to her mirrors to live—sometimes like the schizoid—in a world of her own. "It's you I hate to lose," "Every Day I have the Blues" says, and Monroe may have had the schizoid's worry that, in Laing's words, the "world of his experience comes to be one he can no longer share with other people."

In spite of all their shortcomings, movies were still a bona fide way for Monroe to share at least part of herself with other people. Miller seemed to appreciate movies in that way, for he urged her to face the cameras again, in the hope that she would come to herself in the concentration required to perform for them. He was particularly anxious to go forward with his screenplay of *The Misfits*, a draft of which he finished sometime in the spring of 1957, and which he would continue to work on for the next year. In the meantime, Monroe decided to take the role of Sugar Kane in Billy Wilder's *Some Like It Hot*, which would be ready to start shooting in the summer of 1958.

Miller's counsel carried more weight than ever, since Monroe publicly announced on April 11, 1957 her intention of breaking with Greene. She felt he had misinformed her about contracts and made secret commitments. Their partnership was legally dissolved in April of 1958, after two years of working for the critical acclaim that still eluded her. *Bus Stop* had been a triumph, and she had outshone Olivier, but she measured Greene against the grander goals he had promised to achieve. Her bitter disappointment bewildered Greene, who had devoted himself to her career. Miller would find himself in a similar position a few years later, when her fondest hopes for their marriage and *The Misfits* collapsed.

From the spring of 1957 to the summer of 1958, however, Monroe and Miller were busily involved in a joint career. She could still imagine that they were creatively inseparable, as the cast and crew of *The Misfits* was assembled in nearly magical order: John Huston, her ideal director;

Clark Gable, her romantic childhood image of her father and a Hollywood king; Eli Wallach, a friend and Actors Studio stalwart,; and Montgomery Clift, who was so like herself, Monroe thought. She asked Frank Taylor, an old friend of Miller's who had been one of the first to hear the author read his screenplay, to be the film's producer. With the interim prospect of working with Wilder, a director she admired enormously, Monroe believed she had the elements that could coalesce into a unified persona and career. The Strasbergs believed in Miller's script and were already preparing her for one of her greatest performances in *Some Like It Hot*. She also held on to the hope of another pregnancy. Perhaps her self-fulfillment was not so far away after all.

CHAPTER ELEVEN

Imperʌonationʌ/Repetitionʌ
(Auguʌt 1958–June 1960)

*What am I afraid of? Do I think I can't act? I know I
can act but I am afraid. I am afraid and I should not
be and I must not be.*

On August 4, 1958, the first day of shooting *Some Like It Hot*,
Marilyn Monroe arrived on the sound stage with her usual
assortment of associates, which included not only her husband but her own "hairdressers, make-up man, press representative, a maternal dramatic coach confidante, and untitled others."
Billy Wilder does not seem to have minded her ménage, for he realized
she was a genius when it came to building upon her Marilyn Monroe
image. He had worked closely and amicably with Monroe and Natasha
Lytess on *The Seven Year Itch* and felt the actress had developed a wonderful comic performance, part of which had to be completed during her
wrenching separation from Joe DiMaggio. To be sure, she had held up
production by forgetting lines or showing up late, and she was susceptible to sudden illnesses and prolonged periods of agonizing insecurity.
But the huge success of their previous project and his fundamental faith
in her talent sustained Wilder during what were to be the most miserable
days of his moviemaking career.

Of the three roles in *Some Like It Hot*, Monroe's was actually the
smallest, yet she knew that the quality of her performance and its strategic placement were crucial to the film's success. Wilder knew it, too,
and carefully consulted Monroe and Miller about the role, obtaining her
acceptance of it before he and his collaborator, I. A. L. Diamond (screenwriter of *Love Nest*), finished the screenplay. Monroe was also courted by

With Billy Wilder (1959)

her co-stars, Jack Lemon and Tony Curtis, who were most charming in
the early stages of the planning and filming.

Billy Wilder told Curtis that Frank Sinatra had been Monroe's first
choice for his role. In an April 3, 1958, meeting with her powerful agent,
Lew Wasserman, she said she did not like Curtis for the part and that

she was waiting for Sinatra to "enter the picture." In his memoirs, Curtis recounts an affair he had with Monroe during their early days in postwar Hollywood. Did her history with Curtis affect her judgment, especially now that Miller, present at the meeting with Wasserman, was a much more active participant in shaping her career? Rupert Allan remembered Monroe telling him how solicitous Tony Curtis was. He would drop by her dressing room every day to pay her elaborate compliments. Later, his flattery would become forever overshadowed by his comment that kissing her was like kissing Hitler. In his memoirs, Curtis explains that he made the remark after watching the famous scene in which Monroe virtually smothers him with kisses. He was in a projection room and upset because of the lewd comments of publicists and crew members who he did not think should even be present, and then he became even angrier when he saw that the director favored Monroe's takes, which showed Curtis "wearing down." As he exited the room, the question was shouted out, and he answered, "What do you think it was like, buddy? Like kissing Hitler?"

Jack Lemmon remembered that at their first meeting Monroe grabbed him and kissed him. He couldn't imagine feeling "more wonderful." Like Olivier during his initial encounter with the actress, Lemmon was delighted by Monroe's sweetness and charm. She impressed him with her thorough knowledge of the parts he had played and by her critiques of each one. He was "stunned." She had him "right in the palm of her hand," he confessed. So they got along "beautifully," and he admitted that he "really loved Marilyn very much." She revered Lemmon's talent, Rupert Allan recalled, and as she explained to Allan, she suspected that Curtis's later meanness was linked to her favoring Lemmon.

Working on *Some Like It Hot* should have been a deeply satisfying experience for Monroe, since the cast and crew and her whole entourage started out with complete commitment to the picture. Monroe liked Wilder personally and had enjoyed the work they had done together on *The Seven Year Itch*. The part of Sugar Kane, written expressly for her, had a sensitivity that was lacking in most of her previous roles. To begin with, Wilder took advice from both Miller and Paula Strasberg about improving Monroe's role. It had been two years since Monroe had worked on a film, and now she had an independent production, with a share of the profits—exactly the kind of deal that justified her return to the screen.

Monroe's friends said she wanted to work; she loved the part. Ralph Roberts, John Springer, and Rupert Allan cannot recall her ever discuss-

Some Like It Hot (1959)

ing any misgivings about the role. Yet Arthur Miller characterized Sugar Kane as a "tasteless and characterless ingénue which she had to invest with some life so that it was real. . . . She had so assiduously worked on this small worthless role, and she couldn't get a part worth working on. . . . Underneath it all, it was to her something of an affront." Monroe's behavior on and off the set suggests ambivalence. Almost in spite of herself, she struggled to attain a superlative performance. Perhaps she shared Miller's view—expressed after acrimony developed with Wilder—that her role was of "no consequence. That part was a triumph of comedic inventions. She had made something out of nothing." Nearly every step forward in her acting seemed to require a step backward, a rehearsal of previous mistakes. She was overcome by a compulsion to repeat even as she slowly edged toward her best work. On *Some Like It Hot*, distrust, paranoia, and frustration peaked. Indeed, she seemed to suffer from a sense of dislocation that ultimately estranged her from her closest companion, advisor, and lover: Arthur Miller.

Monroe, now thirty-two and writing notes to herself, was playing, a "gay young hopeful girl," when, in fact, the actress felt "depressed with my whole life." Stymied, she felt the urge to throw a silver plate into a "dark area on the set," but she knew she "couldn't afford to let out anything I really felt." To do so might mean losing all control over herself and her performance. Her salvation, she told herself, was to concentrate: "What I am using is that one Sunday when I was fourteen for I was all these things [gay and young and hopeful] that day."

The ensemble playing of all the main actors is so superb—they have a way of matching each other's brio and bravado perfectly—that it is hard to believe the production was beset by delays in filming. Take after take exhausted the actors—especially Curtis—as Monroe stumbled over dialogue. One brief scene, in which she entered a hotel room, searched through dresser drawers, and asked, "Where's the bourbon!" took fifty-nine takes, as she repeatedly flubbed her one line with such attempts as "Where's the bonbon?" Wilder even taped the single line to the inside of dresser drawers, but nothing helped, and she seemed oblivious to the strain she was putting on everyone.

Sometimes Monroe had difficulty accepting even elementary direction or taking the simplest scenes at face value. For example, Wilder wanted her to act surprised when a concealed whiskey flask drops out of her dress onto the floor of the train while she is rehearsing a song with the band. Monroe thought her character should be frightened—presumably of losing her job, since she had been warned about her drinking. She halfheartedly tried to do the scene Wilder's way. When he cut and asked for more surprise, she immediately went to Paula Strasberg. For fifteen minutes, the two women discussed the scene while the humiliated director waited for Monroe to return. She was refusing to act what she did not feel—a perfectly reasonable reaction in a Method acting class, but terribly disruptive to movie set discipline. Jack Lemmon said her "built-in alarm system" would go off in the midst of a scene that was not working. She would come to an abrupt stop and "stand there with her eyes closed, biting her lip, and kind of wringing her hands. Eventually she would sort out the problems without considering the reaction of anyone else."

Lemmon watched in fascination, apparently adopting a view of Monroe's self-centeredness akin to Josh Logan's and Don Murray's. They all could see how she wanted to know her characters and how her acting had to be all of a piece. It had to come organically out of herself—even the smallest gestures and seemingly innocuous expressions. Sugar Kane could easily have been just a stereotype, a figure in a farce, but in playing her Monroe generated a substantial personality, a wholeness that transcends caricature.

Right from the beginning of her work on Sugar Kane, Monroe was concerned about believing in her character. She wanted to know how she could play a woman who did not discover the true identities of two female impersonators despite being intimately involved with them. Since the film is a farce, and since many other characters are also deceived by Joe and Jerry, the question might seem pointless. But for Monroe there had to be a compelling reason for Sugar's identification with Jerry/Daphne and Joe/Josephine. Lee Strasberg solved Monroe's problem by reminding her that while men always wanted to be close to her, she often had difficulty getting to know women. Now, in the film, two women liked her and wanted to be her girlfriends. Strasberg recalled that his suggestion settled Monroe's doubts. As Jack Lemmon perceived, "[S]he had a good sense of comedy, but she had to bend the characters to herself." For Monroe, every approach to her character was an approach to herself; she was making a profound personal investment in her role.

After seeing the first day's rushes of her opening scene, in which close-ups singled her out as the heroine among a band of female musicians, Monroe and Miller realized that not enough had been done to distinguish her personality from the others. The couple suggested to Wilder what needed to be done, and as a result, when we first see Sugar Kane, she is wearing a sleek black outfit and carrying her ukulele, stepping hurriedly and nimbly in very high heels along the same train platform that Daphne (Lemmon) and Josephine (Curtis) had cautiously and somewhat unsteadily crossed moments earlier. Her entrance is accompanied by a raucous and jazzy horn solo that amplifies the sexy agitation of her walk and sounds a note of interest in her vocalized by Daphne's male half. Daphne/Jerry watches Sugar move on tiny heel and toe points that almost shake and lift her off the ground, then exclaims that her movement is like "jello on springs." At this point, she has already swerved away from the shaft of steam that has hit her rear, and Jerry is studying her, swinging his shoulders in imitation of her, and perfecting his Daphne in ways that will later entice the millionaire Osgood (Joe E. Brown).

The shot of steam is a comic device, a bit of physical humor particularly appropriate to a farce, but it also signals the first male thrust at Sugar Kane. Later Jerry pinches her while they are in the water together after they have arrived in Florida—a trick he says he picked up (from Osgood) in the hotel's elevator. Finally, there is the steam on Joe's glasses during the seduction scene when Sugar has knowingly made him hot. Also, the blast of steam neatly diverts Joe and Jerry from their previous concern. At a stroke, as it were, they are no longer simply running away from Spats Columbo and his gang. They are now chasing Sugar, who is as innocent and unsuspecting as they were when they became witnesses to Spats's Saint Valentine's Day Massacre of the stoolie Toothpick Charlie and his gambling associates.

For the film to be able to withstand so much counterpoint between male and female experiences without seeming just a clever contrivance, the first scene with Sugar has to carry a special charge, catapulting the characters and the audience into an outrageous new realm in which male and female role reversals are not just accepted, but welcome. As Jerry playing Daphne, Lemmon takes on many of Sugar's characteristics; that is, he learns from her how to be a woman, even as he desires her. He also takes on aspects of the movie persona Monroe had developed in earlier films. For instance, in the course of commenting on Sugar's vibrating walk, he blurts out, "It's a whole different sex." The stupid sincerity of his observation is pure Monroe, pure Sugar, in its endearing daffiness. As Stephen Farber observes, Lemmon and Monroe are a team, "two great big dumb innocents, throwing themselves at life with verve and abandon." At the same time, Lemmon as Jerry/Daphne is never entirely feminized, for the actor also parodies the comic mannerisms of Joe E. Brown (Osgood)—especially Brown's wide-open, fulsome, aspirated laugh. Lemmon latches onto Monroe as the female complement to his character in the same way that Brown romances Lemmon playing Daphne. Similarly, Tony Curtis is both the suave male lover impersonating Cary Grant and the sisterly Josephine, who comes on like Jane Russell—"big and sassy," the short bellboy calls him/her. Curtis as Joe restrains Jerry's predatory eyeing of Sugar, just as Russell as Dorothy in *Gentlemen Prefer Blondes* tries to tone down Lorelei's vulgar appraisal of men.

That Sugar's experience parallels Joe's and Jerry's is made explicit when she speaks to Joe's female half, Josephine, explaining that she is running away from male bands—particularly male saxophone players (like Joe) who have exploited and rejected her. "Running Wild," her first song, provides much of the momentum for the film's train sequence. Sugar strums her ukulele and steps in circular yet forward fashion down the aisle in imitation of the locomotive's spinning wheels, which the camera features periodically during the train trip. When the music stops, the bandleader notices bullet holes in what Jerry calls his "bull fiddle," so that the reasons for his running are recalled. When Sugar's liquor flask falls to the floor, Jerry covers for her, as he has always done for his arch male chauvinist partner when Joe was in a jam with a woman. But Jerry, as Daphne, also acts like one woman protecting another, just as Joe, as Josephine, will later act as Sugar's female confidante, advising her that no man—not even himself—is worth her suffering. Later, Sugar will adopt many of Joe's lines when presenting herself as a debutante suitable for marriage to his mockup of a millionaire, going after him with an assurance she has never expressed before. Indeed, the film is full of these repetitions and reversals of behavior, in which males and females impersonate each other and identify with male and female experiences without either sex becoming dominant.

Some Like It Hot presents a world of comic dualism in which Monroe's persona of the dumb blonde is acknowledged but also displaced, since it is Jerry as the blonde Daphne who wins the millionaire, while Sugar settles for the reality of poor Joe. There is a sadness in Sugar—she calls it being blue—and a neurotic quality (she drinks too much and frets over the repetitiveness of her experience) that distinguishes her from Lorelei, Pola, and Monroe's other female impersonations. Like Elsie and Cherie, Sugar seems older than Monroe's previous blondes. Disheartened by male duplicity, she is determined not to make the same mistakes again:

> You fall for them and you love 'em—you think it's going to be the biggest thing since the Graf Zepplin—and the next thing you know they're borrowing money from you and spending it on other dames and betting the horses. . . . Then one morning you wake up and the saxophone is gone and the guy is gone, and all that's left behind is a pair of old socks and a tube of toothpaste, all squeezed out. . . . So you pull yourself together and you go on to the next job, and the next saxophone player, and it's the same thing all over again. See what I mean? Not very bright. . . . I can tell you one thing—it's not going to happen to me again. Ever.

Of course, she has perfectly described Joe and the way he has depleted women like Sugar. Monroe delivers these lines with as much disappointment in herself as in the men who have exploited her. Bitterness is mixed with self-criticism as she catches the recurring rhythm of her experience in a voice tinged with fatigue but finally buttressed with determination and a reserve of energy. Like Monroe herself, Sugar seems an excellent candidate for psychotherapy, caught in her own contradictions and repetitions, a helpless person bent on helping herself. Somehow the actress manages to speak with a voice that is an admixture of experience and injured innocence.

Although certain lines qualify Sugar as a dumb blonde, she is aware of her limitations and has a self-consciousness that suggests some maturity. Indeed, the brilliance of Wilder and Diamond's dialogue is that it encompasses Sugar's paradoxical appeal so simply, directly, and believably. Of male saxophone players Sugar remarks, "I don't know what it is, but they just curdle me. All they have to do is play eight bars of 'Come to Me My Melancholy Baby'—and my spine turns to custard, and I get goose-pimply all over—and I come to them." Monroe manages to be at once ignorant, helpless, sad, resigned, and sexually suggestive by mixing her matter-of-fact delivery with a chronic plaintiveness that is somehow not tiresome but attractive. There is nothing put-on about her speech. She keeps just enough lilt in her voice to suggest vitality when saying how depressed she gets over her compulsiveness—and then hits her head as if either to knock some sense into it or to chastise herself. However one interprets her gesture, her whole stance in the scene in the ladies' washroom reveals an avowal of her limitations. In *The Seven Year Itch*, The Girl also frankly confesses that she gets "goose-pimply all over," but she lacks Sugar's sense of having been abused. The Girl is not dissatisfied with her toothpaste commercial, and she does not feel squeezed out like the tube of toothpaste left behind by Sugar's lovers.

For Sugar, Joe, and Jerry, Florida is, in a way, the end of the line; they are all trying to escape former selves and all trying to fashion lives that will not simply repeat past mistakes. Even Osgood, romancing Daphne, is seeking a marriage partner who will finally bring an end to his long string of divorces. For Joe and Jerry, a repetition of the past would literally mean death. Sugar, on the other hand, senses she'll experience a psychic death, a further diminution of her person, if she continues to work for male bands. Yet it is two men impersonating women who in effect save her from herself—just as she, in a sense, rescues them from the destructive aspects of their maleness, of the murderously masculine world epitomized by the gangsters. Joe, as Josephine, tries to dissuade Sugar from joining the drinking party in Jerry/Daphne's train berth, a

party that began with Sugar's simple wish to thank him/her for protecting her by pretending to have dropped the whiskey flask that would have
cost Sugar her job. At the same time, of course, both men are desperately
trying to figure out ways to seduce her. Their predatory attitude gradually changes as they are put in her place. Thus Sugar says to Jerry, "If it
hadn't been for you, they would have kicked me off the train. I'd be out
there in the middle of nowhere, sitting on my ukulele"—to which he replies, "It must be freezing outside. When I think of you—and your poor
ukulele. . . ." As he empathizes with her, he recapitulates her experience
as his own—which in a way it is, since before getting on the train he had
been out in the cold with his bull fiddle looking for work. All the same,
of course, as Jerry he wants nothing more than to seduce Sugar—reason
enough not to want her out in the cold.

Brandon French terms *Some Like It Hot* a "good-natured dream of
sexuality as a sliding scale from male to female." Her phrasemaking is
particularly apt, considering the way Lemmon modulates his voice between high and low pitches so that it often cracks somewhere between
male and female registers. Similarly, Curtis drops his voice on the word
"really" when he learns Sugar goes for male saxophone players, and Sugar
roughs up her voice to say "some like it hot" when she describes the jazz
the female band plays. This variety of voice and music—from Sugar's coy
boop-boopy-doop song to the mellow bass and brassy horn solos—provide contrasts of character not equaled in any of Monroe's other films.

Unlike Monroe's previous leading men, Lemmon and Curtis are
forced to warm up to her character before they can try to possess her.
Jerry, as a woman, has to allow Sugar to snuggle up to Daphne without making advances. His restraint puts him in a fever, and Sugar tries
to rub the chills out of him. Similarly, Joe discovers that Sugar will not
be responsive to his usual male saxophone player ploys, so he behaves
like a girlfriend, sharing his lipstick with her—and like a mother, offering
tender, supportive suggestions. In his impersonation of a millionaire, he
remains passive and cool, preferring classical music to jazz, and inviting
Sugar to help him recover his potency. In these hilarious scenes, Sugar
is, indeed, the source of energy as well as the fulfillment of male sexual
fantasies. She is like Monroe's past screen personas, but she is also more
maternal. She is more suggestive of life's vibrancy than they ever were.

Once Sugar thinks she has found her millionaire on the beach, one
who is "quiet, bespectacled, intellectual" like The Girl's ideal man in *The*

Seven Year Itch, she manipulates him in the same way Joe has manipulated women. Like Joe, she even uses Jerry/Daphne as her straight man/woman when she wants him/her to support her pretensions:

SUGAR. This is my friend Daphne. She's a Vassar girl.
JERRY. I'm a what?
SUGAR. Or was it Bryn Mawr?

The more Joe puts on his act as aloof millionaire, the more Sugar plays her part as a high society girl, so that her naïve parody of a debutante is the exact equivalent of his simple burlesque of the rich. One caricature begets another.

This coupling and recoupling of characters—Sugar with Daphne, then Sugar with Josephine, then Sugar with the millionaire—is also an escalation of impersonation that reaches a crisis when Jerry/Daphne decides to expose Joe by dashing back to their hotel room with Sugar before Joe can return from the beach to change back to his Josephine getup. When Jerry/Daphne and Sugar arrive, however, Josephine is already in a sudsy bath, singing Sugar's song, "Running Wild." Both figuratively and literally, Monroe's male co-stars assume her role, and it is the role-playing itself that is actually exposed when Sugar leaves the room and Josephine/Joe/Shell Oil millionaire all emerge from the tub. The figure wears Josephine's wig and makeup, the millionaire's blazer and white pants, and Joe's formidable anger as he makes Jerry back away and dumps his yachting cap full of water on Jerry's head. Thus Joe douses Jerry's rebellion against him, and they are no longer rivals for Sugar's love. Now a new act is created in which Jerry as Daphne will woo the millionaire Osgood and help Joe win Sugar by getting Osgood out of the way so that Joe can entertain Sugar on Osgood's yacht.

These plot changes prepare for a reversal of emphasis that puts Monroe's character in charge of the action—as in *The Prince and the Showgirl*, when Elsie begins to dominate the Grand Duke by using the very same seductive tactics he used against her. Midway through the film, the Grand Duke feigns love-struck humility to engage Elsie's sympathy, and then reveals a genuine ineptness and awkwardness as she turns his tricks against him. Similarly, Joe feigns sexual immaturity—he calls himself Junior—and an ineffectualness that proves to be somewhat real when he has trouble with the gears on the small boat he has to drive in reverse to get out to the yacht. He also fumbles around the yacht, opening the

With Tony Curtis in *Some Like It Hot* (1959)

IMPERSONATIONS/REPETITIONS

183

wrong doors and generally acting as blind with his glasses on as Pola acts with hers off in *How To Marry a Millionaire*. It is Sugar who finds the appropriate room for their tête-à-tête. At this point, Monroe takes over the film.

After Junior relates his woeful tale about the causes of his impotence and the futile attempts to revive his sex drive—including sessions with Dr. Freud and a trip to the Mayo Clinic—Sugar asks him if he has tried American girls. Like Elsie, she is presented as having a pure sexuality that will arouse even the most jaded sophisticate to an elemental and profoundly moving passion. Sugar is all over Junior, pressing her flesh against him, running her fingers through his hair, kissing him tenderly, then heavily from several different angles. Like the Grand Duke in the major love scene in *The Prince and the Showgirl*, Curtis's character reclines against plush pillows as Monroe softens him up, using her hands to hold and caress him, to shape him to her desires. Her head is above his, and he has to look slightly upward to follow her cue—like Lorelei's lover boy in *Gentlemen Prefer Blondes*. Then Junior's glasses slide down his nose, only to be removed as all his pretense of cool formality slips away. In response to her first kiss, he kicks his leg abruptly upward in an erection reminiscent of Wilder's sexual signaling in *The Seven Year Itch*. After her second kiss, he loosens his collar. Finally, Monroe encircles him with her arms in the full heat of her kisses and pushes him further down into the pillows, almost smothering him with love. Surely the audience is enjoying Monroe—not Sugar—at this point, though the actress does nothing out of character. It is just that scenes like this one—and like "Diamonds are a Girls Best Friend"—have a fulsome quality not strictly necessary for the development of Sugar's or Lorelei's personalities. That Curtis continues to parody Cary Grant only adds to the audience's awareness that its enjoyment of movie stars and movies is being played with here—specifically those films in which Grant is not the pursuer but the pursued.

Wilder swish pans to scenes of Daphne and Osgood dancing, the lead switching between them, in a perfect matchup with Joe and Sugar, who have also alternated in their pursuit of each other. In fact, Osgood and Daphne bring together the dominant and recessive traits continually exchanged between the main characters in this film, so that male and female qualities are as inseparable as the dance itself. One scene naturally leads into another as sexuality is portrayed as an endlessly variable dance.

For example, Junior/Cary Grant's remark that Sugar's passion has caused a tingling sensation in his toes recalls her rubbing of Jerry/Daphne's feet in the train berth, the earlier scene acting as a warm-up for her erotic ministrations to her millionaire.

Sugar is fragile and poignant, lamenting that she will never love again, but she is also robust and receptive, a "New World" woman, as Sinyard and Turner say. Guided by her compelling candor and unpretentiousness, Joe sheds all his old roles and confesses his true sex by kissing her while he is still dressed as Josephine on the bandstand. It is the perfect way of exposing and accepting his contradictions and of saving Sugar just when she thinks her bogus millionaire has departed to marry a rich woman. Her song, "I'm Through with Love," as many critics have noted, shows Monroe at her best. She puts heartbreak in the lyrics and sings as if on the verge of emotional collapse, a collapse that the actress—in weak physical and emotional health throughout the shooting of the film—undoubtedly felt for both herself and for Sugar, who is the last of the four main characters to reach the small boat that will take them to Osgood's yacht. Osgood has been married twelve or thirteen times—he's not sure, his mother keeps count—so he has been even more disappointed by women than Sugar has been by the saxophone players in six male bands. When Osgood refuses to be dismayed by Jerry's sudden revelation that he is a man and contentedly offers the closing line of the film, "Nobody's perfect," he might as well be speaking for everyone in the boat—especially Sugar, who accepts her lover faults and all.

It is amusing and appropriate that Osgood, the character with the biggest mouth, should have the last word. He speaks for a generosity of temperament that is immensely tolerant of a farcical world. His words arise naturally out of *Some Like It Hot*'s good humor, in which no one is truly demeaned—least of all Monroe—though everyone is shown to have limitations. No one can perform as Monroe's superior for very long in this film, and without her it is hard to see how it could have such drive. Take, for example, her certainty that she is inspiriting when she reacts to Junior's description of the impact of her kiss. "It's like smoking without inhaling," he says regretfully. "So inhale!" she urges him as she bestows on him another kiss. The utter relaxation of her voice and the ease with which she commands him to let go of all inhibitions are inimitable. As Wilder said after Monroe's death, "a whole category of films has been lost with her gone." This is not to minimize the astute performances of the others actors—especially Jack Lemmon, whose versatility and voice and gesture are unmatched. But Monroe is the model for Jerry and Joe; she arouses the action; the steam has to shoot out at her.

Filming of *Some Like It Hot* ended on November 6, 1958, and Wilder held a dinner party to celebrate. Monroe was not invited. He had been cautious with the press during filming, but shortly afterwards he expressed his disgust with her. She had seldom worked a full day, and because of her the production had gone several weeks past its scheduled end, exceeding its budget by about half a million dollars. Wilder took his revenge with a series of sarcastic statements. He was the only director who dared to cast her in two of his films. The Screen Directors Guild should honor him with a Purple Heart. His appetite was improving and he no longer suffered from the back pain that plagued him throughout the filming. His insomnia had vanished, and he could now look at his wife "without wanting to hit her because she's a woman." He was "too old and too rich" to have to undergo the ordeal of directing Monroe again. Two years later, there would be something like a public reconciliation between Wilder and Monroe, but immediately after finishing the film both of them were enraged.

Arthur Miller felt called upon not to mediate—as he done with Olivier—but to support his wife in a series of vehement telegrams. Miller noted the director had been informed by Monroe's physician that she could not work a full day because of a pregnancy that she learned about when starting the movie, and he implied that Wilder was to blame for Monroe's second miscarriage, which began "twelve hours after the last shooting day" in November. She had begun the picture "with a throat infection so serious that a specialist forbade her to work at all until it was cured," but she continued to work out of a sense of responsibility. Now that the picture was going to be such a success—in large part because of her performance—Wilder's attack was "contemptible," and he was "an unjust man and a cruel one."

Wilder sent a telegram replying that reports of Monroe's conduct "would have been twice as vicious" had he not spoken up, and while he was very sorry about her miscarriage, he rejected "the implication that overwork or inconsiderate treatment by me or anyone else associated with the production was in any way responsible for it. The fact is that the company pampered her, coddled her and acceded to all her whims." He insisted on Monroe's inconsiderateness and pointed out her inability to understand "anyone else's problems." The cast and crew, he asserted, would testify to her "overwhelming lack of popularity." And then, in a covert reference to her heavy drinking from a thermos of vodka and orange juice on the set, he closed his telegram by suggesting that if "you had been . . . subjected to all the indignities I was, you would have thrown her out on her can, thermos bottle and all."

Miller followed up with one more telegram defending Monroe's admittedly shaky discipline. He suggested that Wilder was riled by her unwillingness to be obedient, and that gifted actors who were doing their best ought to be allowed to take their own route to an extraordinary performance. Having defended Monroe as both his wife and a great artist, Miller then withdrew from the argument.

Wilder sent a final facetious apology, offering to "acknowledge that good wife Marilyn is a unique personality and I am the Beast of Belsen but in the immortal words of Joe E. Brown quote nobody is perfect end quote." Wilder's humor barely masked the almost insane anger generated on the set of *Some Like It Hot*, an anger that Miller may also have experienced. According to Guiles, Wilder witnessed one of Miller's "killing glances" at Monroe and "and wondered if perhaps Arthur didn't dislike Marilyn more than he did." The director's reference to the concentration camp, Belsen, recalls Curtis's comment about how kissing Monroe was like kissing Hitler. In response to an assistant director who knocked on her dressing room door to tell her that cast and crew were ready for her, Monroe screamed "Fuck you," and went on reading from Tom Paine's *The Rights of Man*. Later Wilder made a joke of this, too, saying, "Maybe she doesn't consider that directors and assistant directors have rights. . . . Or maybe she doesn't consider us men."

Although Monroe's next film, *Let's Make Love*, had almost a calming effect on her, it was an anomaly in what was otherwise a steady escalation of anger that most likely had been suppressed or displaced in earlier stages of her career by periods of depression. She was always capable of making remarkably swift transitions from fury to joy—or to a variety of emotions between those extremes—but displays of anger multiplied in her last years. On the advice of her psychiatrist, she called Wilder to reconcile their differences. Audrey, the director's wife, answered the call and said her husband was not at home. Monroe, stammering slightly, decided to speak with her. The tense actress struggled to express her feelings. After on a few inconsequential words, she lost control and began screaming, denouncing the director, in his wife's words, as "the worse son of a bitch who ever lived." Monroe wanted Audrey to "tell him he can just go and fuck himself, fuck himself, fuck himself. . . ." Then she paused, regained her composure and wished Mrs. Wilder well. Years later, in a section that was edited out of her *Life* interview, Monroe called Wilder "paranoid on Celluloid." She seemed to be joking, but it is difficult not to believe that, like Wilder, she was half camouflaging her hatred. In 1968, he attempted to deflate her legend as a victim and martyr: "I am appalled by this Marilyn Monroe cult. . . . I have never met anyone as utterly mean as Marilyn Monroe."

The actress's wrath may have forced Miller to be uncharacteristically defensive with Wilder. Miller was accusatory in her accents, almost as though he were trying to maintain their bond by identifying with her sense of injury. Anything less than an expression of his total commitment to her she probably perceived as a rejection. Viewed in this light, he was also desperately combating her collapsing faith in herself; all she seemed to have left was her fight with others. Rosten recalled that during this period she was much taken with the hero of Joyce Cary's novel *Mister Johnson*, who "represented to her the spirit of innocence killed by the 'bad guys.' Marilyn would say it was 'them' against 'us' everywhere. The story with its tragic ending left a deep impression upon her." At precisely this time Monroe began to lose much of her hope in Miller. Rosten remembered that "their evenings with friends were often played out in a façade of marital harmony. Miller was more and more living with her in the third person, as it were, an observer."

In early November of 1958 the divide deepened between Monroe and Miller with the loss of their second baby in the third month of pregnancy. She had been elated to be pregnant again and had enjoyed performing during the beach scenes on *Some Like It Hot* because the sunshine and fresh air would be "great for the baby." She took special precautions to avoid needless movement and tried to retire early every evening. When life was again stilled in her, she felt deeply inadequate and lost her equilibrium.

The marriage held together—in part because Miller hoped to save it with *The Misfits*, in part because Monroe could not easily relinquish a helpmate and lover thoroughly bound up in her career and sense of herself. Miller would yet have a hand in choosing her next leading man, Yves Montand, and in rewriting dialogue in *Let's Make Love*, a commitment to Fox Monroe decided to honor before making *The Misfits*. Miller would have to fail her again before she could imagine life without him.

In the winter of 1958–59, Monroe and Miller stationed themselves in

New York City, where Monroe continued to study with the Strasbergs and make new friends, many of whom she first met in the Strasberg home, which served as a secure environment for actors and actresses coping with the rigors of performing. As Estelle Parsons observed, Lee Strasberg "creates an atmosphere that forces you to open and draw the terrors out. This then creates a safety for you and you're comfortable with him. I've been terrified to work for Lee but afterward I felt like a great artist—highly exalted." There is no question that Monroe shared this faith in the way Strasberg could father talent, and so she communed with people in the same orbit of expectation.

A new friend she made at the Strasbergs was to become one of her dearest companions in her last years. Listening to Ralph Roberts speak reverently about her and catching the light in his eyes as he described their first meeting, is to capture the affectionate exuberance he and other friends often absorbed from Monroe's presence. Even before he knew exactly who it was he was meeting at the Strasbergs, he was taken with her glow. If she had felt "used up" after the loss of her second baby, her recuperative powers were awesome, for Roberts's description of that first meeting makes her seem like the principle of light itself.

Others, like Gloria Steinem, have similar recollections. Ellen Burstyn speaks of a photograph of Monroe at the Actors Studio shot in available light, in which she shines against the darker background of other faces. Miller, in the December 22, 1958, issue of *Life* penned a tribute to Monroe no less idealized than Roberts's. Beyond her presence, what Roberts seemed to remember most was her esthetic appreciation of life. They took many long walks together in Brooklyn, in which she took an observant delight. They would occasionally act a scene together, talk over their mutual admiration of Todd's *The Thinking Body*, and discuss her curiosity about art. At one point, she even took a "Famous Artists Painting Course," Copyright 1953. She gave Roberts a copy, bound in a large red book with her name stamped in gold on the cover.

Roberts was an actor making most of his living as a masseur, and in that capacity he would prove especially important in alleviating the actress's tensions. In some way, Monroe found it easier to confide in him than in others, because he was something of an alter ego. Roberts had a commanding physical presence, and yet possessed a quiet gentleness. He measured his words carefully and spoke slowly, sometimes hesitantly, as Monroe herself would often do. His sensitivity and vulnerability made him endearing to her and may have become increasingly apparent as the two actors worked on a scene from *Of Mice and Men*. Roberts played Lennie, a role perfectly suited to his robust frame and mild demeanor. Monroe played Curley's wife, a beauty especially proud of her hair and desperate to attract the attention of men in her deadly dull environment. For some time, Monroe and Roberts struggled with the sense of the scene, with the frustrated woman who wants slow-witted but sensitive Lennie to understand her. Monroe kept feeling that they were not getting it right, that contact between the characters—and between actor and actress—was somehow never quite established. Suddenly it occurred to her that that was exactly how the scene should be played—or as she put it to Roberts, "the fact that we aren't communicating is what it's all about." Monroe's earnest striving for insight made up a large part of Roberts's poignant memories.

She never turned her powerful ability to be disappointed against him as she did against Miller, a fact Miller explained by calling Roberts one of those "neutralized persons" who never actually had to make a life with her. Unlike Miller, Roberts never had to function as her hero. On the contrary, he was Monroe's coworker, and his services to her were therapeutic. Miller, however, was part of her plan of rehabilitation, a Lincolnesque figure helping to heal the deep divisions within herself. After *Some Like It Hot*, Miller was still prepared to play that role, directly using his power as a writer for her glorification.

Miller's writing about Monroe countered the public's perception of her as solely a symbol of sex; his language attempted to rescue her from becoming a cliché. He did not so much directly refute the popular conception of her as a passive, pretty package, a mass-produced commodity of sensuality. Instead, he emphasized images and metaphors that made her appear active, spontaneous, and creative. In the December, 22, 1958, issue of *Life*, he published a brief text to accompany Richard Avedon's photographs of Monroe impersonating movie stars, in which her ability to enter into the artistic aspects of her assignment is apparent. Instead of just looking like stars of times past,

> Marilyn came onto the set . . . and a record player was started. Songs of the '20s burst forth. Marilyn aimed an experimental kick at a balloon on the floor. She said she was ready. Avedon yelled, "Go!" and she pursed her mouth around her cigaret [*sic*] [in a Clara Bow pose], kicked a balloon, shot the fan out forward—and she made a world. I suddenly saw her dancing

on a table, a hundred Scott Fitzgeralds sitting all around her cheering, Pierce-Arrow cars waiting outside, a real orchestra on the stand the Marines in Nicaragua. We all found ourselves laughing.

Her miraculous sense of sheer play had been unloosed. Suddenly she was all angles, suddenly the wig had become her own hair and the costume her own dress.

In watching her work her metamorphoses from Theda Bara to Clara Blow to Jean Harlow, Miller was most taken by her ability to render different personalities—become alternate selves—and yet remain identifiable as Monroe. The creation of these doubles of herself was somewhat like the droll use of masking and mimicking employed in *Some Like It Hot*—except that here the actress was in control and could measure herself, one to one, against Avedon's still camera rather than having to contend with Wilder's motion picture. Later, *The Misfits* would nearly rip away her mask by coming very close to a literal presentation of the off-camera Monroe, who had no one to mimic but herself.

Miller continued to work on the draft of *The Misfits* through the early months of 1959. Monroe hardly seemed heartened by her success in *Some Like It Hot*. The film became an almost instant popular and critical favorite, and she looked magnificent at the premiere on March 29. But in the lobby of the Loew's Capitol Theatre on Broadway, she spoke with her childhood stammer and seemed to lose control over her public persona. In May, she was gratified to receive the David Di Donatello statuette from Italy and a crystal star from the French film industry for her performance in *The Prince and the Showgirl*. In June, she underwent surgery meant to facilitate another pregnancy, but that summer was a considerable strain for her and Miller, and the last half of the year was spent with no great purpose in mind.

In the winter of 1959–60, as she approached the filming of *Let's Make Love*, Monroe roused herself in the company of her co-star Yves Montand and his wife, Simone Signoret, who was the perfect model of the serious actress Monroe wanted to become. Signoret had all of Amy Greene's polish and sophistication, and she was a professional comfortable with her work, sharing stories about it with Monroe without the slightest condescension. As Signoret put it, the women became friends and neighbors, occasionally cooking dinner together, having their hair done as they reveled in the hairdresser's anecdotes about working with

Jean Harlow, and enjoying a harmonious home life. Signoret discovered that Monroe had no stories to tell about her film work, but instead talked about Avedon's series of photographs for *Life* as one of the highlights of her career. Signoret and Montand were providing the kind of backstage culture Monroe had always missed, and she readily fit into the foursome that assembled in adjoining bungalows in February of 1960 for the shooting of *Let's Make Love*.

Miller admired Signoret and Montand's production of his play, *The Crucible*, and both couples shared basically the same political views. Miller had recommended Montand as his wife's leading man when Gregory Peck, dismayed that his co-starring role had been underwritten, bowed out of *Let's Make Love*. Signoret respected Monroe's courage in standing beside Miller during his congressional testimony in spite of threats from her studio. Miller, with his deep sympathy for the underprivileged, and Monroe, with her acute memories of childhood poverty, easily identified with Montand's working class background and his struggle for both his principles and his profession. He first caught Monroe's attention in his highly successful one-man show on Broadway, where he exemplified an elegance she was still striving to attain.

Aspects of Montand, the man and the actor, parallel characteristics in both Miller and Monroe. By the same token, he may have represented those qualities in her husband that Monroe still wanted to admire: an earthiness and intellectuality that epitomized her democratic values and emotions. An article devoted to Montand's return to New York City for his one-man show describes his appeal in terms that apply equally well to Monroe: "[T]hroughout his whole life he has attracted working people and intellectuals alike."

As Sidney Skolsky—who spent several evenings with Signoret and Monroe—saw it, Miller got stuck in the humiliating process of rewriting a poor script according to the producer's deadlines. While Miller's stature was shrinking, Montand's was growing in Marilyn's eyes. And ironically, Montand was drawing Marilyn closer to him by leaning on her for assistance with his English. That she could offer him help, and that he sought her assistance so openly and unaffectedly, was particularly gratifying, perhaps reminding her of the time when Miller had relied heavily on her.

An affair between Montand and Monroe began in earnest after a mid-March break in shooting caused by an actors' strike. Miller decided to take advantage of the interval in the production to travel to Ireland to

Monroe and Montand (1960)

consult with John Huston about the script for *The Misfits* and to visit locations in Nevada that would be used for the film. Shortly thereafter, Signoret was called to Europe to fulfill a professional commitment. In early June, when filming of *Let's Make Love* was about half finished, Miller decided to travel east to be with his children, whom he had not seen in a long time. He could not have missed his wife's increasing reliance on Montand, and although Miller's ostensible reasons for leaving her were good ones, it is difficult not to suppose that he was, in some sense, clearing out, making it easier for them to have each other if that was their wish. According to Montand, the affair began when he was saying good night to Monroe in her bungalow. He bent down to kiss her on the cheek, her head turned, and his lips "went wild. It was wonderful," he told his biographers. "I was half stunned, stammering," and full of guilt but unable to resist an involvement not with a needy woman, but a confident one. He remembered her laugh. "Marilyn's laugh was something," he emphasized. She had a kind of peasant quality that appealed to him. It was not her glamor that attracted him: "She had no need to check the seam of her stocking to give you ideas: when she talked about the rain or the fine weather or the cafeteria menus, she had the same power." She had a god-like inner light, he recalled, "a light beyond the control of those it burns in."

Arthur Miller had said as much in his *Life* tribute to Monroe, and if he was not exactly abdicating his responsibility to keep her intact, he seemed to be confessing his helplessness. Or was his departure an act of selflessness, a giving in to his recognition, expressed to Fred Guiles, that Montand made Monroe happy?

This was not Monroe's interpretation. She believed her husband abandoned her, and she needed the passionate liaison with Montand to survive—especially since she had begun to criticize Paula Strasberg for paying "too much attention to her daughter, Susan." Monroe called in Dr. Ralph Greenson, a close associate of Anna Freud's and a friend of Marianne Kris's. Greenson listened to Monroe's complaints and found himself playing the role of "supportive acting coach." Although Monroe wanted "to go straight on the couch for a session of Freudian therapy," the psychiatrist decided upon a less intense inquiry into "the facts of her day-to-day life."

Greenson seemed to realize that Monroe was not prepared for treatment that forced her to examine her own motivations. She preferred to find fault in others—in particular her husband, who she termed "cold and unresponsive" to her problems, attracted to other women, and "dominated by his mother." She attacked Miller with "venomous resentment," pointing out that he neglected his father and was not "nice" to his children. Greenson was not to believe Miller's side of things, Monroe cautioned, but when the psychiatrist did meet her husband he saw Miller as a father figure "rapidly coming to the end of his rope." Greenson advised Miller to give his wife unconditional love; she could accept nothing less. Greenson believed Miller genuinely wanted to help Monroe but was not able to control an anger that expressed itself as rejection of his wife. Greenson himself would eventually come under similar strains, as the actress demanded his undivided attention and sympathy. No one man, it seems, could satisfy her, since she was looking for an idealized father figure who could be all things to her.

In her few remaining years, Monroe would revel in a pattern of promiscuity that suggests lack of sexual fulfillment and preference for a succession of men who might momentarily serve as substitutes for the loving relationship she could not sustain with Miller. As parts of her past were revealed in sessions with Greenson, she came to dwell more and more on the image of herself as an orphan and waif, and Greenson had to perform the exhausting role of healing father. According to Miller in *Timebends*, it was initially Ben Hecht who encouraged and, in a sense, fathered Monroe's inclination to cast herself as a waif. And yet, Miller also writes that Monroe could enter a room and spot anyone who had grown up an orphan. As so often in Monroe's biography, the line between her life and her role-playing could not be precisely demarcated.

Similarly, how seriously to take the affair with Montand is open to question. Donald Spoto, for example, disputes the standard account that has Monroe deeply in love with her co-star. His Monroe remains more in control of her feelings than in other persuasive accounts (like Barbara Leaming's) and regards the affair as not much more than—well—an affair blown up by her studio to generate some excitement about a weak movie. At any rate, her involvement with Montand seemed more fulfilling than their work on the picture. From the first day's rushes she knew *Let's Make Love* was not going well, and she complained to Greenson that she did not like her part. The pedestrian script did nothing to test her talents or to enlarge her screen persona, for Amanda Dell is a shadow of Monroe's full self, a cloying cliché all sweetness and light. Like most of her films, *Let's Make Love* lags behind Monroe's off-screen self. In *Some Like It Hot*, for example, Sugar was twenty-five, while Monroe was thirty-two. In *Let's Make Love*, Amanda attends classes at night to get a high school diploma and to learn what people are referring to; Monroe took extension courses at UCLA several years earlier. In the first stages of her career, she deliberately shaved a few years off her age, but by 1959, on a trip promoting *Some Like It Hot*, she emphasized her maturity—although the press still used her lines as jokes. "[A] charging pitchman, Marilyn tells Chicago reporters, 'I'm a big girl now—I'm 32.' As newsmen looked puzzled, she said she meant years old."

Let's Make Love sentimentalizes Monroe's persona, without the compensating humor and cynicism of *Some Like It Hot*. As Amanda Dell, Monroe has little to play against, and her voice flattens out. Her gestures and facial expressions—except in her songs—have very little range, and she comes remarkably close to seeming dull. Monroe's face never kindles with the sudden joy she shows in *Some Like It Hot* after Daphne claims the whisky flask. Sugar beams with the glee of a child who has been spared a spanking, or of a kid who has found a pal who will stick up for her. Her face vibrates with happiness; the emotion suffuses her skin with highlights. In *Let's Make Love*, Amanda's face is pasty by comparison.

Monroe worked hard at getting her routines in *Let's Make Love* right, and her professionalism is evident, but the musical sequences do not advance the action or deepen her character as they do in *Some Like It Hot*. Instead, there are weak echoes of her earlier production numbers. "My Heart Belongs to Daddy" is comparable to "Diamonds Are A Girl's Best Friend." She uses the same finger motion to call men to her in both scenes, and there is the sexual wink, the hip swing, and allied maneuvers that are meant to evoke the ambiance of a Marilyn Monroe film. She is all persona here, an impersonation of an impersonation revolving around itself—just as Monroe swings and circles around a small, dimly lit stage that closes her in. The sets, the acting, the direction—all are on a diminutive, redundant scale.

Montand's acting, unfortunately, is no help to her. As the billionaire Jean-Marc Clement pursuing Amanda Dell, loving her for her freshness and her ability to "forget herself," he is stiff and awkward. He is supposed to be, so that Amanda's motility will be especially striking. But Montand has none of the charming clumsiness that Cary Grant suavely insinuates into similar roles. It was Montand's first part in an American film. His poor English made him uncomfortable, and he may not have fully grasped the comic tradition out of which the screenplay developed.

Off screen, Monroe was usually docile in Montand's presence, and on screen she is easily mollified when she discovers that his character has deceived her. True, it is part of Monroe's persona to behave generously, but there is some grit in Cherie, Elsie, and Sugar; they do not like to be pushed around. Amanda's resistance is exceedingly brief; she is the equal of her predecessors only in those scenes where she exhibits the poise of a mature woman dedicated to her craft. And if she is sometimes naïve—dumb seems too harsh a word to use for a character with her keen sensibility—she is not foolish like Jean-Marc, Joe and Jerry, the Grand Duke, or Bo, all those men who blunder about in their masculine mania to have everything on their terms. "Money doesn't mean anything to me," Amanda avers, an accentuation of feelings Monroe also held. The male coarseness of a world of gain repels the female who is famous for all she has to give.

During the early stage of production, before she left for Europe, it was evident to Simone Signoret that Monroe did not like her job very much, and along with Montand she attempted to keep the actress in good humor while Miller was away in Ireland. After one late night session of tale telling, in which Monroe gave Signoret the impression of "a kid who's delaying the moment for lights out," Monroe failed show up at the studio the next day. At first, Montand and Signoret were simply concerned to get her back to work, then they and everyone at the studio became scared as Monroe refused to acknowledge efforts to contact her and acted as though she were dead to the world. With considerable irritation Montand slipped a note under his co-star's door denouncing her capriciousness in hopes of rousing her to work. After a full day and evening of her absence, Miller phoned from Dublin explaining that his wife had called him to confess that she was "ashamed" and did not know what to do. At Miller's instigation, Signoret knocked on Monroe's door. Suddenly she had in her arms "a weeping girl, who kept saying, 'I'm bad, I'm bad, I'm bad. I won't do it again, I promise!" All was forgiven, and it even became a joke with them: "She phoned Dublin so that Dublin would phone her next-door neighbors."

In retrospect, Signoret regards that "lost day" somberly, seeing in it an alarming similarity to Monroe's actual death, an event that did not surprise Signoret when she first heard it announced. She wondered when Monroe "had started to be angry with herself in that silence, that false death." The actress seemed paralyzed, losing contact with the outside world, and feeling absolute despair about reuniting the broken parts of her life. As Fred Guiles remarks, her life seemed more and more like "a series of endings."

The threefold repetition of "I'm bad," and the promise not to "do it again," sounds remarkably childlike. Like all children, Monroe would "do it again," would feel she had disappointed others by not meeting her obligations, by not acting like an adult. Earlier, on the set of *The Prince and the Showgirl*, she had sent for Dr. Kris after learning of Miller's disillusionment with her. Monroe, angry with herself for disappointing others, was out of control on her "lost day," which was expressive of her lost life, or of a life late in arriving. She articulated her biography as a Freudian fate sealed in childhood. Freud stresses that "loss of love and failure leave behind them a permanent injury to self-regard in the form of a narcissistic scar, which . . . contributes more than anything to the 'sense of inferiority' which is so common in neurotics," who are unable to accept themselves. In May 1961, Dr. Greenson wrote of Monroe to one of his colleagues, expressing how appalled he was at the "emptiness of her life" and at her almost total lack of objectivity. Even when he saw signs of improvement, her "narcissistic way of life" troubled him, and he wondered how deep and lasting her recovery would be.

CHAPTER TWELVE

The Film of Her Life
(July 1960–January 1961)

Gable said about me, "When she's there,
she's there. She's there to work." . . . I now live in
my work and in a few relationships with the few
people I can really count on.

T

he Misfits was originally scheduled for shooting in the fall of
1959, but Monroe's agreement with Fox to do *Let's Make Love*
and Clark Gable's work in *It Happened in Naples* put off filming
of *The Misfits* until the spring of 1960. Then the actors' strike
during the filming of *Let's Make Love* and other production delays meant
that Monroe would not be available for another role until the middle of
July. As a result, there was hardly a break between the two films. With
just a few hectic days in New York spent on costume fittings and test
photography for *The Misfits*, she rushed to Reno, Nevada, where a cast
and crew of over two hundred awaited her appearance on the set of what
had been intended as the masterwork of her career and the fulfillment
of her life. Unfortunately, she and Miller had waited too long to consummate their joint vision. Their marriage was dying, and they were forced to
engage in a furious struggle against each other to maintain their integrity
as persons and professionals, an integrity that once seemed as indivisible
as the marriage itself.

All elements of the production—the original screenplay by a major
American writer, the best director for it, John Huston, and the perfect
casting—inspired Frank Taylor, the film's producer, to call *The Misfits*
"'the ultimate motion picture.' Each of them, Marilyn, Clark, Monty Clift,
Eli Wallach, Thelma Ritter, is the person they play." The line between art
and life was perilously thin. Everything about this independent, austere

The Misfits (1960)

movie—characters, locations, stunts, and story—had to be as authentic as possible, deliberately antithetical to machine-made, studio-faked extravagances like *Let's Make Love*. On *The Misfits* there would be no closed set, as there had been on *The Prince and the Showgirl*. James Goode was permitted to write a diary-like version of the filming; Magnum received permission to field a group of photographers on the set; numerous friends and acquaintances of the cast and crew visited, as did other celebrities and the press. It was as if the makers of *The Misfits* wanted intimate contact not only with the Western environment they were depicting, but also with the larger world outside the movie set.

Wallach, Ritter, and Clift described the normal difficulties of film-making they were trying to overcome: no rehearsal before the first day's shooting; lack of ensemble playing between actors who do not know each other's work habits; the distractions of the lights and the crew requiring a concentration more intense than that used in preparing plays; and the minute adjustments the actor must effect to portray the essence of a character. This instant commentary on moviemaking while they were making the movie represented a virtual catalogue of the disruptions and disarrangements of Monroe's replicated life.

Montgomery Clift, in particular, felt the self-reflexive quality that informed his own as well as Monroe's role. In a naked admission of the life-like nature of film (which sometimes attaches itself to the actor's vulnerable person in a way he cannot shake off), Clift commented: "Someone said, 'My God, it's exactly like you.' Now it's just a question of can I do it? It is a wonderful part, and if I don't do it justice I'll shoot myself." Miller denied having written the character specifically for Clift, but like Gable and Monroe, Clift would inhabit his role, making it look like a fusion of art and life.

Huston abetted the actors in achieving an organic bond between themselves and their characters by shooting *The Misfits* in chronological sequence, an unusual and expensive way of filming that furthered the natural evolution of their characters. Monroe had never had the opportunity to develop a role in continuity, except in *Don't Bother to Knock*, in which the director, Roy Baker, followed a rehearsal format resembling that used for a stage play. Huston was well known for his subtle, unobtrusive handling of actors, and ever grateful for his faith in her performance in *The Asphalt Jungle*, Monroe could be hopeful their collaboration would reveal new dimensions of her talent, as it had ten years earlier.

At the same time, Monroe had grave doubts about the script and was angry about Roslyn's "wishy-washy" character, which Miller still had not strengthened after years of work on the script. In desperation, Monroe put in a call to Norman Rosten—as he recalls in his memoir, *Marilyn: An Untold Story*—demanding that Rosten tell Miller, who she put on the phone, that one of Roslyn's speeches needed a complete rewrite. The uncomfortable Rosten said he would give his opinion if Miller asked for it. Miller made no request, but an irate Monroe continued to berate her husband about his awful writing.

Monroe was not alone in rejecting Miller's defective script. As Donald Spoto reports, John Huston had similar doubts, although he expressed them deferentially and in the disguise of Hollywood hyperbole about what a magnificent job Miller had done. Even more telling, Elia Kazan wrote to Miller—full of Huston-like compliments, then delivering the bad news about "thematic finger pointing" and the film's unresolved ending, which did not work because of "the girl, a little too—well too a lot of things, too right, too often too pure, too aware." In *Timebends*, Miller virtually concedes that Kazan and Monroe were right. But he confesses that he could not change his approach to Roslyn, because his vision of her emanated from his futile effort to save his marriage. In other words, to expose Roslyn's shortcomings would mean the end of his effort to repair his rapport with Monroe. Only after Monroe's death, with the production of Miller's play, *After the Fall*, could he reveal the dark side of the Marilyn myth that had enveloped him—just as Ted Hughes dared not probe the overpowering mythology of Sylvia Plath's life and death until the posthumous publication of *Birthday Letters*. In both cases, these writer-husbands present themselves as in the grip of a self-destructive dynamic beyond their resources to remedy.

Like the nameless woman in Miller's short story, "Please Don't Kill Anything," and like the Marilyn Monroe of his *Life* tribute, Roslyn Taber declares her reverence for the permanence of things: "I can't stand to kill anything." Roslyn "claps her hands to her ears" in surprise and profound dismay over the impending capture of the mustangs, just as the woman in "Please Don't Kill Anything" "put her hands to her cheeks" in shock over the sudden capture of the fish that are gathered in the fishermen's net. In *The Misfits*, we see the world as a woman sees it, but in this case Roslyn's modes of perception—and what they stand for metaphorically—are explored and to some extent modified by a complex drama of human relationships only hinted at in the *Life* tribute and briefly sketched in the short story.

In one sense, Roslyn's all-encompassing vision turns her into a vibrant nature symbol—and even into a tender metaphor for life itself. She moves in sensitive solidarity with plants, animals, and people; she offers herself as an exuberant and generous unifying principle of the kind Miller lightly touches on in *Life* when he praises the manifestations of Monroe's beauty and spirit in what might be called her natural, everyday self, "playing with the dog, redoing the cleaning woman's hair, emerging from the ocean after a swim, or bursting into the house full of news." Roslyn is a "golden girl [who] comes busting out of the closet." Gay tells her, "You just shine in my eyes." Guido remarks on how she lights up his house and how she has the "gift of life." As her cowboy companions get to know her, she virtually becomes their source of light, their point of reference, as when Gay tells her, "Honey, when you smile it's like the sun comin' up." The metaphors arising out of seemingly casual speech are meant to render the men's growing sense of discovery that Roslyn has, in Guido's words, "the big connection. You're really hooked in; whatever happens to anybody, it happens to you." Most of these metaphors shift from the concrete impression the males have of her person to rather abstract, even mystical, yearnings. By achieving oneness with her, each would fill the emptiness he feels in his lack of relation to family, to society—to the world at large, where he is regarded as a misfit. Roslyn's gift is to minister to each man equally, even if the help she offers is simply a heartfelt "hello" to Guido at a time when he feels most alienated from himself and others; to Perce a gentle mothering that allows him to probe his disaffections; and to Gay a resolute but pliable sense of her own femininity that persuades him to accept, in a manner similar to Sam's in "Please Don't Kill Anything," the other half of the world, the female side he has always dismissed from his world of permanence and self-sufficiency.

These men ignore and sometimes even fight against Roslyn's adamant defense of life's sacredness. Their contrary urge is to make life a test, as in Perce's rodeo riding and the roping of the mustangs. But Roslyn enforces her will to free the captured misfit mustangs, a family (a stallion, four mares, and a colt) not unlike the misfit family of three men and one woman she joins together. She does so not by arguing beliefs, but by fully responding to life in a manner that justifies the metaphors the men use to describe her. For example, when Perce rides his bull, Roslyn does not hear the crowd roaring, and she is only partly involved in observing him hang on for his prize—for his life really. Her sense of the scene is more organic. She feels the "ground shake as the bull pounds out across the arena." She feels the thunder of its weight and the "resounding answers from deep below the ground." She "nearly goes blind" as her world shakes and seems to fall pieces.

If Roslyn's eyes can seem "larger than life" in the breadth of their vision, and if she seems capable of joining the "sun and earth" in staring at Gay, there is a sense in which she exists not before but after the fall. In her own way, she is just as solitary as the other characters, and her organic grasp of life has not been allowed to develop. She tells Gay, who gardens for her in an Eden of their own making, "I never really saw anything grow before." She has never had possession of herself until, for a moment, she feels his love and is no longer afraid: "[I]t was like my life flew into my body. For the first time."

Roslyn searches for the meaning of life, which often eludes her. Many of her statements are questions and tentative probings of relationships. She has failed at marriage once, and she seems caught in some indeterminate, mystifying stage between childhood and adulthood (Miller suggests something like this about Monroe in *Life*) that provokes Guido to comment: "One minute she looks dumb and brand new. Like a kid. But maybe he [her first husband] caught her knockin' around, huh?" The finest expression of Roslyn's quest for wholeness occurs when "she flies into a warm, longing solo dance among the weeds, and coming to a great tree she halts and then embraces it, pressing her face against its trunk," as Monroe had hugged a tree in Sam Shaw's photograph of her in Connecticut in 1956. Roslyn seeks to steady herself in the grip of nature and in the presence of its creatures, for she also "presses her face against" the dog who quivers during the mustang hunt, just as she quivers when she first realizes that the horses will not only be captured but killed and used for dog food. The dog and the tree save her from solitary suffering. So does the dance toward the tree, her metaphor for life's permanence—as Miller himself had once been for Monroe, when she said meeting him was "like running into a tree."

Roslyn's moment of self-fulfillment, her embrace of the tree, is reminiscent of one of Monroe's own lyric fragments, "To the Weeping Willow":

I stood beneath your limbs
And you flowered and finally clung to me
And when the wind struck with . . . Earth
And sand—you clung to me

The tree in Monroe's poem is both symbol and fact, her friend Norman Rosten pointed out, for it had been "planted under her watchful eye at her country place." Like Monroe's unfinished poem, *The Misfits* takes its tone from the fruition of human and natural relationships, with the female character acting as the erotic magnet drawing the world together.

There are Edenic moments in *The Misfits* when the characters try to make the desert bloom, when Roslyn goes "all out" and seems equal to enjoying life in its fullness, when Gay blesses her for making him feel as if he has "touched the whole world." But those innocent, metaphoric apprehensions of existence are tempered by Roslyn's worries, by her sense of being lost, and by her need for help because she does not know where she belongs. She seeks guidance from Gay but cannot reconcile herself to his gentle, paradoxical insistence—so like Sam's in "Please Don't Kill Anything" and probably like Miller's as well—that, "Honey, a kind man can kill."

The filming of Roslyn's unreconciled state was Monroe's most arduous assignment. On July 21, during the shooting of her character's first appearance, the temperature in the bedroom setting reached one hundred degrees, with Huston, his crew, and their equipment crowded in together with the actress. After Isabelle (Thelma Ritter) is seen calling Roslyn to hurry up, the camera concentrates on a mirror Roslyn uses both to make herself up and to memorize the lines she will deliver in applying for a divorce. Isabelle is rather like the strong-minded but sensitive female coaches and confidantes Monroe relied on; like Natasha Lytess, Paula Strasberg, and Hedda Rosten, she is a woman from an earlier generation helping her young charge compose herself. Even this early in shooting *The Misfits*, Monroe had to have been acutely conscious that this film was limning her life in a new dimension—not simply by making her character late and by giving her trouble with lines, but by revealing the struggle of going through a rehearsal and replication of self. Roslyn, like Marilyn, wants to articulate herself authentically "I can't remember this. It's not the way it was," she says. She resists putting on a face and a dialogue in what might be called this "behind the scenes scene," which in Huston's capable direction gives the lie to earlier backstage and powder room scenes in *Gentlemen Prefer Blondes* and *How to Marry a Millionaire* where Lorelei and Pola are happily content with putting on the roles they play. Instead, Roslyn resents her scripted self and is shown to be on the verge of a hysteria and exhaustion akin to Cherie's frail fretfulness in *Bus Stop*. But Roslyn seems much older and more mature than Cherie and more disillusioned. For once there is less of a gap in age and temperament between Monroe and the character she plays. How much Monroe's own physical fatigue contributed to this scene is hard to gauge. When James Goode asked her whether she would discuss how much energy her acting took, she replied, "No, because I didn't start with any."

As with Cherie, Elsie, and Sugar, experience has taken its toll on Roslyn, and she is wary. But Roslyn is alone in expressing her worry over the ambiguity of human relationships and her doubt that any genuine communication is possible. She knows she is a misfit, and she reacts som-

Gable (1960)

berly to the atmosphere of Reno, the divorce capital, heavy with failure. In part, Roslyn's languid demeanor at the beginning of the film may be an indication of how the divorce has numbed her and made her temporarily incapable of the outgoing emotions and gestures usually associated with Monroe's screen personas. This languorousness perhaps explains why some critics find Roslyn rather remote and amorphous. Only in the course of her awakening is she able to pin down the troubling issues that have made her back away from full involvement with others and from understanding of herself. Somehow Roslyn has escaped most of the cynicism and self-pity Guido harbors in himself, and the mirror shot in Monroe's first scene reflects a rudimentary purity—complicated by disappointment, but expressive nevertheless of an innocence highlighted for the first time when she sees Gay's dog, Tom Dooley. Her affection for animals animates her. Her eyes appear completely open for what seems like the first time during this transitional scene taking her from her divorce to her new life with Guido, Gay, and eventually Perce.

When Gay tells Roslyn she shines in his eyes, he is, to be sure, complimenting her, but he is also commenting, however inadvertently, on her reflective capacity and on his power to measure it—a power the film points up by isolating the glint in his eye. In the film of *The Misfits*, it is obvious that Gable is courting Monroe, and his compliment, not Gay's, confers upon Monroe the status of a cynosure of the screen. In the cinema-novel that Miller wrote based on the movie script, Roslyn's consciousness controls such scenes as the one at the rodeo, where the very ground shakes in accord with her trembling concern for Perce. In their first big close-up, when Gable leans over to kiss Monroe, and she responds by confessing she does not feel "that way" about him. Gable's easy assurance that in time she "just might" is tied to his movie persona as the "King" of Hollywood, who for so many years carried his roles with a bluff, hardy confidence. The aplomb with which he receives Monroe's mild rebuff seems tinged with sly humor over her demurrer before the most romantic, masculine figure the movies have produced, the father-idol of his co-star. Although Gable and Monroe looked to performances in *The Misfits* to prove their prowess as actors, not just personalities, and although neither of them does anything to disturb the consistency of their characters, Gay and Roslyn, the sensation of actors moving in tandem with their screen personalities is undeniable.

It had been Monroe's lifelong dream to play opposite Gable in the movies, but the prospect of performing with him also put pressure on her to be perfect, a pressure he unfailingly and gallantly tried to relieve by taking every opportunity to encourage her—in one instance kissing her after an especially well done scene. John Huston said that in private Gable was nonplussed by Monroe's unprofessional behavior, but in public he remained deferential to her and protective, as if he was willing to impersonate the father-lover she saw in him for the sake of her emotional health and of the tender scenes in *The Misfits*, which reflected her desire to be his consort. Thelma Ritter observed, "[T]his picture is a little unlike any I've done before, because it depends on the personalities and relationship of the actors. . . . We stage actors don't get this kind of jazz. They'd say, 'What's she playing?' There's more emphasis on the stage on roles, not personality." Actors in *The Misfits* could not simply escape into their roles and become their characters; in fact, the film depended on the clash and coordination of personalities, not just on "playing," as stage actors would have it.

From the middle of July to nearly the end of August, Monroe and her three male leads struggled with the cumbersome first half of the script, which required Gable, Wallach, and Clift to vie for the honor of charming her. Each man has to have his turn to dance with her, to woo her, and she has to receive all of them openly without encouraging their advances. She gently probes the reasons for their lovelessness and nurses their sensitivities. At the same time, she is in their care, as they show her how they live in accord with the West's freedom, its frontier mentality. Although the careful approach to personalities provided fine shadings of character, to Monroe *The Misfits* seemed irresolute and Roslyn too elastic, given the enormous demands upon her compassion and her loyalty to each man. Huston and Miller constantly conferred on changes in the script, sometimes debating wording and camera work. In spite of all the planning, the shooting in continuity, the fine cast and crew, the picture lost coherence, and each day was devoted to tinkering with the disordered pieces.

As Monroe reached the center of the film, where Roslyn, Guido, and Gay accompany Perce to the rodeo in exchange for his agreement to join them in the mustang hunt, Monroe had to play Roslyn's hysterical fears for Perce's life, followed by a demanding five-minute scene—the longest take Huston had ever filmed—with Clift just after he is injured at the rodeo. It was necessary to summon all aspects of Roslyn's to soothe Perce's wounded body and spirit. Increasing her intake of Nembutals in the evening, Monroe relied ever more heavily on Ralph Roberts's morning massages and on the ministrations of others who tried to walk her into wakefulness and prop her up with coffee. At night, in Miller's presence, she would sometimes get hysterical, and he would try to calm her with innocuous conversation, but in the middle of the night she would lose control and rage at him. He was close to a breakdown himself, and Nan Taylor, the producer's wife, persuaded Miller to take a separate room. A prolonged fit of anxiety kept Monroe away from the set on August 27 and led to her breakdown, officially announced on August 29 when she was flown for medical care to Los Angeles. The whole production shut down, and shooting did not resume until her reappearance on the set on September 6.

At Westside Hospital in Los Angeles Monroe was gradually weaned off of Nembutal and put in a milder medication. She received visits from Miller, Huston, the Strasbergs, and other friends, including Joe DiMaggio, who began to emerge as one of her dearest supporters. In truth he had never given up the possibility of remarrying Monroe, and in notes to himself in the April 4, 1955 issue of *Sports Illustrated*, he emphasized "forget ego & pride . . . Be warm, affectionate, & Love . . . Be patient—no matter what." He cautioned himself not to be jealous: "Remember this is not your wife. She is a fine girl and remember how unhappy you made her. Happiness is what you strive for—for HER. Don't talk about her business or her friends. Be friendly toward her friends. Don't forget how lonesome and unhappy you are especially without her."

Ten days after her collapse, she visited him briefly before returning to Reno to finish *The Misfits*. To Huston, in the hospital, she seemed to have made great progress, appearing bright and alert. He could see that she was aware that the drugs were destroying her, and she asked his forgiveness. He remembered reassuring her.

In spite of some setbacks, upon her return her acting was stronger, and she had more control over herself. Just before her breakdown she had to do retakes of the rodeo scenes, since her reactions to Perce's dangerous stunts were exaggerated, perhaps a sign of her impending neurasthenic collapse. Now she evinced a new calm in her treatment of Miller. On one occasion they even went on a walk together, and on another Miller danced with her to demonstrate the kind of action he had in mind for one scene. They were not intimate—not even for the sake of public appearances—but the contest between them abated and would not revive until the final tense days of filming.

Monroe resumed work on the five-minute scene with Clift. In speaking to Clift as Perce she was perfectly in tune with herself as Roslyn. Like Roslyn, who complains that her husband was not "there," Perce regrets that his mother, after her remarriage, could not "hear" him. He puts his head in Roslyn's lap to ease the aches of mind and body. She responds to his garrulity, prompted by his drinking and dancing, by trying to quiet him and to smooth over the rough edges he has acquired in proving himself. Just as Gable as Gay acts as her father-lover, so Monroe as Roslyn acts as mother-lover to Clift as Perce—as W. J. Weatherby sensed when he noticed Monroe behaving "like a concerned mother hen" while the reporter spoke with Clift.

Frank Taylor called Monroe and Clift "psychic twins," and Weatherby observed that Clift was "sensitive to any vibes from or around Monroe." The actors shared their insecurities, their drinking and drug problems, and treated each other affectionately from their first shy meeting some time after the completion of *Bus Stop*. As Robert La Guardia, one of Clift's biographers, puts it, "Marilyn could bitch and laugh and feel as uninhibited as she wanted around him." Clift responded in kind, first as himself, then as Perce revealing to Roslyn fundamental misgivings about himself: "I . . . I don't understand how you're supposed to do." On the set of *The Misfits*, Clift spoke to James Goode of the actor's need to "uncallous" himself; the long scene with Monroe accomplishes just that, for it portrays an exquisite exfoliation of Perce's hardened self—the one who does not mind the rousing rodeo stunts and who accepts the hard world of male rivalries. This supreme blending of the actor with his art is what Monroe was always seeking, and what she and Clift manage between them in a setting suggestive of their characters' fragmentary careers: "[T]hey emerge behind the saloon. Trash, a mound of empty liquor bottles and beer cans, broken cartons, are littered about. . . ." In the moonlight (cameraman Russell Metty was actually shooting day for night) Roslyn and Perce articulate the miscellaneousness of their betrayed lives. "Maybe all there really is is what happens next, just the next thing and you're not supposed to remember anybody's promises," Roslyn speculates.

It is impossible to say how many times Monroe and Clift obliterated the thin margins between their on- and off-screen selves while working on their five-minute scene. That more than usual was at stake was clear from the closed set, from Gable's keen interest in being present (he was not even on call to act that day), and from the rehearsal time used before filming. At first, both Clift and Monroe had trouble with their dialogue; then, after several takes, they finished the scene without missing any lines. Monroe complimented Clift on his performance, was herself reassured by Miller, and checked with Paula Strasberg just as Huston decided the scene should be repeated. Two more takes were spoiled—one by Monroe (who thought she had shifted Clift's bandage out of place), and one by Clift, who had trouble with a line. Goode reports that Monroe "clutched him to her in compassion for his mistake." In the next take, she missed a word. Near the end of the day tension mounted, as two more takes were ruined before the final perfect scene was shot. Compared to the multiple takes of much shorter scenes, this long, beautifully modulated exchange between Clift and Monroe was performed with economy and grace.

Clift might have been thinking of this outstanding scene when he commented after Monroe's death that "working with her was fantastic ... like an escalator. You would meet her on one level and then she would rise higher and you would rise to that point, and then you both would go higher." She evidently responded to Clift's sincerity as an actor with an ingenuousness of her own, rarely apparent to other actors—even Jack Lemmon, who admired her, but who noted her "tendency to act at instead of with you." Clift would not have concurred with Lemmon's conclusion: "[Y]ou just got so far with her, and then you could feel a curtain drop—and you didn't go beyond that. I suspect nobody in the world really understood Marilyn."

The second half of *The Misfits* profited immensely from Monroe's recovery and resilience. Both the shooting of the film and the pacing of its scenes quickened from the moment Roslyn feels the dog shivering and begins to inquire into the purpose of the mustang hunt. Like Monroe herself, who at this time became, in Guiles's words, "alive to her surroundings," Roslyn explores her environment with renewed intensity. As her questions become more pointed, the cowboys must confront their own complicity in decimating their dreams of a frontier past, in which mustangs were used to settle a wild country and not to feed dogs, the tamed animals of modern consumer culture.

Roslyn appears helpless not only to stop the hunt, but also to mount an effective objection to it, since, as Gay reminds her, she eats steaks and gives Tom Dooley dog food made of mustang meat. She appears naïve and lacking the courage to accept her own compromises with killing. The momentum of the film is against her, for the men are taking all the risks. Beside them, she seems merely hysterical and belittled by the vast Western landscape. Conceding Gay's victory over the mustangs—"You won," she tells him—she tries to restrain him, but he sweeps her to the ground with his arm. Finally, she breaks out of the frame that Gay, Guido, and Perce have established in the chase sequence by recentering herself at a considerable distance from them. As Nick Barbaro observes, "[S]he is at a totally different depth from the men in the foreground on either side":

They see Roslyn walking. She is heading across the open lake bed.

"Roslyn." Gay takes a step, and halts himself.

She has swerved about. Her shadow sketches toward them. Forty yards away, she screams, her body writhing, bending over as though to catapult her hatred.

"You liars! All of you." clenching her fists, she screams toward their faces: "Liars!"

Unnerved, Gay flinches.

"Man! Big man! You're only living when you can watch something die! Kill everything, that's all you want! Why don't you just kill yourself and be happy?"

She runs toward them, but stops as though afraid, and says directly toward Gay: "You. With your God's country. Freedom!" she screams into his face. "I hate you!"

Unable to bear it, Gay utters. "We've had it now, Roslyn."

"You sure did—more than you'll ever know but you didn't want it. Nobody does. I pity you all." looking from one to another, and beyond them to imagined others. "You know everything except what it feels like to be alive. You're three dear, sweet dead men."

Roslyn is almost out of control, voicing her bitterest feelings and severing her connection with the cowboys even as her shadow, their conscience, approaches them. In the space she has created, she performs what almost amounts to an exorcism, an exhaustion of her hostility. At the same time, she is attacking "man"—as well as these men who serve a rapacious society. The urge to destroy, she implies, is ultimately suicidal. She turns Gay's remarks about having "had it" into an elliptical comment on their former harmony, and implicates herself, as well, in the tragic insight that "nobody" knows how to have it all, to experience the togetherness she and Gay have lost. In spite of her rage, there is compassion in her condemnation of the "three dear, sweet dead men," with whom reconciliation is still possible.

As Huston filmed it, the scene is deliberately awkward, since there is a sudden shift, a break in the action betokening a set piece, an unwieldy supplanting of the exciting chase sequence with Roslyn at the frame's center. Her speech ought to be redundant after so many speeches in this exceptionally talky movie, yet her words work because they are fitted to a frame she is seen to form, however clumsily, and because, unlike all her previous dialogue, these words come up from the pit of suppressed resentment she barely manages to articulate. Her bent-over posture suggests a being divided in two by male and female contentiousness, by love and hate of society, and by life and death. In projecting her profound sense of alienation to Gay, to his male companions, to men in general, and to the whole of existence, Roslyn is both triumphant and defeated. She is the ultimate cinematic embodiment of Monroe's double bind.

Huston and Miller were uncertain about how to prepare for the final scenes between Roslyn and her male companions. Gable had not liked the original ending of the screenplay, in which Roslyn feels compassion for Gay, who remains on the lakebed defeated by the stallion. Huston, on the other hand, was concerned about clearing up what he perceived as vagueness in Guido's character. Frank Taylor wondered whether the screenwriter and the director still had the energy to create a proper ending. The final scene had gone through at least three revisions since March of 1960, and as of the first week of October there were rumors of still more changes—with one version of the ending "awarding" Roslyn to Perce. When Monroe finally had the opportunity to read the scene that made Guido Roslyn's ex-lover, she became hysterical, for it threw the whole picture "out of key," she told Paula Strasberg. Gable, who had the contractual authority to reject script alterations, agreed, and Monroe's supporters felt vindicated. Later, Miller conceded that Gable's judgment was sounder than his own.

In the end, Miller was satisfied that he had achieved the appropriate close to *The Misfits*, and Gable concurred. Gay conquers the stallion Perce has cut loose in deference to Roslyn's feelings, but then Gay frees the stallion and makes his peace with Roslyn. Gable felt his character was not broken, but had acknowledged the necessity of finding "another way of life." Miller thought Gay and Roslyn had compromised and recognized reality. Gay would have to come to terms with "a settled existence, and face the struggle between a personal code and social cooperation." Roslyn would have to accept the "violence in all of us" that existed "side by side with love." This couple would not live happily ever after, but a certain balance had been achieved in their relationship with each other.

Monroe could not accept the logic of the picture because it had not shown the violence in her. She was made to stand too far apart from the men who worshipped her. She did not regard the film in the harmonious terms Huston and Miller had confected. She never cited it as an example of having reached a crossroads in a dramatic part the way she tentatively regarded *Some Like It Hot* as a significant achievement in comedy. Before filming *The Misfits* she quarreled with Miller about his screenplay; after shooting it, she complained about Huston's tampering with the writer's words.

Many viewers of *The Misfits* come away from it feeling the ending has somehow been tacked on, that the troubling ambiguities of Roslyn's relationship with Gay, with the other male characters, and with the world at large have been evaded, even sentimentalized. The ending is also a beginning, however, since Roslyn and Gay have reached a fuller consciousness that precludes seeing them in absolute, unchanging terms. "We see them only in frontal shots and only inside the truck," Nick Barbaro points out. The effect emphasizes "moving on, trying to find their way home," not riding off into the sunset to "live happily ever after." No doubt this was Miller's and Huston's intention, but Gable's utter calm and sureness, and the romantic aura of twilight that bathes him and Monroe mitigates the sobriety of Miller's outlook and Huston's shot selection. Barbaro successfully shows that the end is not just an affected appendage, but he discounts too heavily the way these movie stars radiate in their roles, making the final frames of *The Misfits* verge on cinema cliché.

In late October, when *The Misfits* was nearly completed, Monroe told Miller to get out, which he proceeded to do with the help of Monroe's secretary May Reis, Frank Taylor, and his aide, Edward Parrone. In early November, Monroe became hysterical and incoherent when a reporter called her with news of Gable's death. Reis, Rupert Allan, Patricia Newcomb, and frequently Joe DiMaggio helped her through the next shaky weeks. Allan had recommended Newcomb to Monroe when he was not able to accompany his distraught friend to New York City. Newcomb supervised the Monroe household, screening calls and generally insulating the actress after the announcement of her separation from Miller.

In late December and early January, she sorted out her allegiances, making up a new will that included her half-sister, Berneice Miracle, who she did not know well but with whom she nevertheless felt "family-like." The will also acknowledged May Reis, now much more than an appointments secretary. Reis had become a trusted advisor of exceptional tact and discretion. Monroe felt some ambivalence about Paula Strasberg, probably because Paula, like Natasha Lytess, had become too visible in aggressively championing her charge, and somewhat stifling for a younger woman suspicious of those who came to her aid too readily. Monroe had been generous with Paula, supplying not only a good salary but several gifts, so it was Lee—more instrumental in nurturing the actress's talent, but circumspectly distant from the actual conditions of her employment on movie sets—who was to receive a part her estate and personal belongings.

The everyday business of living defeated Monroe, as she attempted to put her end in order. She was back on heavy doses of Nembutal, even pricking the capsules with a pin for faster effect, as Rupert Allan observed. She made no secret of her pill habit or of her craving for oblivion. Pat Newcomb noticed her employer's fascination with the "murky depths of New York harbor" one day, and moved "close enough to reach out in case of emergency." Monroe spent listless days, only rarely visiting the Strasberg apartment, the source of so much of her inspiration.

On January 20, 1961, in the company of her attorney, Aaron Frosch, and Pat Newcomb, Monroe flew to Juarez, Mexico, to obtain her divorce from Miller, a sad public acknowledgment of her dashed hopes on the very day the country inaugurated a new leader. Pat Newcomb and John Springer, who had been handling Monroe's publicity on the East Coast since early 1959, selected the date in hopes that President Kennedy would get all the headlines.

If Monroe was to survive she had to find new interests. Miller had opened up the world of politics to her, and she became attuned to all the talk about the new direction signaled by the presidential election. During the making of *The Misfits*, as cast and crew followed the presidential debates on television, Monroe told W. J. Weatherby that she wanted to see Kennedy win because of Nixon's association "with the whole [Redbaiting] scene." She may have met Kennedy as early as 1951 in the company of Charles Feldman, one of her agents with close connections to the Kennedy family. Her admiration and affection for Kennedy grew as Adlai Stevenson's supporters failed to secure his nomination at the Democratic convention. She watched the inaugural during a two-hour layover in Dallas on her way to Mexico. She was already responding to the Kennedy charisma, to the novelty of a political figure with the glamour of a movie star. Many people were expecting to participate in an unusual administration, in a new frontier that had all the glitter usually attributed to Hollywood. Just as she had missed her moment of rebirth in *The Misfits* and dropped precipitously into the worst depression of her life, Monroe was storing up energy for one more ascension by reaching out to the society outside herself, to the future that Kennedy represented.

CHAPTER THIRTEEN

The Lady of Shalott (December 1960– August 1962)

And moving thro' a mirror clear
That hangs before her all the year,
Shadows of the world appear.

I n a series of intermittent discussions with W. J. Weatherby in New York from late 1960 to some time in January 1961, Monroe latched onto his phrase, "a pattern of selves," to argue against the idea of a single self persisting through an entire lifetime. She favored "fragmentary changing natures." In his presence, her moods changed quickly. Her contradictoriness and fatiguing awareness of her divided feelings were driving her toward collapse and hospitalization. Weatherby sensed she was struggling to control herself.

One time, in the bar they used for their talks, Monroe appeared tentative, nervous, and "rather distant"—and sloppily dressed. As she had with Margaret Parton, who interviewed her in mid-March of 1961, Monroe skirted her past, refusing to discuss her childhood rape story. But she did reveal her mirror obsession: "I sit in front of the mirror for hours looking for signs of age." She was attracted to old people, to the sense of completion age may bring: "I want to grow old without face-lifts. They take the life out of a face, the character. I want to have the courage to be loyal to the face I've made." In the next breath, however, she conceded that sometimes "it would be easier to avoid old age." She claimed control over the depiction of her person: "When the photographers come, it's like looking into a mirror. They think they arrange me to suit themselves, but I use them to put over myself." But how much character did she have, she wondered, when she was killing the truth by killing photographs harmful to her public image? Was she in charge of her body, or simply infatuated with it? She was not sure. Compared to the beauty that could be perpetuated in a stage career, her attractiveness on screen seemed ephemeral: "You can go on forever in the theater. The distance, the footlights, the makeup—it all helps to create whatever illusion you wish."

In their last few meetings, Weatherby detected a new strain in Monroe's demeanor, perhaps anxious anticipation of the mixed reception *The Misfits* would indeed receive. In early February, when he mentioned a Steinbeck character who commits suicide, "she seemed to draw back in her seat," asking why the character did it and admitting she had tried to kill herself once and was "kinda disappointed it didn't work." She looked depressed and worried she did not have "what it takes" to carry out her plans. She was afraid to be alone. She showed up at their final meeting with unwashed hair and "a faint body odor." All "worked up," she aggressively maintained a "person's privilege" to commit suicide. "I don't believe it's a sin or a crime . . . . Although it doesn't get you anywhere," she said in reaction to Hemingway's suicide. She found it hard to trust people, to see that she had made any progress in her life. She speculated about a "weak-minded quality" inherited from her mother and appeared confused, embarrassed, and tired—almost totally enveloped in self-doubt and doped up with sleeping pills.

The winter of 1961 was a bleak season for Marilyn Monroe. The lilt was gone from her blurred and weakened voice, and she was more depressed than Norman Rosten had ever known her to be. Often she was heavily sedated or in a state of high nervous tension. She saw few friends and put herself, it seemed, at considerable remove from the world. By early February, she was on the verge of total collapse and agreed with Dr. Kris's decision to hospitalize her.

Dr. Kris accompanied her patient to the Payne-Whitney clinic in New York without explaining that it was a mental institution. Monroe supposed it would be like other hospitals to which she had retired for secluded rest. Much later, Dr. Kris admitted to Ralph Roberts it had been a terrible mistake sending her patient to Payne-Whitney, for Monroe immediately panicked. A nurse present during Monroe's admission to the hospital ward recalled for Richard Meryman how Monroe froze when she heard the "grim snap of a lock closing behind her." "She stood there endlessly repeating, 'Open that door! Just open that door! I won't make any trouble, just let me out! Please! Open that door!'" A letter she hurriedly wrote to the Strasbergs emphasized her desperate circumstances:

> You haven't heard from me because I'm locked up with all
> these poor nutty people. I'm sure to end up a nut if I stay in this
> nightmare—please help me Lee, this is the last place I should
> be—maybe if you called Dr. Kris and assured her of my sensi-
> tivity and that I must get back to class so I'll be better prepared
> for "rain" [the Somerset Maugham play planned for television
> production with Strasberg as director]. . . . P.S. forgive the spell-
> ing—and theres nothing to write on here. Im on the dangerous
> floor its like a cell. Can you imagine—cement blocks. They put
> me in here because they lied to me about my calling my doctor
> and Joe [DiMaggio] and they had the bathroom door locked so
> I broke the glass and outside of that I haven't done anything [to]
> be uncoperative!

With her family's history of mental illness, it is not surprising that Monroe was frightened and resistant. According to Rosten, she became exasperated with a young doctor who kept asking her why she was so unhappy. In anger she struck back: "I've been paying the best doctors a fortune to find out why and you're asking me?" To Alan Levy she denied rumors of disrobing and playing "other scenes of high drama in the hospital." She laughed and said she wished she had done so just to get something out of her system. She was proud of having told the staff to have their heads examined. She later told Patricia Newcomb, "If they were going to treat her like a nut, she would behave like one." The letters she wrote to the Strasbergs and to Ralph Greenson demonstrate that no matter her distress, she had not lost her ability to observe her own behavior. Indeed, it is clear she modeled some of her actions on her performance in *Don't Bother to Knock*. But the line between her acting and her own experience remained blurred.

In three days, she was out of Payne-Whitney thanks to the help of Joe DiMaggio. She was moved to Columbia Presbyterian Hospital, where she spent nearly three weeks withdrawing from her pill habit. She recuperated at home in New York, followed up on her plans to do *Rain* on television, and granted an interview to Margaret Parton, who wrote an admiring, sensitive profile rejected by the *Ladies Home Journal* because its editors believed the journalist had been "mesmerized" by her subject.

It was typical of Monroe to come out of her deepest depressions and hysterical episodes full of vigor and intelligence—and just as typical for her renewal to be greeted with skepticism.

When NBC refused to accept Lee Strasberg as her director (he had no experience in television), Monroe canceled plans for *Rain* and accepted DiMaggio's invitation to join him in Florida in late March. The change of scene refreshed her, and she was able to see her half-sister, Berneice Miracle. Naturally, the press buzzed about the resumption of a Monroe-DiMaggio romance, but the couple called themselves just friends. As she had done with Miller, Monroe needed to draw on DiMaggio's strength. As Norman Rosten would have it, "[S]he gravitated toward power. This type of [stern] figure gives you security and absolution." Rejuvenated, she returned to New York to resume her career.

Even so, March and April were not easy months for Monroe. On March 9 she was photographed in a black mink leaving the funeral of Arthur Miller's mother, with whom she had remained close after the divorce. This was a death in the family for Monroe, as she indicated by taking a seat with the Millers at the services. After returning from Florida, she was shattered by a press report that Clark Gable's wife, Kay, had said, "*The Misfits* helped to kill him. But it wasn't the physical exertion that did it. It was the waiting, waiting, waiting." According to Skolsky, Monroe took Kay Gable's remarks to be an indirect reference to her tardiness on the set. Rupert Allan, who was in especially close contact with Monroe during this period, says Kay Gable told him she never made the critical statement and that she remained a friend of Monroe's after her husband's death, even inviting the actress to the christening of Clark Gable's son. In any case, Gable's death afflicted the actress with great guilt, both Weatherby and Skolsky report. The latter recalls her asking, "Was I punishing my father? Getting even for all the years he kept me waiting?" She was feeling suicidal, and friends persuaded her to close up her New York apartment temporarily. In the late spring of 1961, she flew to Hollywood to rest and to diet in preparation for a gallbladder operation scheduled for late June in New York City. In California, under the supervision of Dr. Hyman Engelberg, her internist, and Dr. Greenson, who took over complete responsibility for her psychiatric care, she began in mid-July the agonizing process of putting her life back together.

From the spring to the autumn of 1961, Monroe made little progress. Greenson had earlier noted "symptoms of paranoia and 'depressive reaction.'" Now he observed "signs of schizophrenia." In May, he wrote to a colleague that Monroe was still trying to "escape into the drugs or get involved with very destructive people, who will engage in some sort of sado-masochistic relationship with her." He was apparently referring to Frank Sinatra and his Las Vegas friends, whose parties she frequented. Greenson wrote like a disapproving father, referring to the actress as an "adolescent girl who needs guidance, friendliness, and firmness." Although Monroe said she relied on Greenson, this did not prevent her, in Greenson's words, "from canceling several hours to go to Palm Springs with Mr. F. S. She is unfaithful to me as one is to a parent." At the same time, Monroe became frightened—almost terrorized—by her father's attempt to communicate with her, feeling that it was "too late" to hear from him. She hardened herself against his second effort to reach her.

In these six moths, she began to see signs of aging and worried about flabby breasts, stretch marks, the beginnings of crow's feet, and brown spots on her hands (some of this deterioration can be glimpsed in Bert Stern's photographs). From Marjorie Stengel, employed as Monroe's s secretary during this period, Mailer draws a picture of his subject's aimlessness. She was uncommunicative and in disarray, rising late, wandering about her New York apartment in a "slightly soiled" nightie, and spending a long time on the phone with Dr. Greenson. Her apartment was nondescript, except for a mirror on the ceiling—her "major touch," Mailer calls it. In the living room "all was white": walls, rug, piano, couch, transparent leaves in a vase—even a Cecil Beaton photograph showed her in a white gown. This is the white dream home described in *My Story*, the one Gladys promised but could not deliver to her daughter. Except for Joe DiMaggio, friends did not visit.

Across the continent, in November of 1961, Eunice Murray saw Monroe in another apartment, emerging from her six-month ordeal. Dr. Greenson helped her withdraw from barbiturates, and his patient now seemed ready for more independence after months of "round-the-clock" nursing care. Murray, who was to serve the actress—with Greenson's encouragement—in several capacities, was immediately fascinated by a radiant Monroe, without makeup and in every way different from the drab described by her secretary, Marjorie Stengel. Only the bedroom with "huge floor-to-celling mirrors" linked Monroe's Los Angeles and New York lives.

In the last year of her life, Monroe traveled between New York and Hollywood without surcease, as if her identity were indeed bi-located. Evidence can be compiled to demonstrate that now she meant New York, now Hollywood, to be her home. She was of two worlds. Most of her friends in one realm had little knowledge of her friends in the other, for she usually liked to segregate her intimates. Anthony Summers traces just how complicated she made her life by swinging between circles of friends in show business, politics, and perhaps (through Sinatra) the Mafia. Consequently, radically different impressions of her personality and plans, of her commitment to the East and West coasts—and to the stage and the screen—were common among her friends and acquaintances, who were perhaps not fully aware of how much Monroe tended to act the chameleon, to play up or play down her connections to the Kennedys and other famous figures.

Monroe attempted to pattern life after her psychiatrist's suggestions. "By late 1961, for Dr. Greenson, Marilyn was both patient and ever present family friend," Summers notes. She "took great offense at the slightest irritation on his part," for, in his own words, he had become one of those "ideal figures in her life" from whom she expected perfection. By February of 1962, she found a house—similar in style to his own—and was trying out his idea of a stable, rooted existence.

With Murray's help, the actress began slowly to furnish and remodel her home. A trip to Mexico, where she purchased furniture and other items for her household, concentrated her mind wonderfully. Murray remembered that her employer was particularly interested in meeting politicians and actually preferred doing so to invitations to meet members of the artistic community. Fred Field, an American expatriate living in Mexico, saw a great deal of Monroe (she had come with an introduction to him from mutual friends in Connecticut) and remembers her vehement support for civil rights for blacks and for the government in China, and her anger at all forms of Red-baiting. J. Edgar Hoover was singled out as an object of hatred. Judging by her conversations with Weatherby, by her comments on politics in portions of the *Life* interview that were not printed, and by the material in her FBI file, Monroe looked to the Kennedys to set things right. They would finally bring about a more just world of equal opportunity for the abused and for abandoned minorities—among whom Monroe counted herself. Greenson observed that she could not seem to survive without these heroic examples in her life.

In the spring of 1962, the Rostens, visiting Monroe in Los Angeles, were invited to the Greenson home, where Norman immediately sensed his friend's "complete relaxation." With his patient's consent, Dr. Greenson described in general terms his treatment of her. He told Rosten that she was "some years" away from becoming an "analytic patient," even though she needed "psychotherapy, both supportive and analytical." He encouraged her familiarity with his family in order to supply the attachment she had been lacking "from childhood onward." To some biographers, such as Donald Spoto, Greenson's unorthodox measures, which obliterated the traditional boundaries between therapist and patient, were reckless and actually weakened any effort Monroe might have made to strengthen her sense of independence. But Monroe, it seems to me, was skillful in her ability to manipulate Greenson and all of her therapists, and nothing in her biography suggests that she herself could conceive of an alternative to the psychiatrist's care. As Greenson explained to Maurice Zolotow in 1973, he was taking a "desperate measure—because previous forms of therapy had failed." It seems likely that Monroe was suffering from what Greenson, in a paper published in 1958, called "a defective formation of the self image, an identity disorder" that explained why she was "not ready" for psychoanalysis. He may have regarded her as one of his "screen patients," although he does not identify her by name in any of his writings.

A screen patient is anxious about how well he or she communicates. Like such patients, Monroe seemed warm and giving, ready to recite her life history, "despite anxiety or shame." She had been successful, yet she belittled her accomplishments. In spite of her talent, her productivity had been "sporadic and unreliable." Like other screen patients, she was unduly concerned about her popularity and her ability to entertain, prone to severe mood swings and exhibitionism, yet chronically optimistic about her career. Enthusiastic and sentimental, impressionable, suggestible—even gullible—she tended to exaggerate to the point of lying, almost like a swindler, although she was "sensitive, perceptive, and empathic." In fact, like Greenson's other screen patients, she was "psychologically minded" and could spontaneously arrive at important insights, but had "great difficulty in integrating those new insights effectively."

Monroe evidently followed a pattern that Greenson detected in his other screen patients. She developed "a strong, positive transference." This technical term, about which Greenson published a great deal, describes the process by which the patient becomes irrevocably committed to the analyst and sometimes "morbidly dependent" on him. In its first stages, transference can be remarkably helpful because, as in Monroe's case, the patient is eager to rebuild her life along the lines the analyst suggests. Unfortunately, in its later stages transference can thwart the resolution of neurotic conflicts, because patients identify totally with the analyst and lash out at others, displaying, in Greenson's words, "a markedly different set of character traits at work and at home, with their family or with strangers." Monroe would demonstrate this kind of irrational, contradictory behavior when she began work, in the late spring of 1962, on *Something's Got to Give*.

Like other screen patients, she was not able to assimilate or clearly comprehend her past: "[A]lmost all the important people of their past lives are remembered as essentially black or white figures." This "rather disturbed relationship to time" promotes a blurring of past and present, with the past remaining so alive in patients' minds that they project "a youthful quality and their self picture is many years younger than their chronological age." In movies, Monroe was screened in precisely this way; that is, she was literally screened or blocked off from her true age, from a character who should have been maturing. Just like other screen patients, Monroe's characters had to be created anew. Off the screen, as well, each phase of her life was conceived as a beginning, not a continuation of what was already in place. Screen patients, Greenson points out, have to feel fresh and have the ability to "awaken new hopes." But since such personalities cannot be old, and cannot be seen to carry a past with them, they are essentially suspended in a nowhere—like Sugar Kane, whose behavior can be compared to the "imperative, urgent, and repetitive quality" Greenson identified in screen patients.

Screen patients feel favored, like "the lucky ones," and exhibit "feelings of omnipotence and expansiveness. This occurs in moments of triumph or in rage." At other times, as in Monroe's "lost day" with the Montands, their megalomania may manifest itself as "monumental self-punishment with which no one may interfere." Their reason for such drastic psychic alternation, Greenson submits, is that "these people confuse the wish to be favorites with the feeling that they are the favorites. Frequently such people change their names, undergo plastic surgery, and, in general, hold themselves together by manufacturing self-gratifying visions of their appearance as substitutions for deprivations in childhood associated with their mothers as unreliable givers." To feel intact, they must be looked at as though they were on stage. At home, where nobody could see her, the actress "might not be able to put herself together very well," Greenson wrote to a colleague. Monroe, he pointed out, thrived on the public perception of her as a beautiful woman, "perhaps the most beautiful woman in the world." He concludes, "Whereas the ordinary patient coms to anal-

Something's Got to Give (1962)

ysis because he does not like who he is these patients come to analysis to find out who they really are." Such language echoes Monroe's confessions of self-doubt, from *My Story* to her last recorded interview for *Life*.

By the time *Something's Got to Give* went into full production on April 23, 1962, the actress was facing a lifetime of failed enthusiasms. Although both Dr. Greenson and Mrs. Murray (acting now as the actress's house-keeper) believed she was making significant progress, she felt profoundly ambivalent about going back to work. She had not been able to cope well with her buried paranoia, feelings of persecution, frustration, and rage. It is not as if she avoided dealing with her traumatic memories; instead, such memories, as Greenson says of other screen patients, "may serve a screening function for a more severe trauma" the patient is somehow powerless to get at.

Monroe did take certain measures that might relieve her anxieties about her role. Before the shooting date, she consulted Nunnally Johnson, who was writing the script, a remake of a 1940 comedy, *My Favorite Wife*, starring Cary Grant and Irene Dunne. Johnson had worked on *How to Marry a Millionaire* and *We're Not Married*. Her first words to him, "Have you been trapped into this too?" were a fair indication of her distrust of the studio and of her suspicion of any project it might propose. She was fulfilling her commitment to Fox, negotiated during Milton Greene's tenure as her business partner, and it is unlikely she felt inspired by her role. Dr. Engelberg was treating her for a viral infection she may have picked up in Mexico. Her energy level was low, but it rose immediately, stimulated by Johnson's assurance that he had chosen to write the screenplay rather than accept other projects offered to him. When she realized he was not talking to her merely out of a sense of obligation, she became enthusiastic about the film, exploring questions of casting and plot development. He was so taken with her sharp perceptions, he regretted every harsh word he ever said against her and became her unabashed admirer.

Monroe's main worry then became the director, George Cukor, who told Johnson how much he "loathed" Monroe. He had directed her in the lame *Let's Make Love*, and he was on her list of approved directors. He owed Fox a picture, and so did Monroe. Cukor seemed to want to make the best of it, according to his biographer, Patrick McGilligan. Cukor vowed, "It's gonna work. We're gonna do it."

When Cukor began to revise the script, his actions were tantamount to challenging Monroe's hard won convictions, for this was a script she could believe in. The revisions were an attack upon her—especially since, according to Johnson, Cukor had similarly sabotaged her performance in *Let's Make Love*. Cukor, who had suffered the trauma of being fired as director of *Gone With The Wind*, always made pleasing the studio his priority. And the studio wanted to get a picture, any picture, out of Monroe as soon as possible, figuring that her reign as sex symbol was about to expire, as she reached the age of retirement that ended Betty Grable's career nearly a decade earlier The studio did nothing to allay Monroe's doubts about script changes that arrived almost daily.

Walter Bernstein, the last of six writers to work on *Something's Got To Give*, recalls that the studio catered to Monroe's every whim. She complained that the script had her chasing a man, when just the reverse should be true in a Marilyn Monroe movie. But why should this have been a surprise? It was the same for Cary Grant, and for other leading men and women, who realized that as stars they should only take roles in which they were pursued. Bernstein, who was plainly disgusted with Monroe, does not see that after Johnson's departure she regarded all changes as assaults on her personal integrity. Consequently, she took every opportunity to make her image immaculate. Once her artistic vision of the film was violated, she reacted like a politician or a general, making sure her power remained intact. "Sometimes she would refer to herself in the third person, like Caesar. 'Remember you've got Marilyn Monroe,'" she said to Bernstein when she wanted to wear a bikini in one scene. "You've got to use her," she instructed the screenwriter.

Such comments reveal how difficult it was for the actress to jettison her screen personality. If Fox would not use it properly, she would find other ways to get the attention she deserved. On Friday, May 18, she traveled to New York to sing "Happy Birthday" to President Kennedy on Saturday evening. She promised to return to work Monday. She considered her appearance in Madison Square Garden a "Command Performance," Guiles states. That it caused her considerable anxiety is apparent in the taped but not published transcript of her *Life* interview.

In a paper published in 1974, Dr. Greenson—identifying Monroe only as "an emotionally immature young woman patient, who had developed a very dependent transference to me"—mentions her "major concern about the period of my absence [to attend an international congress in Europe] was a public appearance of great importance to her professionally." She felt the event ratified her existence and defined her both as a star and as one of "the people"—as she put in in the *Life* interview. By singing to "the people," she was singing to herself, to her fantasy of watching herself at center stage from way above, "under one of those rafters, close to the ceiling." In fact, film of her during the Madison Square Garden event shows her shielding her eyes with her hands, which act as a visor but also as a kind of salute to the audience in the rafters, where she was

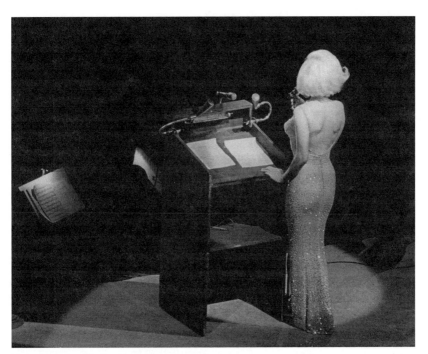

Happy Birthday, Mr. President (May 18, 1962)

placing herself. Marilyn Monroe, she was demonstrating, was everyone's dream of democratic success. In the tape-recorded *Life* interview, she can be heard, again and again, marveling that the sound of her voice did get out. It is as if the child in her feared some stifling of the sexy birthday song she had practiced for weeks—sometimes in the presence of Ralph Roberts and others—and planned for in elaborate fittings of a skin-tight dress with "hundreds of strategically place brilliants [that] shimmered and glittered so brightly that the body was clothed in reflected light."

This last description, by Mrs. Murray, who helped the actress with her wardrobe, is reminiscent of the studio's description of Monroe's outfit for *There's No Business Like Show Business*. It is also similar to the outfit the studio decided not to use in *Gentlemen Prefer Blondes* because of Monroe's flamboyant sexual display at an awards ceremony, and the flaunting of her femme fatale appeal in *Niagara*. The times had changed—or rather, the times had caught up with Marilyn Monroe, and she could now show herself in her own production.

The scene of her singing to JFK is often reproduced in documentaries side-by-side with excerpts from her movies, for the scene was directed to play for the screen. After Peter Lawford's joking introduction of the "late" Marilyn Monroe and her delayed entrance, she glides forward with small steps, adjusting her fur wrap as she approaches Lawford. With one arm she covers her shoulders with the stole and smiles, bringing the fur closer to her neck as she greets him. She flicks a finger at the microphone, then grabs it with her hand, raises her arms and hands—forming that visor in the bright lights which is also her own framing device—as she puts the audience into the picture of her life. Languidly and suggestively, she begins to sing—thus inspiring Kennedy's subsequent joke about retiring from politics now that Miss Monroe had sung "Happy Birthday" to him in such a wholesome way. She starts a second chorus of the song by shifting out of her seductive pose, vigorously waving her arms like a conductor, and jumping up and down on the stage like the president's most enthusiastic cheerleader. As in a classic Marilyn Monroe movie, the performance is as innocent as it is seductive.

Politics and show business, on this night, were more closely allied than ever before in American life. After all, the "birthday salute"—as it is called in an advertisement extolling the "most exciting program ever staged!"—included a "Spectacular Array of the Worlds Greatest Talent." The actress craved this kind of attention, and her association with the Kennedys completed an ambitious profile of herself initiated by her marriage to DiMaggio and confirmed by her marriage to Miller. She was the screen actress as politician, situating her image in the public's eye, and allying herself with an administration that prided itself on its high production values.

As with Greenson's other screen patients, Monroe's life had to have a high gloss, and the Kennedys, with their Hollywood connections, fit comfortably into her endless efforts to polish her image. John Kennedy reveled in Hollywood gossip, and his brother Robert was interested in movie personalities like Monroe and Judy Garland. Their father, Joseph, had once been active in Hollywood film production, and their sister Pat was married to Peter Lawford. The Lawfords, who lived nearby, became friends of Monroe's, and the actress would see the Kennedys on social occasions. They enjoyed her wit and seemed bothered very little by the gossip that linked her sexually with both John and Robert. And while Monroe felt complimented by being invited into their company, she was also drawn to Robert's commitment to civil rights and political freedom. The Kennedys were important to the actress because they represented a stage on which to perform that was so much greater than what her current film offered.

The set of *Something's Got to Give* (1962)

Rejuvenated by her Madison Square Garden performance on May 21, she returned to the set of *Something's Got to Give* and sparkled in scenes with Wally Cox and Dean Martin. In discarded footage, Cukor's voice can be heard calling on her to do take after take in scenes that show no deterioration in her timing or in her patient repetition of lines that are part of the wear and tear of moviemaking. None of the surviving footage supports Cukor's claim that Monroe "acted in a kind of slow motion" that made the director say he did not believe she could complete the picture. On the contrary, her vitality is apparent in the impromptu nude swimming scene, in which Monroe shed her flesh-colored suit and frolicked in a pool as if to enliven the film's hackneyed plot—and to remind the world of her nude calendar work, now that she was again the 119-pound beauty she had been sixteen years earlier. She realized that photographs of this scene would seize the attention of the world press, and at least momentarily shift attention away from the extraordinary attention focused on Elizabeth Taylor's romance with Richard Burton during the making of *Cleopatra*. That Fox did not realize how much the free publicity helped to promote the studio and its picture is astounding. Monroe appeared on magazine covers around the world, momentarily obliterating the press's obsession with the Taylor-Burton affair. Lawrence Schiller writes in *Marilyn & Me* that Monroe's deal with him to publish his nude shots of her included the proviso that none of the magazines using his work could also carry a story about Taylor and Burton.

But such triumphs were short-lived. As Arthur Miller observes in *Timebends*, there was something sad and alarming about Monroe's resort to nudity, which seemed a desperate move, not a triumph. She seems to have realized as much when Schiller found her resistant to Hugh Hefner's proposal that she do more nude work for *Playboy* involving a kind of peek-a-boo sequence designed for both the front and back covers of the magazine. Visiting Monroe in late May, Rosten found her edgy and irritable. When they made a visit to Greenson's home, the actress was abrupt and even belligerent with the psychiatrist, goading him to interpret a Rodin statue of two lovers she had just purchased. Her voice was shrill and strident, and she repeatedly asked the analyst to tell her what the statue meant. Was the man "screwing" the woman or was it a "fake"? Her interpretation seemed to reflect her own ambivalence: "Look at them both. How beautiful. He's hurting her, but he wants to love her, too." Monroe's words call to mind Greenson's correspondence with a colleague, in which he identified "her inability to cope with any sort of hurt" as one of the "decisive factors that led to her death."

Did the statue reflect a gap in herself, what Alexander Lowen calls "a break in the personality, which fixates the individual at a certain pattern of behavior he cannot change?" What cannot get changed gets repeated. Monroe's actions recall Freud's use of the term "repetition compulsion" to describe the personality's return "to the situation where it got stuck, in the hopes of someday getting unstuck." Monroe was losing patience and approaching the despair of many patients who cannot help themselves and do not see therapy providing the relief it initially promised.

By June 1, Greenson had left for Europe and Rosten had returned home to Brooklyn. Owing to Monroe's demands on him, the psychiatrist was perilously close to admitting defeat. When she "threatened to fall back wholly on drugs, his sessions with her would last four or five hours," Summers reports. Greenson confessed to having become "a prisoner of a form of treatment that I thought was correct for her, but almost impossible for me." In a later letter he confided to a friend that "at times I felt I couldn't go on with this."

Sick again, Monroe missed several shooting days on *Something's Got to Give*. Bernstein suggests she was not the studio's idea of a star, "Sprightly and sexy and full of fun." By the middle of June, the studio had fired her, and she spent the next few days first crying, then in a stupor, and finally angrily defiant. Cukor claimed that she could not be directed: "[Y]ou couldn't reach her, she was like underwater." But Monroe had acted this way with other directors she deemed unsympathetic. Perhaps the most telling refutation came from Dean Martin, who refused to do the picture with Lee Remick, Monroe's replacement. He had signed to do the movie with Marilyn Monroe, and as far as Martin was concerned, she was irreplaceable. In truth, as Donald Spoto documents, the studio mismanaged its dealings with Monroe, and she, in turn, had to deal not only with a script that was changing daily, but with a studio administration that also changed owing to a corporate reshuffle, as Fox floundered with a huge budget overrun on *Cleopatra* and other bad business decisions. Eventually Darryl Zanuck, who had departed the Fox lot to produce motion pictures in Europe, returned to take control of the corporation and to begin negotiations with Monroe to resume work on *Something's Got to Give* in September.

Although Monroe seemed perfectly capable of rallying herself for her art and turning in a fine performance in yet another mediocre picture, she was also, in Rupert Allan's words, facing the "dark tunnel of her career." There is no better authority on Monroe than Allan, who first met her when he was a young writer working on a profile of her for *Look*, and then became her publicist and confidant. He had watched her age and observed her need to make the transition to roles reflecting her maturing appearance and talent. She worked again at Actors Studio, this time on a one-act play, an adaptation of a short story by Colette. Once again her sensitivity impressed the Strasbergs and others, and hopes were high for her stage career, until an unsettling mood sent her back to Dr. Greenson in California. In his view, she had come to identify with him as her "white knight," her "protector," her "talisman" serving to avert "bad luck or evil." In his absence, he says she experienced the "terror" of a "child who has lost her security blanket."

In a final conversation with Weatherby, perhaps sometime in late June, Monroe seemed to be making plans to stay in California, more or less permanently. When he asked her about the Actors Studio, she shrugged in answer. In fact, she had written to Lee Strasberg proposing that he become part of a new production company she was thinking of organizing. No record of his answer has surfaced, but it is likely he knew all too well how that kind of proximity to Monroe would overwhelm him—as it had engulfed Milton Greene, Arthur Miller, Ralph Greenson, and others.

Monroe told Weatherby that her psychiatrist advised her to concentrate on "fun" movies for the time being, and she teased the reporter about her affair with a famous married politician, even as she enthused about President Kennedy as "another Lincoln," about whom she would brook no criticism. She should stick to the movie audience of millions, her politician friend advised her. Ralph Roberts is the key source for the claim that Monroe had sex with President Kennedy. According to Roberts, the president himself spoke to the masseur on the phone while in a bedroom with the actress at Bing Crosby's home. Monroe, Roberts averred, had told Kennedy that the masseur could give him sound advice on how to manage his back problems.

From late June to early August, the actress was under terrific stress, seeing Dr. Greenson almost every day and calling Ralph Roberts—sometimes in the middle of the night—for massages to relieve tension that had her saying, "I'm about to jump out of my skin." At the same time, George Barris's photographs of her—especially the shots of her on the beach—suggest a sturdy personality. In conversation with Richard Meryman and during photographic sessions with Bert Stern, she let go of more of herself, offering not just a reprise of her career, but articulating herself more precisely and creatively than ever before. If her persona demanded repetitions of her successful poses, so that she operated perilously close to cliché, it is remarkable how much energy remained for one more go at originality.

Monroe's moods were mercurial, Stern recalled. His photographs almost seem to chart the rise and fall of her temperature, of the fever to create. Through Pat Newcomb she requested that he have on hand three bottles of her favorite champagne, Dom Perignon, for the modeling assignment arranged by *Vogue*. He bought a whole case, and in the first session on June 23, he kept shooting for twelve hours—which perhaps accounts in part for the tired, even drunken look she wears in some of her poses. In one series, she seems narcotized in a playful happiness verging on melancholy. She puckers her lips, bites on a strand of pearls, partly covers her mouth with her fingers, puts her hands around her head and neck while her eyelids drop. All of this framing of herself is done as though she were half-conscious—on the edge of an awakening or a very deep sleep.

Monroe projects an identity that wavers between extreme states even as she is in complete touch with her body. As Greenson put it in one of his letters, "[T]he main mechanism she used to bring some feeling of stability and significance to her life was the attractiveness of her body." She had lost considerate weight, and her breasts are not nearly so prominent as in her 1950s heyday. It is as if a new decade has shifted concern to other aspects of her body, other areas of the self. The thinness of her shoulders, arms, face, and torso tones down the lushness exhibited in earlier poses. À la Milton Greene, wisps of her mussed hair trail down her forehead, glance past her right eye, and make the left eye seem larger and clearer in a bifurcated Marilyn Monroe pose. Stern stimulated her taste for psychologically intriguing poses. She is wiry, taut, and sharp—but at the same time gauzy, available in outline only, as she covers her body with the transparent fabrics Stern supplied.

In some of the photographs she smiles broadly, allowing her upper gums and her facial wrinkles to show. The actress plays with a string of beads, clutching part of it to her breast with her left hand, while holding out another part of it with her extended right arm. This pose suggests an alternation between her introverted and extroverted impulses, played here for humor with a more honest edge than in "Diamonds Are a Girl's Best Friend." Far more riveting and disturbing is the shot of Monroe with her fingers seemingly penetrating her forehead in great anguish, the tongue askew in her mouth; she seems about to let go or about to summon great concentration.

As each new pose worked itself out, there was very little talking. "[W]e would go a step higher," Stern says, echoing Montgomery Clift. One photograph resembles Monroe's bent-over screaming scene in *The*

Misfits; she drops her scarf for "one glimpse, one stolen frame," out of a series of frames masking various parts of her body. In the fugitive frame she looks convulsed and vulnerable, a slight figure—naked, not nude, with her traumas slipping out of her in a setting no longer squared off by the scarf. There is only the tense fabric of Monroe's own person.

Just as Bert Stern was impressed by how thoroughly the actress prepared for her "last sitting," Richard Meryman marveled at her professionalism in her last interview. She asked to see his questions in advance, thought about them for days, and refused to essay any answer she had not pondered. He noted the excellent taste of the furnishings and art work in her new house, and he responded enthusiastically to her keen intelligence. He saw her in many different guises: a sweet little girl, a low-key hysteric—frightened and not convinced of her abilities, and a perceptive critic of her own work and that of others. Most important of all, however, was her skill at presenting an ideal Monroe. She turned her best side to him, he was sure, going about the interview in a mature, systematic manner. She was pleased with the edited tape, which she saw in print two days before her death. Her conversation with Meryman is the closest she came to a final testament. He ended the interview feeling somewhat troubled about her seclusion, in which her home functioned as a bulwark. She chose it for its privacy—it was at the end of a cul-de-sac—and sometimes she gave the impression of retreating behind its high walls.

Like the last months of her life, Monroe's last days are filled with contradictory evidence about her physical and mental health. In *Marilyn & Me*, Lawrence Schiller presents her as a consummate professional, carefully selecting his nude swimming scene photographs for publication. For him, her death would seem unaccountable and surely an accident. Meryman recalled that "she looked terrific," but when examined closely her skin was "pasty and lifeless-looking," and her hair "had no body to it, like hair that has been primped and heated and blown a thousand times." Her face "was kind of cardboardy." She was not sleeping well, and she was under constant psychiatric care. Her final hours, from some time around 7:30 p.m. until about 3:30 a.m., August 5, when her lifeless body was discovered, are open to endless speculation—even though the Los Angeles District Attorney's office found no reason to doubt the original finding of "probable suicide" as the result of a drug overdose. Pills that for the longest time failed to supply her with enough sleep now disoriented her. In the past, she had built up great tolerance for massive doses, but recently she had been able to get along with fewer sedatives. Perhaps she misjudged how much her body could absorb on an empty stomach. She was not drinking, and her death was nothing so simple as an accidental overdose. It was, rather, part of a pattern of self-abuse and self-absorption that she could not overcome.

At her most fragmented moments she inhabited, like the Lady of Shalott, an intensely private domain, full of a personal mythology, impenetrable to the outsider—even to her psychiatrist perhaps, if one is to judge by her poem that prefaces Rosten's reminiscence of her. It is about a rootless child with a doll in a carriage that goes "over the cracks" (that break a mother's back?) traveling far away from home. The child in the poem comforts her doll ("Don't cry / I hold you and rock you to sleep"). But the poem ends with a plea for "help," as the child feels "life coming closer / When all I want is to die"). The child and the adult vie for attention as the actress attempts to become her own mother, to give herself the feeling of a mother—the mother she never had, the mother who died, more than once, inside of her.

As in the lives of many suicides, a terrible isolation enclosed Monroe's every move, an isolation that was broken by attempts to escape from past failures by assuming glorious roles and dwelling on the grand possibilities of the future. There was a feverish desperation in her plans, a "fluctuation between physical vanity and self-injury" and an "outlandish mixture of the profound and the trivial" that, in Leslie Farber's view, is a common characteristic of the suicide. Much has been made of telephone logs showing that Monroe called the Justice Department several times during her final days. Read biographer Anthony Summers, and you may believe that the brevity of those calls exacerbated Monroe's feeling that she was a woman spurned. Read Donald Spoto, and you will have the impression that Robert Kennedy simply did not have the time any longer to indulge Monroe's questions about his work, even though in more relaxed circumstances he had entertained her with answers. One does not have to believe in murder conspiracies to see that at the slightest provocation this woman, with her fragile psyche, would begin to feel abused by the Kennedys and resentful that she could no longer share the spotlight with them.

Monroe's reliance on drugs to alleviate anxiety made her less and less capable of resuming her search for a sound identity and a substantial role. Temporary stimulants debilitated her, and she could not find the natural dynamic of her life. It became impossible to cope with the frustrations of her career without the lift or the tranquility provided by her pills. Under such circumstances, the will becomes paralyzed, and the whole personality is susceptible to exhaustion, derangement, and depleting illnesses. She seemed caught between her ragged endings and beginnings, and divided by disturbing and contrary impulses. Fragmentary notes to herself suggest she was stymied and sometimes even angry with herself. She could not sustain a loving relationship with a man. She felt less than a whole woman.

Some found the actress too fey, like the fairy Lady of Shalott, laboring under a curse, weaving a magic web around herself that was certain to be unraveled by reality. George Cukor called her death "a nasty business . . . Her worse rejection. Power and money in the end she was too innocent." He was apparently referring to the rumors, already rampant, about her affairs with both John and Robert Kennedy. Dr. Greenson, who publicly denied that his patient was involved with either Kennedy, nevertheless told a member of the suicide team investigating her death that on her last evening she sounded "drugged and depressed," because her meeting with one of the "very important people" she had been seeing was canceled. He also noted that she had found it gratifying to have a "close relationship with extremely important men in government." The relationship was "sexual," and the men concerned were "at the highest level." Dr. Robert Litman, the suicide team member to whom Greenson gave his report, told biographer Anthony Summers that it was clear Greenson was referring to the Kennedys, although they were not named—perhaps, as another suicide team member suggests, because "discretion entered into it." Greenson had been concerned about Monroe's romantic involvement, but did not feel he could oppose it so long as it supplied such a badly needed sense of her own importance. On her last night she was feeling let down. The most beautiful woman in the world, she told her psychiatrist, did not have a date. She was feeling "rejected by some of the people she had been close to," Greenson concluded.

Sooner or later Monroe's mind, like a crystal mirror, would crack. Constance Collier, who briefly served as Monroe's acting teacher, was fascinated by her pupil's "flickering intelligence. . . . It's so fragile and subtle it can only be caught by the camera." Collier and Greta Garbo agreed Monroe would make an "exquisite Ophelia," perhaps because like Henri Cartier-Bresson, they viewed her as an "apparition in a fairy tale," with "something extremely alert and vivid in her, an intelligence . . . something very tenuous . . . That appears disappears quickly, that appears again." John Huston said, "What really counts in film acting is that rare moment—just a flickering when through the eyes you get a glimpse of the real meaning of the character. It is not technique or professionalism, just truth. Garbo had it. Monroe had it." Some, like Arthur Miller, believed that with "a little luck" she might have survived, for she had a worldly side and a tenacity, a faith that "you're always as good as your potential," a certainty that never deserted her until that last moment.

In tape recordings of the Richard Meryman *Life* interview, the actress's voice is strong, full-bodied, and active, ringing with laughter. One person can be heard in the laughter, energizing her listeners as well as herself. The woman with this robust laugh, this woman momentarily at one with her mature self, was never seen on the screen. The laughter sounds like it comes from the core of her being, the core for which she searched. The laughter justifies her claim that on screen and off she had more to express than her roles permitted. If she went to pieces at the last, she still seems to be calling, entreating her audience to "find me, find me, / complete this form."

Afterword

The Murder of Marilyn Monroe

So much has been written about Marilyn Monroe and the Kennedy brothers—much of it based on stories that cannot be verified and on conflicting accounts—that it is nearly impossible to filter out fact from fiction. The Los Angeles coroner's office ruled her death in the early morning hours of August 5, 1962, a "probable suicide" after an autopsy revealed substantial amounts of the barbiturate Nembutal and chloral hydrate in her body, and after conducting an investigation that disclosed her previous attempts to end her life. Even so, rumors persisted that she had been the victim of foul play. Conspiracy theorists noted discrepancies in the accounts of Monroe's final hours given by her housekeeper, Eunice Murray, as well as the suspicions of a Los Angeles policeman called to the death scene at Helena Drive. He believed that Monroe's body had been moved. Exactly how long Monroe had been dead before the police arrived, who was in the house on the night of the 4th, and who stood to benefit from her murder all became part of the catalogue of conjecture in books purporting to expose the plot to silence Marilyn Monroe.

Similar kinds of conspiracy theories had surfaced after the mysterious death of Jean Harlow's husband, Paul Bern, and after Harlow's own shocking early demise, but these precedents pale in comparison to the mystique that soon attached itself to the death of Marilyn Monroe. She became the blameless victim and her death the annihilation of American innocence. She had become involved, it was alleged, in the nefarious underworld of organized crime, the clandestine activities of the CIA, and the seamy side of Camelot, where the Kennedys used women and whatever else came to hand in order to promote their political ambitions and their private pleasures.

This transformation of Marilyn Monroe from a movie star to an icon situated at the very epicenter of American political and cultural life began virtually hours after her death. In Monroe's FBI file, a July 9, 1963, memorandum reports that Walter Winchell's *New York Mirror* column the previous day claimed that Martha Donaldson's *Photoplay* article,

"One Year Later Marilyn Monroe Killer Still at Large," practically named the murderer. Winchell, a famous gossip columnist and purveyor of sensationalist news, liked to affect an insider's knowledge of mysterious events. In this case, he claimed to know the identity of the married man "involved" in Monroe's death, and that like other members of the press, he "hinted at the name." In fact, as the FBI memorandum pointed out, the *Photoplay* article "comes nowhere near identifying anyone. The only 'clues' to the identity of the alleged married man who had an affair with Marilyn and 'caused' her suicide when he rejected her could apply to any number of prominent individuals." Of course, this is precisely why such articles work: They create an air of innuendo and intrigue that proves irresistible, giving a flimsy story a cultural currency because of the public's interest in the behind-the-scenes lives of the famous.

The *Photoplay* article is striking because it establishes so many key elements in the Marilyn Monroe murder myth: Her married lover is world famous; a family man, he never dreamed of falling in love with Monroe when he was at the height of his powers and she was in the depths of her career; his dilemma is that he is an "honorable man" who must disappoint Monroe's hopes that he will divorce his wife and marry her; his final call to her on August 4 breaking off their affair is what drives her to commit suicide. This last detail—that she commits suicide by taking an overdose of sleeping pills—would be turned into murder in the next phase of conspiracy theories. But the article left even this possibility open by reporting that Eunice Murray had disappeared (not true), and that Monroe's married lover had to cope every day with his guilty role in her death.

On October 23, 1964, an FBI field agent filed a report from an unattributed source alleging a romance between Robert Kennedy and Marilyn Monroe, begun after Kennedy's sister, Patricia Kennedy Lawford, introduced him to Monroe at the home of her husband, actor Peter Lawford. During the latter half of 1961 and early 1962, Kennedy is supposed to have seen Monroe while meeting with producer Jerry Wald and others about a film based on his brother's heroism in World War II. A deeply emotional Kennedy promised Monroe he would divorce his wife and marry her. Eventually Monroe realized that he had no intention of marrying her, and then he had broken another promise by not bothering to pressure Fox to reinstate her contract. Her repeated calls to him led to unpleasant words between them. Monroe threatened to make their affair public. With the collusion of Eunice Murray and Patricia Newcomb, Monroe's personal press agent and secretary, a prescription for barbiturates (sleeping pills) was put beside Monroe's bedside table. In her distraught condition, the conspirators were certain that she would take the pills and, following her usual pattern, call out for help and expect her stomach to be pumped. This time, however, no one came to her assistance. The report implied that her psychiatrist, Ralph Greenson, might also have been aware of the plot, since he did not enter her home until after her death, even though she had called him about the overdose. Within forty-eight hours of Monroe's death, Patricia Newcomb was flown to the Kennedy compound in Hyannisport, Massachusetts, to join Peter Lawford, who was evidently also part of the cover-up. Joe DiMaggio, somehow aware of the plot against Monroe, vowed to kill Kennedy after he left office.

The FBI report, labeled as unverifiable, also recounted sex parties that John Kennedy had attended in Hollywood. Los Angeles police chief William Parker had records of the Kennedys' involvement with other women, but kept this material in a safe and helped to rig the inquiry into Monroe's death so that the details of her affairs would not be made public and the Kennedys would not be implicated in her death. Tape recordings of the Kennedys having sex were also supposed to be in the possession of a Los Angeles detective agency.

FBI files are notoriously unreliable. They are simply collections of all the "intelligence" agents collect in the field. No efforts are made to corroborate the material; instead, such reports become part of a watch list, so to speak, a practice that became standard during J. Edgar Hoover's leadership of the FBI. Marilyn Monroe had become a person of interest as soon as she stood by Arthur Miller, supporting not only his HUAC testimony, but generally endorsing his left wing politics.

Just how deeply the mystique surrounding Marilyn Monroe's death had penetrated into the popular imagination by the mid- 1960s is apparent in a letter to Hoover from a woman living in a trailer park in Winter Haven, Florida. On January 20, 1965, Mrs. Alta Melton, "Americanism Chairman" of Mothers of World War II, Inc., announced her campaign to "suppress untrue rumors." She wanted Hoover's opinion on a pamphlet she had been handed. "Suicide or Murder" connected the "former Attorney General" to Monroe. "Such reading can do much to undermine one's character, and I would like to know if there is any truth to any of it. It mentions Communism also and that is why I am interested." It is not surprising that Mrs. Melton wrote to Hoover, famous for alerting the country to the dangers of subversives—communists posing as good

Americans—and the author of a best-selling book on the subject, *Masters of Deceit.* Hoover replied on January 26, 1965, expressing his desire to help Mrs. Melton, but indicating that the FBI as a strictly investigative agency made no evaluations and drew no conclusions as to the "character or integrity of any organization, publication, or individual." So he could not answer her question. Instead, he enclosed several of his articles about the communist conspiracy.

The role of intelligence agencies like the FBI and the sensationalism of newspaper columnists and magazines like *Photoplay* produced a paranoid climate in which the death of Marilyn Monroe could easily be exploited. The first books alleging some sort of conspiracy to murder Monroe that involved the Kennedys appeared toward the end of the 1960s, the product of right wing authors seeking to discredit the Kennedy legacy. But these publications drew almost no attention from the mainstream press, then mainly preoccupied with the many books alleging a conspiracy to assassinate President Kennedy.

Reputable biographers shied away from the unseemly and uncorroborated aspects of the Monroe-Kennedy saga, but friends of Monroe began to speak with biographer Fred Lawrence Guiles, who published the first full-scale biography of Monroe, *Norma Jean: The Life of Marilyn Monroe,* in 1970. Wary of what he could not substantiate, Guiles referred to Robert Kennedy as "The Easterner," and placed Kennedy in Monroe's Helena Drive home on at least one occasion—without indulging in the conspiracy theories of earlier books and articles. For many years, Guiles's book remained the most thorough and respected account of Monroe's life.

When Norman Mailer published his controversial biography of Monroe in 1973, he relied heavily on Guiles and included a chapter speculating on murder conspiracy theories that involved the Kennedys' desire to eliminate Monroe because she was planning to hold a press conference exposing secrets they had told her about the Bay of Pigs invasion of Cuba and other sensitive national security matters. Although Mailer did not endorse such stories, he promoted them, so they became the subject of network television coverage and documentaries.

Interest in a Monroe-Kennedy liaison broadened in 1974, when Robert Slatzer published *The Curious Death of Marilyn Monroe,* claiming that his friend Marilyn had confided to him the story of her involvement with the Kennedys and her anger over their decision to drop her from their circle. By way of asserting intimate knowledge about Monroe,

Slatzer revealed that he had been briefly married to her before she wed Joe DiMaggio. Slatzer could produce no proof, saying the marriage had taken place on October 4, 1952, in Mexico and been dissolved there a few days later after Monroe had second thoughts. Other than a few photographs showing him with Monroe, Slatzer had no documentation of their relationship, and several friends close to Monroe, who had never heard of Slatzer, doubted his story. Donald Spoto's biography of Monroe includes a devastating demolition of Slatzer's claims.

But Slatzer's detailed account, beginning with him meeting the aspiring actress in 1946, provided the first fully worked out rationale for her involvement with the Kennedys. He portrayed the young Marilyn as a conscientious, self-educated person, who cared deeply about public affairs and was flattered by the attention that both John and Robert Kennedy paid to her—until they suddenly withdrew from contact with her, leaving the actress in a vulnerable state in the last summer of her life, when she was trying to restore her confidence after Fox had fired her.

Since the appearance of Mailer's and Slatzer's books, a slew of biographies have appeared purporting to reveal the conspiracy to murder Marilyn Monroe. Some accounts suggest involvement by the Mafia, with Monroe getting caught up in the Mob's revenge against the Kennedys for their investigations of organized crime. Other books contend the CIA was also involved—as well as Jimmy Hoffa, who had his own animus against Robert Kennedy for initiating the prosecution that led to Hoffa's incarceration in federal prison.

And so the suspicion of a vast conspiracy against Marilyn Monroe persists. But that, of course, is the problem: The conspiracy would have to be intricate and call upon participants with conflicts of interest to collaborate in keeping a secret. Successful conspiracies are, by definition, successful because they do not come to light. Even when the conspirators are named—as they often are in books about Monroe's "murder"—the so-called evidence never leads to a conviction, except in the writers' minds. But, then, there is an explanation for this result too: It is not in the interest of the authorities to act on the evidence of crimes that will embarrass or otherwise compromise the powers that be. The world of conspiracy theories is self-contained and utterly satisfying to those who believe in conspiracies. It is, in sum, a tautological world.

Monroe's fame endures, in part, because of this conspiratorial literature. No biographer of Marilyn Monroe can give a public talk or interview without addressing the question of whether she was murdered.

The penchant for dwelling on the deaths of famous people has always been part of what perpetuates their fame. "We take some share, and even some satisfaction in their deaths," Tom Payne argues in his book on fame. Death is a part of the way our icons give themselves up to us. And so we want to know the details of their deaths, no matter how gory. It is a form of participation in the icon's glory that is as old as Homer, Payne reminds us. Grieving for the dead icon "brings us together in a way that makes us civilized, however odd that might seem."

Some of Monroe's iconic appeal is due to the desire of those who want to regard her as suffering for the sins of a corrupt society that encompasses entertainment and politics, Hollywood and Washington, D.C. One of the little ironies of Monroe's biography is that David Conover, the army corporal photographer who discovered her in an airplane factory, was given his assignment by Ronald Reagan, a movie star then in the army, and later to become president of the United States. Monroe's continuing appeal owes at least something to these kinds of connections, which make her life a fabulous network of associations with America's postwar history. She first appeared in the mid-1940s, at a time of great promise, with the country emerging victorious from World War II, and with Hollywood films reaching their peak attendance. A good deal of her trouble also coincided with an industry in decline—not merely losing its audience, but also its monopoly over the entertainment industry. And then Hollywood was devastated by charges that some of its actors, directors, and writers had been disloyal, members of a conspiracy determined to subvert American freedoms and gradually surrender the country to Soviet propaganda—and even, perhaps, to a communist government. Stars like Monroe had to be watched, an FBI file established on them, and kept in line by their studios. That Monroe rebelled against her studio and took progressive stands on the issues of her time makes her all the more central to the postwar period, so that she becomes something larger than just a 1950s sex symbol.

Donald Spoto notes that Monroe's ascent to stardom coincided with the controversy over *Sexual Behavior in the Human Female* (1953), Alfred Kinsey's controversial study, which appeared just as audiences were watching *Gentlemen Prefer Blondes*, featuring an orgasmic "Diamonds Are a Girl's Best Friend" musical number that had a consort of tuxedoed men quite literally falling at Monroe's feet. In nearly twelve thousand interviews with women, Kinsey dealt directly with female orgasm and suggested that women had an interest in sex that the "pretenses of Puritan-

Victorian moralism" had denied. Civic, school, and church groups—not to mention the Legion of Decency and the Production Code—attacked Kinsey's report, even as Monroe on screen reveled in the sexuality that Hollywood no longer wanted to keep under wraps. (Although Fox hedged its bets by replacing the diamond-studded gown Monroe was supposed to wear with a much more sedate, if elegant, dark pink gown with a high neckline. A version of that jewel-encrusted dress would not appear again until Monroe sang "Happy Birthday to JFK" in 1962). In other words, Monroe and her studio skirted the mores of the 1950s by presenting, in Spoto's words, a "quietly aggressive," if "frankly carnal creature. Vulnerable and frightened though she was (and often appeared on screen), there was yet something tenacious and independent about her." Above all, "she seemed a woman with a strong sense of her body's power, she was an exponent, a summary of the postwar American woman Kinsey reported—and like Kinsey's woman, she could not yet be taken seriously." It would take the culture decades to catch up with Kinsey and Monroe, Spoto suggests, because both represented the "unfulfilled dreams and the personal (not merely sexual) maturity both longed for and feared in the American woman."

Sociologist S. Paige Baty observes that Monroe assumes the "traces of the decades." She is a "poster girl for the 1950s," evoking nostalgia for a bygone and seemingly innocent era, representing somehow a safer world that was destroyed by President Kennedy's assassination. But she is also "'shorthand' for the confusion, mourning, nostalgia, and loss . . . the marks of a common contemporary condition," and one of the unsolved mysteries of the 1960s for those who ask, "Who Killed Marilyn Monroe?" For virtually all those who are attracted to her, she embodies "a nostalgia that recalls the difficulties of the American self," the quest to invent or re-invent an identity in a land entranced with the idea of the self-made man and woman.

As Andy Warhol demonstrated in his multiple silk-screen images of Monroe, she is, in Baty's words, "powerful, in part, because she can be made up again and again, in so many different ways." Like many myths, and the icons who embody those myths, she is a collection of opposites that can be read as emblematic of American history. So Baty contends, "We are a nation narrated by characters with double histories and identities. What circulates on one page as sunny life, liberty, and the pursuit of happiness may flip to reveal a history of corruption, mishandling, theft, and loss." Monroe is an example of hope and hazard, Baty concludes,

Sources

My acknowledgments give complete information on my interviews. The notes below specify sources not clearly identified in my narrative. Wherever possible, I have cited page numbers for articles and books, but in some cases e-books and articles retrieved from clipping files at various archives, including the New York Library for the Performing Arts and the Academy of Motion Picture Arts and Sciences, do not contain page numbers. Epigraphs after chapter headings are from Richard Meryman's August 3, 1962, *Life* interview. All other quotations from Monroe are from *My Story*, first published in book form in 1974 by Stein and Day, but available in England in 1954 as a series of articles (published May 9–August 1) written in close collaboration with Ben Hecht for *Empire News*. The autobiography must be used with caution, since it sensationalizes aspects of the actress's life and contains errors, such as identifying the University of Southern California rather than UCLA as her night school. Certain biographers, especially Norman Mailer and Donald Spoto, distrust *My Story*. Nevertheless, other biographers, including Fred Lawrence Guiles and Lois Banner, have been able to authenticate many of the incidents described in *My Story*, and the book is true to many of the feelings about her life Monroe expressed to friends and associates I interviewed, as well as to what Arthur Miller recounts in *Timebends*. Both Maurice Zolotow and Stanley Flink, friends of Ben Hecht's, testify persuasively to Hecht's intense interest in the actress he got to know well while helping to write the script of *Monkey Business*. Anthony Summers interviewed Hecht's widow, who remembered Monroe correcting the manuscript of *My Story* and expressing enthusiastic approval of the way "Benny had captured every phase of her life." Exactly when the autobiography was written is not clear, although *MM—Personal* (Abrams, 2011), p. 135, provides a copy of the contract with Hecht that Monroe signed on March 18, 1954. In the October 1954 issue of *Motion Picture*, Erskine Johnson states that Hecht wrote *My Story* during the time Monroe was on suspension from Fox—in other words, in late 1953. Work on the manuscript seems to have ceased in early 1954, since the last chapter is about the actress's trip to Korea shortly after her marriage to DiMaggio. Apparently DiMaggio objected to having the book published, and relations between the actress and her biographer "soured," according to Summers. Monroe left no notes or marks on the manuscript that she gave to Milton Greene for safe-keeping, and it is not clear whether she had plans to finish it. The 1974 edition of her autobiography, and a new edition that includes Milton Greene's photographs of Monroe, contain several passages that did not appear in *Empire News*, passages that could have come only from the manuscript Milton Greene briefly described to me.

Chapter One: Childhood

Lois Banner, *Marilyn Monroe: The Passion and the Paradox* (Bloomsbury, 2012), discovered that Monroe's foster families were not strangers to her. They were friends of Grace McKee, who enjoyed Gladys's confidence. Even so, to a child these constant changes of scene could well have seemed disruptive and destabilizing. If Banner, who has done the deepest investigation of these foster families, detects no insecurity in an apparently placid and accepting Norma Jeane, that conclusion does not discount Monroe's view of her upbringing as traumatic. Banner believes that Norma Jeane was probably the victim of childhood abuse—not rape, but fondling by a male who is identified in *My Story* as "Mr. Kimmel." Banner adduces from Monroe's later behavior the signs of one who has been sexually molested, but of course that kind of analysis must remain speculative. Some rather cryptic comments by Monroe in *Fragments: Poems, Intimate Notes, Letters* (Farrar, Straus & Giroux, Kindle edition, 2010), suggest she may have been sexually abused as a child. Marilyn Monroe treated her childhood as a Dickensian story. There may have been at least a brief period when Gladys and Norma Jeane enjoyed something like a normal life together. *MM—Personal* includes a letter, dated August 15, 1962, from Harry C. Wilson to Berniece Miracle, Monroe's half-sister, describing a visit during Christmas 1935 to Gladys, who asked Norma Jeane to sing for him: "Gladys had a Christmas tree all decorated and Norma Jean [*sic*] stood between the tree and us and sang a pretty song. I was entranced by it . . . After Norma Jean left to go to bed I talked about it to Gladys. I told her I was very much in love with her and her little girl. It was less than a month later when tragedy struck. I almost lost my mind over it." Wilson is apparently referring to Gladys's mental breakdown, but he has the date wrong, since by September 1935, Norma Jeane was in the orphanage.

"strongly sexed feeling since a small child": *Fragments*, Kindle edition.

"I loved everything": Richard Meryman, "Behind the Myth of Norma Jean," *Life*, August 3, 1962.

Grace McKee: Banner provides the fullest biography of Norma Jeane's sometime guardian and mentor.

Mrs. Dewey: Fred Lawrence Guiles, *Norma Jean: The Life of Marilyn Monroe* (Bantam, 1970), 30–31; Maurice Zolotow, *Marilyn Monroe* (Bantam, 1961), 17.

Alice Miller, *Prisoners of Childhood* (Basic Books, 1981), 32.

R. D. Laing, *Self and Others* (Penguin, 1971), 50–51, 119.

A letter from Mrs. Dewey: J. Randy Taraborelli, *The Secret Life of Marilyn Monroe* (Grand Central Publishing, 2010), Kindle edition.

Ana Lower and Christian Science: Banner provides the most complete and insightful account of the religion and Ann Lower's profound impact on the maturing adolescent who would become Marilyn Monroe.

Laing: Self and Others, 51, 137.

Chapter Two: Adolescence to Adulthood

The first paragraph is based on Monroe's own account of her adolescence in *My Story* and in her *Life* interview.

"her lover, husband, and father": James Dougherty, *The Secret Happiness of Marilyn Monroe* (Playboy Press, 1976), 73–74.

"my relationship with him": *Fragments*.

"she panicked": See R. D. Laing, *The Divided Self* (Pelican, 1965), 54–57, for a case similar to Norma Jeane's.

"interim identity": Mailer, *Marilyn: A Biography* (Grosset & Dunlap, 1973), 46.

"just as an infant manipulates images of itself duplicated in a mirror": Jacques Lacan, *Ecrits: A Selection* (W. W. Norton, 1977), 1–7; Norman Rosten, *Marilyn: An Untold Story* (Signet Books, 1973), 47; "Patricia Rosten on Marilyn Monroe," *Closeups*, edited by Danny Peary (Workman, 1978), 321.

De Dienes photographs: Mailer, 40, 51; Edwin P. Hoyt, *Marilyn: The Tragic Venus* (Robert Hale, 1967), 42.

Burnside: Anthony Summers, *Goddess: The Secret Lives of Marilyn Monroe* (Macmillan, 1985), 24–29.

Chapter Three: Early Career

Modeling: Zolotow, *Marilyn Monroe*, 38, 40; Guiles, *Norma Jean*, 61–63.

"Such changes"; Zolotow, *Marilyn Monroe*, 39–40; Guiles, *Norma Jean*, 73.

Screen test: Zolotow, *Marilyn Monroe*, 44; Louella Parsons, *Tell It to Louella* (Putnam's, 1961), 213.

Publicity shots of the period 1946–48: John Kobal and David Robinson, *Marilyn Monroe: A Life on Film* (Hamlyn, 1974), 38–39, 42–43, 46–49; Sam Shaw, *In the Camera Eye* (Hamlyn, 1979), 133–34, 136–38; Mailer, 66–67.

"How do you become a star?": Interview with Rose Steinberg Wapner; see also Shelley Winters, *Shelley* (William Morrow, 1980), 91; Parsons, 214; Robert Stack, *Straight Shooting* (Berkeley, 1981), 104; Hoyt, 65.

Ryman recalled: Richard Natale, "MGM Vet Lucille Ryman Carroll Recalls the Reel Adventures of Liz, Rock, Marilyn and Nancy," *People*, November 2, 1987, http://www.people.com/people/archive/article/0,,20097488,00.html.

John Engstead remembers: John Engstead, *Star Shots: Fifty Years of Picture and Stories by One of Hollywood's Greatest Photographers* (Dutton, 1978), 195–96.

"she used sex as a way of saying thank you": See Summers for the most detailed account of Monroe's sex life. To journalist W. J. Weatherby, *Conversations with Marilyn* (Mason Charter, 1976), she confessed to going through a period of trading sexual favors for career advancement. Donald Spoto, *Marilyn: The Biography* (HarperCollins, 1993), 140, reports that Monroe even engaged in a brief career as a Hollywood Boulevard hooker.

Natasha Lytess: Natasha Lytess, "My Years with Marilyn," a twenty-eight page manuscript deposited in the Maurice Zolotow collection, Humanities Research Center, University of Texas at Austin; see also Jane Wilkie, *Confessions of an Ex-Fan Magazine Writer* (Doubleday, 1981), 4–5, 172–87; Sidney Skolsky, *Marilyn* (Dell, 1954), 42, 49.

Ladies of the Chorus: Baltimore Sun, February 11, 1949, 12; Joan Mellen, *Marilyn Monroe* (Pyramid, 1973), 63–66; Janice Anderson, *Marilyn Monroe* (Crescent, 1983), 27–29; Michael Conway and Mark Ricci, *The Films of Marilyn Monroe* (Citadel, 1964), 29.

"She was just a baby then": John Kobal, *Movie-Star Portraits of the Forties* (Dover, 1977), 443, 448.

worked briefly as a stripper: Richard Lamparski, *Hidden Hollywood: Where the Stars Lived, Loved and Died* (Simon and Schuster, 1981), 87.

Nude calendar: Guiles, *Norma Jean*, 112.

Johnny Hyde: Fred Lawrence Guiles, *Legend: The Life and Death of Marilyn Monroe* (Stein and Day, 1984), 145; see photograph of Hyde and Monroe in James Spada and George Zeno, *Monroe: Her Life in Pictures* (Doubleday, 1982), 24–25.

John Huston: Guiles, *Legend*, 120–21. Spoto, 160, notes that Huston had another actress in mind, Lola Albright, and that the director took too much credit for immediately recognizing Monroe's talent.

Nunnally Johnson: Hoyt, 74–75.

Celeste Holm: Rudy Behlmer, *America's Favorite Movies: Behind the Scenes* (Frederick Ungar, 1982), 206.

Dana Andrews: Columbia University Oral History Office: Dana Andrews interview.

Flink and Allan: interviews; see also Rupert Allan, "Marilyn Monroe: A Serious Blonde Who Can Act," *Look*, October 23, 1951.

Film personality: Cavell, 27–28.

"kind and soft and helpless": Sidney Skolsky, *Don't Get Me Wrong—I Love Hollywood* (Putnam's 1975), 124; Steffi Sidney interview.

"the most mysterious property of a factoid": Mailer, 63.

On Miss Caswell and Monroe, compare Skolsky, *Marilyn*, 42 with Joseph L. Mankiewicz and Gary Carey, *More About All About Eve* (Random House, 1972), 222.

"but somehow she never understood": Mankiewicz and Carey, 96–97.

In the minds of Joseph Mankiewicz and others: Mankiewicz and Carey, 77; Hoyt, 86; Garson Kanin, *Hollywood* (Viking, 1974), 315–20.

she would weep: Barbara Leaming, *Marilyn Monroe* (Crown, 1998), 6.

Kazan, Miller, and Monroe: Leaming, 7–10.

Chapter Four: Becoming a Star

"women get accustomed to chopped-up images": Kennedy Fraser, "On and Off the Avenue (Feminine Fashions)," *New Yorker*, November 9, 1981, 52.

June Haver: Hoyt, 89–90.

"think I'm no good": *Fragments*.

"no attitude": *Fragments*.

"Other women": Guiles, *Legend*, 178–79.

Acting on movie sets: Interview with Ellen Burstyn.

In her class notes: *Fragments*.

Let's Make It Legal: Conway and Ricci, 66.

UCLA: Monroe, 109–10; *Fragments*.

Chekhov: Monroe, 133–35; Guiles, *Norma Jean*, 142; Jane Corwin, "Orphan in Ermine," *Photoplay*, March 1954, 45; Weatherby, 57; Michael Chekhov, *To The Actor: On the Technique of Acting* (Harper & Row, 1953), chapter 1, 22–25, 30–31; 74–83, 103.

Mabel Elsworth Todd: *The Thinking Body: A Study of the Balancing Force of Dynamic Man* (Paul B. Hoeber, 1937); interview with Ralph Roberts.

"no looks": *Fragments*.

Lee made the striptease: Rachel Shteir, *Gypsy: The Art of the Tease* (Yale University Press, Kindle edition, 2009).

Monroe-DiMaggio relationship: Monroe 124–30; Zolotow, *Marilyn Monroe,* 85, 120–29, 134, 146–47, 186, 195, 195, 202–211; Guiles, *Norma Jean,* 150–51, 154–55, 163, 166–67, 171–73, 179–81; Mailer, 95–107, 111, 116–22.

The publicity solidified her appeal: Zolotow, *Marilyn Monroe,* 104–8, "Marilyn 'Hurt' by Army Ban on Photo," *Los Angeles Times,* September 2, 1952, 2; Hedda Hopper, "Marilyn Tells the Truth to Hedda Hopper," *Photoplay,* January 1953, 85; Mailer, 95.

"psychological gesture": Chekhov, 76–77.

To Hedda Rosten: interview with Hedda Rosten.

Bancroft and Widmark: Guiles, *Legend,* 205.

Robinson: Kobal and Robinson, 16, 9.

Nunnally Johnson: Hoyt, 94; Tom Stempel, *Screenwriter: The Life and Times of Nunnally Johnson* (Barnes, 1980), 168–69.

Chapter Five: Fame

Details of Marilyn's life with the DiMaggios are derived from June DiMaggio with Mary Jane Popp, *Marilyn, Joe & Me* (Penmarin Books, 2006), 75, 79, 85, 112, 114.

"Zanuck was never smart about women": John Kobal, *People Will Talk* (Knopf, 1986), 613.

Photoplay awards dinner: Hoyt, 125–26; Zolotow, *Marilyn Monroe,* 186–88; Monroe, 113–14.

Kilgallen letter: George Carpozi, *Marilyn Monroe—Her Own Story* (World Distributors, 1961), 87–88.

Goslar: Guiles, *Legend,* 221–22, 232.

Todd: 1, 174–75, 281, 295.

"goddam dumb," Kobal, *People Will Talk,* 496.

"Darryl, you're making realism": Kobal, *People Will Talk,* 496.

The line was added: Spoto, 229.

Monroe as put-on: Jacob Brackman, *The Put-On* (Bantam, 1972), 19; Mailer, 106.

Truffaut: *The Films in My Life* (Simon and Schuster, 1975), 72.

Johnson: Stempel, 170.

Lauren Bacall: *By Myself* (Knopf, 1979), 208.

Negulesco: Zolotow, *Marilyn Monroe,* 191–93.

Johnson: Hoyt, 116–17. June DiMaggio points out in *Marilyn, Joe & Me,* 95, that Marilyn was very nearsighted and wore glasses when at home with the DiMaggios, but would take them off when anyone she did not know entered the room.

Winters: *Shelley*, 450–54; Otto Preminger, *Preminger: An Autobiography* (Doubleday, 1977), 128.

Korea: Monroe, 141–43; C. Robert Jennings, "The Strange Case of Marilyn Monroe vs. the U.S. Army: A Reminiscence," *Los Angeles*, August 1966; Guiles, *Norma Jean*, 180–82; Skolsky, *Marilyn*, 82.

"she appeared in a low-cut": *MM—Personal*, 114–15.

A Cold War symbol: Lois Banner, *MM—Personal from the Private Archive of Marilyn Monroe* (Abrams, 2011). For the best coverage of Monroe's Korea trip, see Spoto, 264–67.

Chapter Six: Half-Life

"Sitting next to Mr. DiMaggio": Tarraborelli.

Jimmy Cannon: Leaming.

Monroe's co-workers: Interview with Rose Steinberg Wapner.

Monroe's costume: Twentieth Century-Fox publicity release in the files of the Academy of Motion Picture Arts and Sciences.

Monroe's illness: Zolotow, *Marilyn Monroe*, 218–19; Hoyt, 140–41; Carpozi, 106; interview with Rose Steinberg Wapner.

Pills, fears of insanity: Summers, 85, 109–12.

"the silent treatment": DiMaggio, 131.

Susan Strasberg: *Bittersweet* (Putnam's, 1980), 41.

Monroe-DiMaggio breakup: Guiles, *Norma Jean*, 186–91; Zolotow, *Marilyn Monroe*, 222–25; Skolsky, *Don't Get Me Wrong*, 224.

Winters: Lewis Funke and John E. Booth, *Actors Talk About Acting: Fourteen Intimate Interviews* (Avon, 1963), 156.

Ken Darby: Hoyt. 135.

The Beatles: John Lahr, "The Beatles Considered," *New Republic*, December 2, 1981.

Milton Greene: Interviews with Milton Greene; Rupert Allan, and Steffi Sidney.

Chapter Seven: Search for Self: The Method

Interviews with Milton Greene, Rupert Allan, Susan Strasberg, Ralph Roberts, John Springer, and Stanley Flink inform my understanding of Monroe's life and career in this chapter.

Monroe's thoughts, dreams, and notes to herself in 1955: *Fragments*, 71–85.

Strasberg and Guiles: tape-recorded interview (January 17, 1967), courtesy of

Fred Lawrence Guiles. Unless otherwise noted, my account of Strasberg and his comments on Monroe come from this interview.

Black-and-white sequence: Mailer, *Of Women and Their Elegance* (Simon and Schuster, 1980), 218–30.

Amy Greene: Helen Bolstad, "Marilyn in the House," *Photoplay*, September 1955; Mailer, *Of Women and Their Elegance*, 72–74, 79–84, 88–89, 284; Summers, 123.

Dr. Siegal: Summers, 123.

Greenson: Summers, 188.

Person to Person: Mailer, *Of Women and Their Elegance*, 99–122.

Chronology of events leading to meeting with Strasberg: Zolotow, *Marilyn Monroe*, 244–45; Guiles, *Norma Jean*, 206.

Reading Stanislavsky: Hoyt, 152; Zolotow, *Marilyn Monroe*, 257; Pete Martin, *Will Acting Spoil Marilyn Monroe?* (Doubleday, 1956), 56.

Strasberg's class: Dwight Easty, *On Method Acting* (House of Collectibles, 1980), 159.

James Dean: David Dalton, *James Dean: The Mutant King* (Straight Arrow Books, 1974), 92.

Stella Adler: Cindy Adams, *Lee Strasberg: The Imperfect Genius of the Actors Studio* (Doubleday, 180), 178.

Strasberg: For a recent harshly critical view of Strasberg, which is heavily influenced by Donald Spoto's biography of Monroe, see Rosemary Malague, *An Actress Prepares* (Routledge, 2012). Malague indicts the director for his autocratic, patriarchal, and misogynistic behavior. She shows that he was especially hard on women, often making them break down in front of him to prove their sincere and authentic approach to their roles. But she ignores the instances with Monroe in which he deviated from this abusive pattern, treating the actress with tenderness and compassion. Monroe's crying during and after performances with him was hardly a response to Strasberg alone. Indeed, her dependence on him—which Malague attributes to Strasberg's machinations—is a repetition of Monroe's search for a father figure, a point Malague concedes but does not build into her narrow analysis of the Strasberg-Monroe dynamic.

Ellen Burstyn: interview.

Helen Hayes: Funke and Booth, 71.

Arthur Miller on the Method: *The Theatre Essays of Arthur Miller*, edited by Robert A. Martin (Penguin, 1978), 274.

As Strasberg put it to Maurice Zolotow: *Marilyn Monroe*, 246.

Wilder on Monroe's acting: Zolotow, *Marilyn Monroe*, 259–60, 321.

Strasberg with a student: Adams, 210.

Strasberg on psychoanalysis: Robert H. Hethmon, ed., *Strasberg at the Actors Studio* (Viking, 1983), 5, 30.

Strasberg's classes: Zolotow, *Marilyn Monroe*, 247; Guiles, *Norma Jean*, 208.

Steinem's meeting with Monroe: Gloria Steinem, "Growing Up With Marilyn," *Ms.*, August 1972, 35.

One observer: Easty, 159.

Kitten: Adams, 125.

Classic Stanislavsky exercise: *An Actor Prepares* (Theatre Arts, 1942), 86.

Stanislavsky's approach: *Building a Character* (Theatre Arts, 1949), 279.

Character embodiment: *An Actor Prepares*, 96.

Sing a popular song: Zolotow, *Marilyn Monroe*, 248; Hethmon, 224–26, 242.

Gestureless movements: V. I. Pudovkin, *Film Technique and Film Acting* (Grove Press, 1976), 334.

Clurman, introduction to Odets: *Golden Boy: A Play in Three Acts* (Random House, 1937), ix–xii.

Meryman and Flink: interviews.

Strasberg and Stanislavsky and Monroe's preparation or scenes at the Actors Studio: Adams, 107; *An Actor Prepares*, 49, 242; *Building a Character*, 108, 114.

One male studio member: Adams, 261.

Kim Stanley: John Kobal, "Dialogue on Film: Kim Stanley," *American Film*, June 1983.

Cheryl Crawford: Adams, 261–62.

Maureen Stapleton: Summers, 145.

Monroe's reaction to her performance: Adams, 261–62.

Fred Stewart: Guiles, *Legend*, 272.

One reporter: recorded on *Marilyn Monroe: Rare Recordings 1948–1962*, Sandy Hook Records, 1979.

Logan's reactions to Monroe: Josh Logan, *Movie Stars, Real People, and Me* (Delacorte, 1978), 43–48, 52, 55–56; Zolotow, *Marilyn Monroe*, 275.

Don Murray: Guy Trebey, "Don Murray," *Inter/view*, Volume 37, 1973; Debra Levine, "Don Murray Held Marilyn Monroe Close in *Bus Stop*," *HuffPost Arts and Culture*, http://www.huffingtonpost.com/debra-levine/why-niceguy-don-murray-ma_b_707796.html.

Stanislavsky's legacy: Easty, 49.

Lester Markel: Summers, 218–19.

Stanislavsky: see *Building a Character*, chapter 2.

James Dean: Dalton, 101.
Mellen: 112–21.
"Be your own Stanislavsky": Hethmon, 255.
Anne Bancroft: Funke and Booth, 196.

Chapter Eight: The Poet of Her Aspirations

Focus; Skolsky, *Don't Get Me Wrong*, 213.
Snapshot of Miller: Jim Cook, "Marilyn and Her Man," *New York Post*, July 8, 1956, 4M.
Lytess: Alex Joyce, "Marilyn at the Crossroads," *Photoplay*, July 1957, 98.
Skolsky: *Don't Get Me Wrong*, 213.
Odets: "To Whom It May Concern," *Show*, October 1962, 136.
Alan Levy: Edward Wagenknecht, ed., *Marilyn Monroe: A Composite View* (Chilton, 1969), 18.
Stanislavsky: *An Actor Prepares*, 294–95.
Ralph Roberts: interview.
Miller and the Rostens: interviews with Norman and Hedda Rosten.
Miller's impressions of Monroe: Jack Hamilton, "Marilyn's New Life," *Look*, October 1, 1957, 10.
Miller's ebullience: Cook, 4M.
Monroe's surprise: Rosten, *Marilyn*, 34; interview with Rupert Allan.
Miller's HUAC testimony: Eric Bentley, ed., *Thirty Years of Treason: Excerpts from Hearing Before the House Committee on Un-American Activities, 1938–1968* (Viking, 1971).
Levy: Wagenknecht, 19.
Monroe's identification with Miller: Olie and Joe Rauh, as told to Harriet Lyons, "The Time Marilyn Monroe Hid Out at Our House," *Ms.*, August 1, 1983, 15–16.
Monroe's conversion: Rosten, *Marilyn*, 38.
Hoyt: 178.
Guiles: *Norma Jean*, 240–41.
Paula Strasberg: quoted in "Marilyn," *Look*, May 29, 1956, 74.
Miller in 1969: Guiles, "Marilyn Monroe," *This Week*, March 2, 1969, 7.
Laing: *The Divided Self*, 37.
Rosten: *Marilyn Monroe*, 36–38.

Chapter Nine: The Prince and the Showgirl

Monroe's uncertain reception: Dorothy Manning, "The Woman and the Legend," *Photoplay*, October 1956, 98.

Meeting Olivier: Earl Wilson, "The Things She Said to Me!," *Photoplay*, May 1956, 84; Winters, 313.

Accounts of the planning and production of *The Prince and the Showgirl*: Guiles, *Norma Jean*, 253–64, *Legend*, 319–24; Zolotow, *Marilyn Monroe*, 296–311; Mailer, *Marilyn*, 160–66, *Of Women and Their Elegance*, 178–206; Hoyt, 178–86; Carpozi, 139–45; Martin, 116–22; Rosten, *Marilyn*, 42–45; Olivier, 205–13; Spoto, 366–70, 372–75, 378–80, 388–90; Colin Clark, *The Prince, the Showgirl and Me: Six Months on the Set with Marilyn and Olivier* (St. Martin's Press, 1996).

Vivian Leigh: John Cottrell, *Laurence Olivier* (Prentice Hall, 1975), 281–82; for a different view, see Clark.

Olivier's first meeting with Monroe: Laurence Olivier, *Confessions of an Actor: An Autobiography* (Simon and Schuster, 1982), 205.

The press conference: Martin, 120.

Schizoid: Olivier, 205; interview with Milton Greene; Laing, *The Divided Self*, 17.

Hutchinson: Tom Hutchinson, *Marilyn Monroe* (Exeter, 1982), 69.

Rosten: *Marilyn*, 43.

Olivier and the Method: Olivier, 207.

Winters on the Method: Funke and Booth, 147–48.

Olivier's honesty: Robert Daniels, *Laurence Olivier: Theater and Cinema* (Barnes, 1980), 136.

Hedda Rosten: interview.

Paula Strasberg: Strasberg, 67.

Milton Greene: Summers, 166–67.

Rosten: *Marilyn*, 45.

Logan: 67.

Conflicting evidence of Olivier's behavior: Cottrell, 282–84; Michael Korda, *Charmed Lives: A Family Romance* (Random House 1979), 447; Foster Hirsch, *Laurence Olivier* (Twayne, 1979), 114; Clark.

Olivier's pride: Cottrell, 284.

Eyewitness account: Thomas Kiernan, *Sir Larry: The Life of Laurence Olivier* (Times Books, 1981), 257.

Hedda Rosten: interview.

Monroe's notebook: *Fragments*, 115, 119.

Anna Freud: quoted in Steven Poser, *The Misfit*, Kindle single.

Resistance to acting: Cottrell, 280.

Thorndyke: quoted in Mailer, *Marilyn*, 164; Clark.

Critics: Mellen, 123; Janice R. Welsch, *Film Archetypes: Sisters, Mistresses, Mothers and Daughters* (Arno Press, 1978), 202; Hirsch, 116–17.

Chaplin: Welsch, 202; Logan, 56.

Mellen: 123.

Hirsch: 113–17.

Logan: 66–67.

Chapter Ten: Home Life

Dr. Marianne Kris: Poser.

"the survival of an unprotected shrub": Rosten, *Marilyn*, 70–71.

"My nightmare": Wagenknecht, 32.

"becoming obsessively concerned": Guiles, *Norma Jean*, 266.

"temporarily putting films aside": Rosten, *Marilyn*, 47.

"make believe": Rosten, *Marilyn*, 44–46.

Abortions: Summers, 148, 285–86.

Fred Karger's doubts: Monroe, 78.

Suicide: Rosten, *Marilyn*, 75; Summers, 6, 23–24, 48–49, 193, 197.

Monroe's poetry: Rosten, *Marilyn*, 55.

"In one": Strasberg, 51.

Monroe's drawings: interview with Norman Rosten.

"I am sure": interview with Norman Rosten.

bushels of fan mail: interview with Norman Rosten.

"no makeup": Rosten, *Marilyn*, 11–12.

"Can I really be": Truman Capote, *Music for Chameleons* (Random House, 1980), 238.

"a firm core": Laing, *The Divided Self*, 42–43.

Chapter Eleven: Impersonations/Repetitions

"hairdressers, make-up man . . . : see Maurice Zolotow, *Billy Wilder in Hollywood* (Putnam's 1977), for a full account of the director's point of view on the making of *Some Like It Hot*.

Curtis: *MM—Personal*, p. 82, includes Monroe's personal note about Curtis: "There is only one way he *could* comment on my sexuality and I'm afraid he has never had the opportunity!"

Rupert Allan: interview.

Jack Lemmon remembered: Walter Wagner, *You Must Remember This* (Putnam's, 1975), 303.

Monroe's friends say she wanted to work: interviews with Rupert Allan, John Springer, and Ralph Roberts.

"a tasteless and characterless ingenue": Guiles, *Legend*, 355.

"gay, hopeful, young girl": *Fragments*, 151.

"built-in alarm system": Don Widener, *Lemmon: A Biography* (Allen, 1977), 170.

Farber: Leslie Farber, *Lying, Despair, Jealously, Envy, Sex, Suicide Drugs, and The Good Life* (Basic Books, 1973), 370–71.

French: Brandon French, *On the Verge of Revolt: Women in American Films of the Fifties* (Frederick Ungar, 1978), 147.

Sinyard and Turner: Neil Sinyard and Adrian Turner, *Journey Down Sunset Boulevard: The Films of Billy Wilder* (BCW Publishing, 1979), 220–21.

Critics: Gerald Mast, *The Comic Mind: Comedy and the Movies* (Bobbs-Merrill, 1978), 278; Bernard F. Dick, *Billy Wilder* (Twayne, 198), 235.

"without wanting to hit her": Guiles, *Norma Jean*, 287.

Audrey Wilder: Zolotow, *Billy Wilder in Hollywood*, 271.

Wilder in 1968: Zolotow, *Billy Wilder in Hollywood*, 272.

Miller and Wilder: Zolotow, *Billy Wilder in Hollywood*, 265–67.

Mister Johnson: Rosten, Marilyn, 78.

Estelle Parsons: Adams, 210.

Ralph Roberts: interview.

Ellen Burstyn: interview.

Ralph Roberts: interview.

"neutralized persons": Guiles, "Marilyn Monroe," 7.

Signoret: Simone Signoret, *Nostalgia Isn't What It Used To Be* (Penguin, 1979), 335.

"throughout his whole life": Moira Hodgson, "Yves Montand—From the Musical Hall to the Met," *New York Times*, Arts and Leisure, September 5, 1982, 14.

Skolsky: *Don't Get Me Wrong*, 228.

Montand: Yves Montand with Hervé Hamon and Patrick Rotman, *You See, I Haven't Forgotten* (Knopf, 1992), 324–25.

Greenson: Summers, 188–89, 205–6.

The press: "Walk Like This, Marilyn," *Life*, April 20, 1959, 104.

Signoret: 336–39.

"a series of endings": Guiles, *Legend*, 324.

Freud: 42.

Greenson: Summers, 205–6.

Chapter Twelve: The Film of Her Life

See Goode for the most complete account of the filming of *The Misfits*. Unless otherwise noted, quotations from those involved in the film come from Goode's book. George Kourvaros, *Famous Faces Yet Not Themselves: The Misfits and Icons of Postwar America* (University of Minnesota Press, 2010), suggests that *The Misfits* reflects and helps to promote a changing conception of the movie star, a conception that includes an iconography extending "beyond the [star's] role on screen."

"Miller denied": Robert La Guardia, *Monty: A Biography of Montgomery Clift* (Arbor House, 1977), 211.

Monroe's doubts about Roslyn: Rosten, *Marilyn*, 85–86.

"Lee Strasberg told Fred Guiles": interview with Fred Guiles.

Sam Shaw's photograph of Monroe hugging a tree: Mailer, *Marilyn*, 156.

"To the Weeping Willow": Rosten, *Marilyn*, 59–60.

"John Huston says": John Huston, *An Open Book* (New York: Ballantine, 1982), 325.

"To Huston": Huston, 323.

Monroe's breakdown: Biographer Donald Spoto suggests Monroe's relatively quick recovery is an indication that more was at stake than her health when the film shut down. Huston's huge losses at the Reno gambling tables had exceeded what investors had allotted him, and he used the cover of Monroe's hospitalization to raise the necessary funds to keep the production going. His own unprofessional behavior, according to members of the crew, included falling asleep during takes. See Jeffrey Meyers, *John Huston: Courage and Art* (Crown, 2011), 249.

"In spite of some setbacks": Jon Whitcomb, "Marilyn Monroe—The Sex Symbol vs. The Good Wife," *Cosmopolitan*, December 1960, 53.

"retakes of the rodeo scenes": Alice T. McIntyre, "Waiting for Monroe or Notes from Olympus," *Esquire*, March 1961, 76.

"like a concerned mother hen": Weatherby, 67.

"psychic twins": Patricia Bosworth, *Montgomery Clift* (Bantam, 1979), 352.

"Marilyn could bitch": La Guardia, 310.

Jack Lemmon on Monroe's acting: Widener, 170; Wagner, 304.

Monroe's double bind: for more comment on this scene, see Joel Oppenheimer, *Marilyn Lives!* (Delilah, 1981), 80.

Revisions of *The Misfits*: Goode, 215–16, 306; Weatherby, 33; Guiles, *Norma Jean*, 338; George P. Garrett, O. B. Hardison, and Jane R. Gelfman, *Film Scripts* (Merideth, 1972), 202–382, contains an early version of the movie.

Monroe on *Some Like It Hot*: Wagenknecht, 33.

"Huston's tampering": George Barris and Theo Wilson, "Marilyn Speaks," *Philadelphia Daily News*, August 20–25, 1962.

"Reis, Rupert Allan, Patricia Newcomb": interview with Rupert Allan.

"Monroe told W. J. Weatherby": Weatherby, 73–75. See also Summers, 206, 215–16.

Chapter Thirteen: The Lady of Shalott

Epigraph: Tennyson, "The Lady of Shalott." See also Murray, 152.

Monroe's meetings with Weatherby: Weatherby, 25, 143–51, 166–70, 182–89.

She was more depressed: Rosten, *Marilyn*, 90–92.

Dr. Kris and Ralph Roberts: interview with Ralph Roberts. Dr. Kris, described as a "pioneer psychoanalyst and teacher," specialized in the treatment of children, and was "founder and first president of the International Association for Child Psychoanalysis." See her obituary in the *New York Times*, November 25, 1980, D23.

"the grim snap of a lock": Meryman, "Behind the Myth," 54.

Monroe's letter to the Strasbergs: reprinted in *Fragments*.

"she gravitated toward power": Rosten, *Marilyn*, 92.

"other scenes of high drama": Levy in Wagenknecht, 27.

To Patricia Newcomb: Guiles, *Norma Jean*, 346.

According to Skolsky: Skolsky, *Don't Get Me Wrong*, 230.

Rupert Allan: interview.

Kay Gable: "Shocked Disbelief," Spada and Zeno, 176.

"symptoms of paranoia": Summers, 189, 231–32.

Marjorie Stengel: Mailer, *Marilyn*, 216.

Eunice Murray: Eunice Murray, *Marilyn: The Last Months* (Pyramic, 1975), 13–14, 16.

Norman Rosten: interview.

Fred Field: Summers, 254.

"complete relaxation": Rosten, *Marilyn*, 100–1.

Greenson to Zolotow: Maurice Zolotow, "Marilyn Monroe's Psychiatrist: Trying to Untarnish Her Memory," *Chicago Tribune*, Section 5, September 16, 1973, 2.

Screen patients: Greenson, 115–16, 118–23, 126–31.

Greenson wrote to a colleague: Summers, 206–8.

Nunnally Johnson: Stempel, 173.

Walter Bernstein: Walter Bernstein, "Monroe's Last Picture Show," *Esquire*, July 1973, 105–8.

"a Command Performance": Guiles, *Norma Jean*, 360.

"hundreds of strategically placed brilliants": Murray, 101–2.

Practicing sexy "Happy Birthday" song: interview with Ralph Roberts.

Association with the Kennedys: Wills 22–26, 28–30, 34–35. For accounts of Monroe and the Kennedys, see Martin, *A Hero of Out Time*; Skolsky, *Don't Get Me Wrong*; Wilson, *Show Business Laid Bare*; Schlesinger, *Robert Kennedy and His Times*. Both Anthony Summers and Lois Banner believe in Monroe's close connection to the Kennedys, and both draw on eyewitness testimony putting Robert Kennedy at Monroe's house on the last day of her life. But these eyewitnesses are reporting what they think they saw from afar. Spoto found no way to document a sexual involvement with Robert Kennedy and does not deem the "evidence" cited in other biographies for an RFK-MM affair credible.

"she acted in a kind of slow motion": Bernstein. Patrick McGilligan, *George Cukor: A Double Life* (St. Martin's Press), accepts Cukor's view of Monroe's acting. I'm grateful to Peter Brown, who co-authored with Patte B. Barnham, *Marilyn: The Last Take* (Dutton, 1992), for sending me several hours of footage from *Something's Got to Give*. Nowhere in this material do I see any evidence of the "slow motion" acting Cukor described.

Was the man "screwing": Rosten, *Marilyn*, 112–14.

"a break in the personality": Alexander Lowen, *Fear of Life* (Macmillan, 1980), 47, 62, 186.

Greenson's last visits to Monroe's home: Summers, 269.

"sprightly and sexy": Bernstein.

"dark tunnel of her career": interview with Rupert Allan.

Final conversation with Weatherby: Weatherby, 210.

George Barris's photographs: Mailer, *Marilyn*, 241, 243, 245–46.

Stern: *The Last Sitting* (William Morrow, 1982), 10–11, 14–16, 23, 41, 55–59, 61–69, 71, 88, 146, 186. See a related sequence of photographs in *Eros*, Autumn 1962, 6–7, where the more casual, middle range of Monroe's emotions in contrast to the almost stately ones in Stern's book.

"the main mechanism": Summers, 189.

Meryman's impressions of Monroe: interview with Richard Meryman; Summers, 276.

Leslie Farber: Farber, 61, 66–70, 79, 117, 197.

Greenson's comments on the Kennedys: Summers, 308.

Collier and Garbo: Capote, *Music for Chameleons*, 140.

Henri Cartier-Bresson: Goode, 101.

John Huston: Axel Madsen, *John Huston: A Biography* (Doubleday, 1978), 228.

"Find me, find me / complete this form": lines from Julie Suk's poem, reprinted in Oppenheimer, 55.

Afterword

Marilyn Monroe's FBI file is available at various websites.

Tom Payne, *Fame: What the Classics Tell Us About Our Cult of Celebrity* (Picador, 2010), Kindle Edition, "A Certain Sacrifice."

S. Paige Baty, *American Monroe* (University of California Press, 1995), "Ecce Signum," "In Medias Reas," Google Books edition.

Filmography

Index

Truffaut, François, 72
Turnabout Theater, 67
Turner, Lana, 19
Twentieth Century-Fox, 6, 16, 19, 20, 38, 47, 53, 66, 69, 74, 83, 87, 98–100, 104, 119, 138, 156–58, 188, 199, 225, 226, 230–31, 240, 243, 245, 247

UCLA, 44

Van Doren, Mamie, 84
Vicky (*There's No Business Like Show Business*), 88–89
View from the Bridge, A, 139, 148
Vogue, 232

Wagner, Robert, 103
Wald, Jerry, 240
Wallach, Eli, 170, 199, 201, 208
Wapner, Rose Steinberg, 19, 91, 92
Warhol, Andy, 64–65, 245
Wasserman, Lew, 173
Wayne, David, 53, 77
Weatherby, W. J., 210, 215–17, 232
Welsch, Janice, 154
"We're Just Two Little Girls from Little Rock," 93. See also *Gentlemen Prefer Blondes*
We're Not Married, 53, 57, 94, 159, 225
"When Love Goes Wrong Nothin' Goes Right," 93. See also *Gentlemen Prefer Blondes*
Widmark, Richard, 55, 57
Wilder, Audrey, 187–88
Wilder, Billy, 71, 87, 96, 104, 108, 170, 171, 172–77, 180, 184, 185, 186–87, 188
Williams, Tennessee, 115
Winchell, Walter, 239–40

Winters, Shelley, 78, 97–98
Woolf, Virgina, xvii

Zanuck, Darryl, 47, 52, 54, 66, 69, 80, 156, 231
Zernial, Gus, 48
Zolotow, Maurice, xiii, xiv–xv, 107, 127, 222, 247